LEARNING AND TEACHING ENGLISH GRAMMAR, K–12

BARBARA M. BIRCH
California State University, Fresno

PEARSON

Merrill
Prentice Hall

Upper Saddle River, New Jersey
Columbus, Ohio

Library of Congress Cataloging in Publication Data

Birch, Barbara M.
  Learning and teaching English grammar, K-12 / Barbara M. Birch.
    p. cm.
  Includes bibliographical references and index.
  ISBN 0-13-048834-8
    1. English language—Grammar—Study and teaching (Elementary)—United States. 2.
  English language—Grammar—Study and teaching (Secondary)—United States. I. Title.

LB1576.B4962 2005   2004044852

Vice President and Executive Publisher: Jeffery W. Johnston
Editor: Linda Ashe Montgomery
Editorial Assistant: Laura Weaver
Development Editor: Dawne Brooks
Production Editor: Mary M. Irvin
Production Coordination: Amy Gehl, Carlisle Publisher Services
Design Coordinator: Diane C. Lorenzo
Cover Designer: Ali Mohrman
Cover Image: SuperStock
Production Manager: Susan Hannahs
Director of Marketing: Ann Castel Davis
Marketing Manager: Darcy Betts Prybella
Marketing Coordinator: Tyra Poole

This book was set in Palatino by Carlisle Communications, Ltd. It was printed and bound by R. R.
Donnelley & Sons Company. The cover was printed by The Lehigh Press, Inc.

Pearson Education Ltd.   Pearson Education Australia Pty. Limited
Pearson Education Singapore Pte. Ltd.   Pearson Education North Asia Ltd.
Pearson Education Canada, Ltd.   Pearson Educación de Mexico, S. A. de C.V.
Pearson Education—Japan   Pearson Education Malaysia Pte. Ltd.

10 9 8 7 6 5 4 3 2 1

ISBN: 0–13–048834–8

This book is dedicated to Hannah, Susan, Elena, and, of course, my Jim.

Preface

Because of mandated standards and high-stakes assessments for students, teachers, and schools, there is more pressure on English and language arts teachers to know about English grammar than there has been in the recent past. The goal of this textbook is to present teachers-to-be with three ways to look at grammar. We begin by looking at where future teachers need to be at the end of the book and comparing it with where students usually are at the beginning.

The End Point

The first perspective is a **panoramic** one that surveys the issues and concerns relevant to the teaching of grammar. Teachers need to know the following:

- What the individual and societal attitudes and policies toward language and dialects are
- Who the learners are, what they know, and what they need to know
- How grammar instruction has evolved and what is to be taught
- How to incorporate English language and usage instruction into the English or language arts classroom

The ability to teach grammar depends on having at least two bodies of knowledge: knowing how English works as a system and knowing the conventional usage in Standard Written English and Academic English.

The **microscopic** perspective in Section 2 deals with parts of speech and common usage errors related to each part. The **macroscopic** perspective on English grammar in Section 3 incorporates the parts of speech learned in Section 2 into simple, consistent, dynamic, and learnable grammatical patterns and systems. It also presents common sentence-level usage problems. By the end of Section 3, you will feel confident enough to begin teaching grammar and usage in your classroom.

The Starting Point

If that is the ending point, what is your starting point? What do you know right now? When someone says the word *grammar* to you, what do you think of? Former students of mine wrote the following answers to that question:

> When I think of the word "grammar," I think of all of the rules associated with proper English language usage; I don't think of "grammar" in a bad way, but rather in a way that requires a lot of work. (In being judged to be "right" by others.)

When I first hear the word "grammar," I often think about my friends. You see, they always seem to have bad grammar. I'm not saying mine is the greatest, but when I hear people say "they seen me at the store" instead of "I saw them at the store," it drives me nuts.

What comes to my mind when I hear "grammar" is speaking correctly. Knowing the difference between verb, adverb, pronouns, etc. Being confused by them all.

Grammar = the correct use of words, punctuation, and spelling. Also, boring, dry, and analytical in a meaningless way.

When I hear the word "grammar," I think about being in elementary school, rehearsing over and over on pronunciations and spellings of words. Also, practicing the usage of words on worksheets comes to mind.

It is easy to see that for many students, grammar is uncreative, tedious, and meaningless, and learning grammar is a confusing and frustrating process of memorizing rules and doing worksheets. Therefore, this book has three simple but very ambitious goals:

- ◆ To persuade students that grammar is a creative, interesting, and meaningful subject
- ◆ To make learning grammar clear and doable
- ◆ To motivate students who are future teachers to teach grammar in a better way

The Learning Process

In order to get from your starting point to your ideal ending point, it is important for you to keep several things in mind while assimilating information from this book:

- ◆ Grammar learning is cumulative; it adds up, detail by detail, until there is a critical mass. When the critical mass is achieved, the details fall into place as a system. It is at this point that you will feel that you have learned something.
- ◆ While grammar knowledge is accumulating, it is easy to get overwhelmed by the details. There are a lot of facts, terms, and abstract concepts to learn, but no one can learn them all at once. Keep your eye on the goal: to integrate the details into a coherent whole.
- ◆ Memorization is a good way to store information in memory so that you can recall and recognize it in language analysis activities. It is impossible to recall and recognize information unless it is stored in memory.
- ◆ Hands-on activities with grammar facilitate the integrative and cumulative process. Get your hands "dirty" with language analysis and cooperative class projects. The more actively you learn, the more knowledge you will transfer from the book to your head, and the better you will apply your knowledge to language in the world. To this end, your instructor may ask you to keep a Language Notebook, a loose-leaf binder in which you note observations about language and do your written assignments.
- ◆ The best way for you to learn grammar is to teach it in your own classroom to your own learners. This book is not comprehensive, but it will give you a sound

basis for teaching grammar, and once you start, you will learn even more. As you work through this book, visualize yourself teaching the topic in your own classroom.

Acknowledgments

I appreciate the helpful comments from reviewers Peggy Albers, Georgia State University; Harold Nelson, Minot State University; Larry Andrews, University of Nebraska, Lincoln; Anna Bolling, California State University, Stanislaus; Margaret R. Moulton, University of Nevada, Las Vegas (Emeritus); Lynn Gordon, Washington State University; Helen R. Abadiano, Central Connecticut State University; Debra P. Price, Sam Houston State University; Wanda G. Breedlove, University of South Carolina; Roberta Murata, University of Nevada, Las Vegas; Carol P. Jamison, Armstrong Atlantic State University; Susan M. Blair-Larsen, The College of New Jersey; and Kyoko Sato, California State University, Northridge and editors Linda Montgomery, Dawne Brooks, Mary Irvin, and Amy Gehl. Any errors are, of course, mine. Many patient linguistics students have helped me and encouraged me throughout the years, and I thank them all. I am also grateful to my colleagues at California State University, Fresno, for the productive working environment we enjoy.

Brief Contents

Contents

Chapter 3   Grammatical Approaches and Curriculum   41

Chapter 4   Creating the Multidimensional Classroom   60

SECTION 2: The Microscopic Perspective 85

Chapter 5   Word Categories and Words   86

Chapter 6   Words and Word Formation Procedures   105

Chapter 7   Nouns and Noun Phrases   120

Chapter 8   Determiners and Pronouns   138

SECTION 3: THE MACROSCOPIC PERSPECTIVE   207

Chapter 12   Declarative Sentences   209

Chapter 13   Transformed Sentences   231

Note: Every effort has been made to provide accurate and current Internet information in this book. However, the Internet and information posted on it are constantly changing, and it is inevitable that some of the Internet addresses listed in this textbook will change.

SECTION 1

The Panoramic Perspective

Grammar is an object of study in academia, but it does not exist in a social vacuum. Grammar, like many other aspects of human behavior, stimulates controversy. The English-only movement and the Ebonics debate of the latter part of the 20th century showed that sociopolitical contexts affect our attitudes toward grammar. Everyone, from the most erudite literary scholar to your neighbor down the street, has an opinion about grammar. People judge others by the way they speak or write. Language attitudes form the basis for language policies in communities and schools.

This social and political panorama surrounds the learning and teaching of English grammar. Chapter 1 responds to the following questions: How are teachers to understand the sociopolitical and educational context for grammar instruction? How do teacher attitudes toward the learners language affect successful grammar instruction?

Chapter 2 addresses questions of grammar learning throughout the life span of an individual. Native speakers of a language acquire an unconscious knowledge of grammar that allows them to speak, listen, read, and write informally, but these abilities are not enough for academic tasks in high school and the university. Nonstandard speakers and English language learners face even greater challenges. Learning theory spells out how people learn and use knowledge actively.

Chapter 3 deals with the curricular context for grammar instruction. Teachers must consider the grammatical approach to take and the purpose of instruction, both of which differ for Standard English speakers, speakers of other varieties of English, and speakers of other languages.

Chapter 4 describes effective grammar instruction in a language arts or English classroom. Teachers make grammar instruction meaningful, communicative, and cooperative. They employ effective instructional methodologies and ensure that grammar learning happens by writing and carrying out multidimensional lesson plans.

1

Language Attitudes and Policies

There are thousands of languages in the world, and many of these languages are spoken within the borders of the United States. Each language is composed of a group of dialects. In American English, the typical pronouns in Georgia (*y'all*) are different from those used in Maine (*you*). Older people in rural areas use different phrases (*reckon, fixin' to*) from young people in inner cities. Even the same individual uses different words and grammar in a locker room and in a house of worship. People respond to variation in language in different ways, but variation is normal.

LANGUAGE IDEOLOGIES

An ideology is a complex, semicoherent set of ideas, beliefs, and values that determine the way we think about the world. Our ideas, beliefs, and values surrounding the notion of language variation can be described in terms of two competing ideologies: the **colonial/imperialistic** and the **ecological** (Phillipson, 1992, 1998; Skutnabb-Kangas, 2000). The tension between these two ideologies explains some of the controversies surrounding language issues in the United States today, such as the bilingual education debate or the Official English movement (see Figure 1.1).

The Colonial/Imperialistic Ideology

People who hold the colonial/imperialistic ideology believe that English is "better" than other languages and that Standard English is "better" than other varieties, such as Cajun, Pennsylvania Dutch, or African American English. "Better" may mean more logical, more pure, more comprehensible, more useful, more expressive, or more economically advantageous. They think that because English is the dominant language, everyone should learn it in order to take advantage of the benefits and opportunities of our society. To them, speaking English is a sign of loyalty or patriotism, and the right to speak a different language or dialect is not, and should not be, a basic human right like other human rights (e.g., participation in government, access to education, access to jobs, or freedom to travel).

In this ideology, it is "normal" for people to speak just one language, and therefore minority languages and dialects are superfluous. A bilingual or bidialectal society is a "problem." Advocates of this ideology cite the cost of printing voting materials or

Figure 1.1 *Two language ideologies.*
Source: Pennycook, Phillipson, & Wiley (1998). See also Phillipson (1992), Skutnabb-Kangas (2000).

Colonialism/Imperialism	*Ecology of Language*
People do not have language rights.	People have language rights.
One language is better than others; it should be used exclusively.	Languages are equal in value but may have different social functions.
Monolingualism is the norm; everyone should learn the dominant language.	Multilingualism is the norm for societies and individuals.
Laissez-faire or "survival of the fittest" is the attitude toward minority languages.	Minority languages are protected and maintained.
Multilingualism is a problem.	Multilingualism is a resource.

driver education materials in other languages as a disadvantage. They complain that people do not understand each other at work and that miscommunications occur. They see Canada and India as common examples where multilingualism is divisive. Unfortunately, this ideology caused the near complete extermination of many Native American languages in the United States.

The Ecological Ideology

People who agree with the ecological ideology think that the right to speak one's native language or dialect is a basic human right like the freedom to practice one's religion or the sociopolitical and economic equality of the races and sexes. To be "normal" in the global context is to be multilingual. Therefore, although people can learn the dominant language of their nation, societies should value and maintain their minority languages and dialects.

Even though each language or variety enjoys equal status, it may have different social functions. The Amish continue to speak German among themselves and English with outsiders. Many African Americans speak African American English some of the time while using Standard English in other settings. People may prefer one dialect for newspapers, television, and classroom instruction, but they may consider a second dialect more suitable in the neighborhood church. People may have one standard for academic writing, but they may accept a different standard for informal writing or popular songs. The point is that all dialects and languages are valued for what they offer as a "resource" to a culture. Switzerland, Spain, and Belgium are countries where multilingualism is the norm.

A Continuing Debate

The debate about bilingual education is not a debate between English speakers and non-English speakers. Rather, it is a debate between those who hold largely colonial/imperialistic views (including many minority language speakers themselves) and those who hold mainly ecological views (including many majority language speakers). Opponents of bilingual education see native languages, including their own, as superfluous and believe that to succeed in the United States, one must speak English. They also believe that bilingual education has not succeeded in teaching children English and therefore should be halted.

Proponents of bilingual education feel that children can become fluent in English while maintaining cultural and linguistic ties to their homeland, including the use of their familial language. They accept that not everyone in a society will become perfectly fluent in English. For them, it is okay for people to have varying degrees of fluency in English because it is not necessary to speak English in order to be a loyal and productive citizen. They believe that bilingual education can be more successfully implemented in a society where language diversity is valued and respected.

Language ideologies become educational policy when people vote them in and out of legislation. However, the dichotomy between the two ideologies often raises more questions for the language arts or English teacher than it resolves. How fluent should English learners become? What standards of accuracy in Standard English should be required to graduate from high school? How permissive should a teacher be toward usage errors in the classroom? A more fine-grained approach is a continuum of four language attitudes that people hold toward dialect variation: equality, description, prescription, and prejudice. However, before we can discuss these attitudes, we need to understand what the standard language is.

VARIETY IN THE STANDARD

Although it seems like a contradiction in terms, there are in fact several standard dialects and not just one (Wolfram, Adger, & Christian, 1999, pp. 14–17).

Standard American English

The term for the dialect that has traditionally dominated over others in the United States is Standard American English (SAE). This dialect differs from many other regional and social dialects. SAE does not allow double negatives, which some other varieties allow. SAE has characteristic pronoun use (*themselves*, not *theirselves*) unlike some working-class or rural dialects. SAE has certain forms of the verb *be* (*isn't*, not *ain't*), which cannot be eliminated in sentences such as *He is a big man,* but some nonstandard dialects permit these verbal phenomena.

Historically, a dialect becomes the standard because the most powerful social group in the area speaks it. When it becomes the standard, it is used as the measure against which other dialects are compared. People consider the phrases and grammatical patterns of the other dialects "usage errors" that must be corrected. They insist that K–12 schoolteachers correct children's divergent speech and writing in school. However, the term "Standard American English" will not help educators know what usage to correct, whom to correct, and when to correct. Instead, educators need to think of the following four possible standards.

Standard Spoken English

The acceptable way of speaking that may not follow all grammar rules in the books is called Standard Spoken English (SSE). Because it has some regional dialectical variation from north to south and from east to west, SSE is composed of several **local standards** that people understand everywhere from Florida to Washington. SSE might include words such as *gonna* or *wanna*. Sentence fragments are a normal syntactic structure. Of course, there is no punctuation or capitalization.

Standard Written English

Standard Written English (SWE) is not localized to one region in the United States, and it has different grammatical features from SSE. For example, in SWE all sentences have subjects and predicates. Only subject pronouns can be used (*I*, not *me*) as subjects of sentences. Subjects and predicates must match each other in number agreement. Sentences begin with a capital letter and end with a period. In style, SWE generally allows sentences to end with a preposition. It allows split infinitives, such as *to boldly go*. SWE is commonly used in fiction and news reporting (even in spoken news reporting).

Academic English

Academic English (AE) refers to a more formal style of SWE used both in public academic speaking and in academic writing. AE generally follows most conventional rules of grammar, but it has some other characteristics, such as **passive voice** (*is expected to, is understood as*), **complex noun phrases** (*institutionalized government operations*), and **prepositional phrases** (*in quantitative measurement, against the norm*). It has a particular **register,** or choice of words, that is common in the university setting but rare in other settings (*maximal projection, statistical analysis, syllabus*). To succeed in high school and university work, learners need to master spoken and written AE with some fluency.

Proper English

Many people are familiar with the term Proper English (PE), but in some ways PE is little more than a myth. It is a rigid speech or writing style to which some aspire but extremely few achieve. In PE, every grammatical rule that has come down through the ages must be strictly observed, and any deviations are strictly censured. You must say *an historic occasion.* You must say *it is I.* You must not end a sentence with a preposition. You must not split an infinitive. You must use *among* rather than *between* if you are speaking of a group that has more than two members.

FOUR LANGUAGE ATTITUDES

The attitudes toward dialect diversity range over a continuum, from **language equality** on one extreme, through **description** as practiced by linguists, to **prescription** as many language arts or English teachers must adhere to, and to the opposite extreme

TABLE 1.1

Attitudes Toward Language in Society

	Language Equality	Description	Prescription	Language Prejudice
What is grammar?	Grammar is people's systematic usage in a community.	Grammar is a psychological system of rules, a body of knowledge in a person's mind.	Grammar is a body of public usage rules, a convention that people agree on.	Grammar is a code of proper conduct.
What is the standard?	There is no true standard; it is a cultural myth.	A standard dialect is a variety that has undergone standardization.	The standard is the variety that is acceptable in most public situations.	The standard, PE, is a meterstick against which other varieties are measured.
Is correctness absolute or relative?	There is no standard of correctness; it is a myth.	Correct speech or writing is relative to a speaker's situation.	Correct speech or writing is relative to a speaker's situation.	Correctness is absolute; rules must be followed no matter what the setting.
What or who is the authority for grammar standards?	There are no grammar standards; there is only the usage of the people.	The authority is the knowledge that an "ideal" native speaker has of his or her native language.	The authority for good usage comes from recognized practitioners of the language.	The authority for correctness comes from grammar books, "experts," and dictionaries.

of **language prejudice** as we sometimes see exhibited in letters to the editor or judgmental media commentaries about language (see Table 1.1).

Language Equality

As the most radical form of the ecological ideology, the language equality position holds that different varieties, including all nonstandard varieties, are resources for the individual and the society that enjoys them; thus, they are positive and to be nurtured and encouraged. For example, Oprah Winfrey's speech is always perfectly standard, yet at times she slips into a dialect with a slight African American or southern flavor when she wants to poke fun at someone or show solidarity with a guest or audience member. This is an important resource for her; it is a resource that not everyone has.

From the equality perspective, people have a right to speak the way they want. It is similar to racial, gender, or other types of equality based on human characteristics. If we substitute other human characteristics for the word *dialect(s)* in certain questions (e.g., Is *racial* diversity "normal?" Do the *sexes* have equal status?), we get a sense of the logic that underlies this attitude.

Language Description

Language description is carefully neutral; it is an objective stance adopted by linguists in order to examine languages impartially. This attitude holds that language varieties differ but that they can be described neutrally, with neither a positive nor a negative evaluation. Equality and description may appeal in principle to many English or language arts teachers, but they are ultimately not totally satisfying because society holds teachers accountable for their learners' language usage. Therefore, the teacher's job, to teach SWE and AE, is in conflict with both of these positions.

Language Prescription

This position resolves the conflict for many teachers. *Prescription* is the label for a position that all languages and varieties have merit and can be described without evaluation but that, whether we like it or not, people accept one variety of English in more public situations (e.g., school, the workplace, and writing) than others. This situation exists because of sociohistorical reasons and not because the standard dialect is better. Prescription combines what the linguist knows about language in society with the pragmatic realism of the high school English teacher facing a classroom full of minority dialect speakers.

The prescriptive point of view is based on the belief that dialectical variation is a changeable human characteristic (as opposed to race, gender, ethnicity, sexual orientation, and so on) and therefore that people may choose to adapt their dialects if they can. However, prescriptivism must be carefully distinguished from language prejudice.

Language Prejudice

To judge by critical comments in the media, language prejudice is still acceptable and even laudable at a time when other forms of prejudice have diminished or at least become more covert. In fact, it is not just minority language or dialect speakers who face language prejudice. People who internalize the idea that others speak or write PE perfectly and disparage their own speech or writing because they do not follow all the rules fall victim to prejudice as well.

Language prejudice is toxic because it sometimes masquerades as "standards" but insidiously excludes some portions of our population. It permits and even encourages judgment of the individual or social group whose language or variety differs from the standard. If not overtly racist or classist, it certainly begs the question of privilege because the closer someone's home language or dialect is to that of the school and the workplace, the more advantage he or she has over those who must learn the language. The farther someone's home language or dialect is from the standard, the more remediation he or she requires for academic success.

However, few people hold only one coherent attitude toward variation. Most linguists, for example, combine elements of language equality, description, and prescription. Naive armchair language critics probably combine elements of prejudice and prescription; for example, their attitudes may differ with respect to speech (prescription) or writing (prejudice). In addition, there is an important distinction between

TABLE 1.2 ▬▬▬▬▬▬▬▬▬▬▬▬▬▬▬▬▬▬▬▬▬▬▬▬▬▬▬▬▬▬▬▬▬▬▬▬

Attitudes Toward Language Variation

	Language Equality	Description	Prescriptivism	Language Prejudice
Is variation "normal" and valued?	Yes, variation is normal and valued as a resource for societies and individuals.	It is normal and inevitable.	It is normal and inevitable.	Some variation is "local color," but some should be eradicated by remediation.
What determines a variety's acceptance?	All varieties are equal; therefore, all are acceptable.	Varieties are acceptable if they are appropriate to the situation.	Varieties are acceptable if they are appropriate to the situation.	Varieties are acceptable to the extent that they are close to PE.
Could varieties have the same functions?	Each variety could be used in any setting.	Theoretically, any language can communicate any message.	The standard has all functions; other varieties are more restricted.	PE should be used exclusively by everyone.
Does variation reflect privilege?	In an ideal world, the variety used in a setting reflects the speaker's choice.	Dialect variation reproduces social distinctions.	In the real world, use of the standard is a key to socioeconomic mobility.	Variation is not a question of privilege because everyone can learn PE.

overt and covert attitudes. People may overtly display prescription and yet covertly hold prejudicial beliefs. People may overtly espouse one goal of prejudice (maintenance of a standard for the purposes of clarity) while subconsciously agreeing with another covert goal (maintaining the power status quo) (see Table 1.2).

Teachers' Attitudes Toward Speakers of Dialects

One's attitude toward a language or dialect usually manifests as an attitude toward speakers of that language or dialect. For example, if people believe that everyone can learn PE, they might look down on someone who hasn't succeeded in mastering every grammatical nuance and think that he or she did not try very hard.

On the other hand, if people believe that all dialects are equal, then they realize that the dialect someone happens to speak does not say very much about intelligence, sense of humor, or moral character. Many people have family members whose grammar is nonnative or nonstandard but who are wise, witty, and full of integrity. On the other hand, there are those who speak and write a dialect very close to PE, but the ideas they express so well are faulty, boring, or malicious. In fact, people's language or dialect has more to do with place of origin, socioeconomic class, and education than it does intelligence, creativity, or morality.

TABLE 1.3

Attitudes Toward Speakers of Language Variants[a]

	Equality	Prescription	Prejudice
Do people have dialect rights?	People have the right to speak and write in their native dialect or language. Language is a basic human right.	Yes, but there are social consequences for use of nonstandard.	No, only PE speakers have dialect rights. Others must adapt to the standard.
Is dialect related to intelligence?	It is related to ethnicity, region, education, setting, and socioeconomic class.	No, people can be intelligent no matter how they speak or write.	1. Yes 2. No, but improper usage creates the impression of stupidity or ignorance.
Is dialect related to morality?	It is related to ethnicity, region, education, setting, and socioeconomic class.	No, "bad" grammar does not make someone morally suspect.	1. Yes 2. No, but improper usage creates the impression of slovenliness or lack of character.
Is dialect related to productivity?	It is related to ethnicity, region, education, setting, and socioeconomic class.	No, productive citizens speak in many different ways.	1. Yes 2. No, but improper usage creates the impression of carelessness or disrespect.

[a] The description attitude is omitted because it is neutral with respect to teachers.

This is where attitude becomes very important for the English or language arts teacher. A negative attitude toward the way a learner speaks or writes may unconsciously be part of a negative attitude toward the learner or the learner's background or group. Others, including learners, perceive this negative attitude no matter how much the teacher tries to hide it. In short, if teachers have a negative attitude toward their learners, it cannot help but affect their relationship, their ability to teach, and their learners' motivation (see Table 1.3).

In Andersson and Trudgill (1990), we find a quote that sets out the three attitudes and their repercussions for nonnative or nonstandard speakers of English and their instructors:

Prejudice against lower-class dialects is not dissimilar to racial and sexual prejudice. We believe it is highly undesirable and that it is our job as linguists to work against ignorance about dialect differences and for greater dialect tolerance. Unlike racial and sexual prejudice, however, it is possible to guard oneself against dialect prejudice by changing one's dialect, or by mastering an additional dialect, if one wishes. In an ideal and truly egalitarian and democratic society, it would not be necessary to do this. In our society, however,

many people are under considerable pressure to do so. Teachers are therefore entirely jus-
tified in teaching pupils who do not use Standard English how to write this dialect so that
they can protect themselves against this prejudice and advance socially, educationally, oc-
cupationally and economically if they wish. We do not want children to leave school only
to suffer as cannon fodder in the job market. (pp. 122–123)

Language Policies in Education

People who held the colonialist/imperialistic ideology had an adverse effect on bilingual
education in California when they passed a voter initiative severely limiting it. The public outcry over the proposed use of Ebonics, or African American English, in schools
caused the Oakland School Board to reverse its policy decision allowing Ebonics in the
classroom. It is clear that the ideologies and attitudes affect teachers and learners when
they are converted into policies for the school or classroom. Policies ultimately become
curricula (see Table 1.4). For more information, see the language policy Web site at
www.language.policy.org.

School policies under the language equality position would hypothetically dictate
that language arts or English teachers have very little to do. They would not need to instruct their students on the niceties of usage or style; at most, they would focus on the
clear expression of ideas. At the other extreme, under the language prejudice position,
educational policies would theoretically mandate remediation for almost everyone,
nonnative and native speakers alike, because very few people under the age of 18
speak or write PE these days. The teacher would spend a lot of time doing grammar
drills and correcting compositions with red pens. A more reasonable alternative, prescriptivism, is consistent with SWE and AE as realistic goals instead of PE. In fact, learners study and use nonstandard speech in the classroom to heighten their interest in
language.

TEACHING TO THE STANDARDS AND THE TESTS

The language ideologies and attitudes of legislators and educational policymakers
reach the classroom and the classroom teacher by means of language arts standards
and language arts assessment.

Grade-Level Curriculum Standards

All states set up grade-level language standards that form the basis for curricula in the
schools and the content of textbooks. For example, California has English–Language
Arts Content Standards for kindergarten through grade 12. These standards are the
same for English speakers and for English language learners. To cite the document,

Nearly 25 percent of children in California enter school at various ages with primary
languages other than English. The standards in this document have been designed to
encourage the highest achievement of every student. No student is incapable of

TABLE 1.4

Attitudes Reflected in School Policies[a]

	Equality	Prescription	Prejudice
What is the language goal of the language arts curriculum?	The curriculum should increase language awareness and appreciation for diversity.	The goal is to empower students to gain access to education if they choose.	The goal is to maintain clarity, beauty, and logic of PE (and status of PE speakers).
What is the teacher's role?	Teachers are advocates for equality.	Teach SWE with respect for native dialects and varieties.	The teacher should teach proper usage.
What is the teacher's attitude toward variation in the classroom?	Teachers inform students about variation.	Teachers inform students about variation and encourage bidialectalism.	The teacher tries to eradicate grammar errors.
Should schools allow variation?	Yes.	Yes, it should be allowed for the purposes of learning content or SWE.	No, it is racist; it implies that some cannot learn proper usage; it condemns students to low status.
Can language standards be changed?	Yes, they should be close to the way people use language.	Yes, they should be changed to reflect current usage, if necessary.	No, it is dumbing down and an erosion of culture.
What is the language arts curriculum?	Literacy with no focus on accuracy or style in writing; clarity of expression is the only ideal.	SWE with some remediation for some students with some grammatical features.	Remediation for everyone in mechanics and usage.

[a] The description attitude is omitted, as it generally attempts to be apolitical.

reaching them. The standards must not be altered for English language learners, because doing so would deny these students the opportunity to reach them. Rather, local education authorities must seize this chance to align specialized education programs for English language learners with the standards so that all children in California are working toward the same goal. Administrators must also work very hard to deliver the appropriate support that English language learners will need to meet the standards. (p. vii)

In California, each grade level has specific standards in the same categories, as seen in Box 1.1. Specific grammar standards for various grade levels are shown in Boxes 1.2, 1.3, and 1.4.

Box 1.1   California Standards Categories

Reading
    Word analysis, fluency, systematic vocabulary development
    Reading comprehension
    Literary response and analysis

Writing
    Writing strategies
    Writing applications

Written and oral English language conventions
    Students write and speak with a command of English conventions appropriate to this grade level

Listening and speaking
    Listening and speaking strategies
    Speaking applications

Reprinted, by permission, from the California Department of Education, P.O. Box 271, Sacramento, CA 95812.

Box 1.2   California Grammar Standards for Grade 3 (p. 19)

Sentence structure
1-1   Understand and be able to use complete and correct declarative, interrogative, imperative, and exclamatory sentences in writing and speaking.

Grammar
1-2   Identify subjects and verbs that are in agreement and identify and use pronouns, adjectives, compound words, and articles correctly in writing and speaking.
1-3   Identify and use past, present, and future verb tense properly in writing and speaking.
1-4   Identify and use subjects and verb correctly in speaking and writing simple sentences.

Punctuation
1-5   Punctuate dates, city and state, and titles of books correctly.
1-6   Use commas in dates, locations, and addresses and for items in a series.

Capitalization
1-7   Capitalize geographical names, holidays, historical periods, and special events correctly.

Reprinted, by permission, from the California Department of Education, P.O. Box 271, Sacramento, CA 95812.

Box 1.3   California Grammar Standards for Grade 7

Sentence structure
1-1   Place modifiers properly and use the active voice.

Grammar
1-2   Identify and use infinitives and participles and make clear references be-
       tween pronouns and antecedents.
1-3   Identify all parts of speech and types and structure of sentences.
1-4   Demonstrate the mechanics of writing (e.g., quotation marks, commas at
       end of dependent clauses) and appropriate English usage (e.g., pronoun
       reference).

Punctuation
1-5   Identify hyphens, dashes, brackets, and semicolons and use them correctly.

Capitalization
1-6   Use correct capitalization.

Reprinted, by permission, from the California Department of Education, P.O. Box 271,
Sacramento, CA 95812.

Box 1.4   California Grammar Standards for Grades 9 and 10

Written and Oral English Language Conventions

Students write and speak with a command of Standard English conventions.

Grammar and Mechanics of Writing
1-1   Identify and correctly use clauses (e.g., main and subordinate), phrases
       (e.g., gerund, infinitive, and participial), and mechanics of punctuation
       (e.g., semicolons, colons, ellipses, and hyphens).
1-2   Understand sentence construction (e.g., parallel structure, subordination,
       and proper placement of modifiers) and proper English usage (e.g., con-
       sistency of verb tenses).
1-3   Demonstrate an understanding of proper English usage and control of
       grammar, paragraph and sentence structure, diction, and syntax.

Reprinted, by permission, from the California Department of Education, P.O. Box 271,
Sacramento, CA 95812.

High-Stakes Testing

Testing is "high stakes" if the positive or negative outcome of test has an impact on the
test takers' future opportunities: promotion to the next grade, high school graduation,
college entrance, college graduation, and professional success.

Standardized Testing

In many states, standardized tests begin in the elementary grades to measure how well
learners are achieving the curriculum standards. For example, California uses the

> **Box 1.5   Questions Similar to California High School Exit Exam (CAHSEE) Based on the State's Curriculum Standards**
>
> Choose the answer that is the MOST effective substitute for the underlined part of the sentence. If no substitution is necessary, choose "Leave as is."
>
> 1. Job requirements are <u>stocking shelves, sweeping and mopping the floor, and assisting customers</u>.
>   A. stocking shelves, sweep and mop the floor, and assisting customers.
>   B. to stock shelves, sweeping and mopping the floor, and assisting customers.
>   C. to assist customers.
>   D. Leave as is.
>
> Choose the answer that is the MOST effective substitute for the underlined portion of the sentence. If no substitution is necessary, choose "Leave as is."
>
> 1. The foothills of the Sierra Nevadas are dry and golden <u>in summer however in winter they are wet and green</u>.
>   A. in summer, however in winter they are wet and green.
>   B. in summer; however, in winter they are wet and green.
>   C. in summer: however in winter, they are wet and green.
>   D. Leave as is.
>
> Choose the word or phrase that best completes the sentence.
>
> 2. The chef baked Joan's birthday cake for her mother and _____.
>   A. I
>   B. she
>   C. her
>   D. he

Stanford Achievement Test (SAT 9), which has objective reading, language, writing, spelling, and listening tests that measure learning of the language arts standards within a language context (SAT 9, 1999).

The SAT 9 has alternative language subtests, one of which tests knowledge of grammar and usage. This subtest is a traditional grade-appropriate test of mechanics (capitalization, punctuation, and usage), sentence structure, content, and organization. For example, at a high school grade level, to succeed in this test, learners need to be able to recognize and correct an error in subject–verb agreement, fragments, run-on sentences, and awkward constructions, such as nonparallel structure, redundancies, and misplaced modifiers.

Massachusetts also has grade-level language standards based on the *Massachusetts Curriculum Frameworks,* which can be found at *www.doe.mass.edu/frameworks.* The achievement of grade-level standards is measured each year with the Massachusetts Comprehensive Assessment System (MCAS, 2002). The English Language Arts

---

Box 1.6   California Exit Exam Results, 2002

Gender
   59% of girls passed.
   50% of boys passed.

Ethnicity
   74% of white students passed.
   60% of Asian students passed.
   46% of African American students passed.
   42% of Hispanic students passed.

Language background
   64% English-only students passed.
   63%–66% English-proficient students passed.
   28% English learner students passed.

Economics
   64% of non-economically disadvantaged students passed.
   40% of economically disadvantaged students passed.

(ELA) exam includes a reading test during which students read a passage and answer grade-appropriate questions about meaning, vocabulary, usage, part of speech identification, font, and punctuation. Its writing test is a two-session response to a writing prompt. Test takers use the first session to write a first draft of a composition; after a short break, they revise their first draft and submit the second draft to be scored.

High School Exit Exams

Many states have high school exit exams with English/language arts as a content area to be tested. For instance, the Massachusetts Comprehensive Assessment System exam described previously is also a high school exit exam because students must achieve a certain score on the 10th-grade test in order to graduate from high school.

California has a specially drafted exit exam (CAHSEE, or California High School Exit Exam [CAHSEE, 2002]) for 10th-grade high school students, including English language learners. If they do not pass, they may take the test up to seven more times, and anyone who does not pass receives "supplemental instruction." The test includes questions on grammar and usage, punctuation, and capitalization. Box 1.5 shows some sample questions based on the test. Some interesting results published for the CAHSEE are shown in Box 1.6.

Beginning in 2004, North Carolina 11th-grade students need to pass a high school exit exam consisting of a single test of 100 questions on four domains, one of which is English, reading, and grammar (NC High School Exit Exam, 2002). English language learners may have special accommodations (including extra time) to complete the test. To assess grammar, punctuation, spelling, and usage, the test has a multiparagraph reading passage with errors to which the six questions following the passage are directed. See Box 1.7 for a sample adaptation.

Box 1.7   Another Format for High School Exit Exam Questions

To assess grammar, punctuation, spelling, and usage, the North Carolina High School Exit Exam has a multiparagraph reading passage with errors, to which the six questions following the passage are directed. Here is an example question of that format.

Ms. Jean Smith, CEO
Denton Enterprises
6770 First St.
Black Mountain, NC 27033

Dear Ms. Smith:

(1) I am a high school student at Jefferson High with a background in art and ceramics. (2) I am very interested in your corporations marketing department because I would like a career in business administration in the arts and crafts area. (3) I would also like to work in sales. (4) And, I have very good people skills. (5) Which is what people tell me all the time. (6) I would like to call you next week to talk to you about setting up a partime internship program that I could do during my senior year. (7) I have a lot of ideas to discuss with you. (8) We can set up a business or sales internship that would be as good for your company as it would be for me.

1. Which correction should be made to sentence 2?
   A. Change your to *you're*

   B. Change corporations to *corporation's*

   C. Change arts to *art*.

   D. Change business administration to *Business Administration*

2. Which of the following is a fragment?
   A. I would also like to work in sales.

   B. And, I have very good people skills.

   C. Which is what people tell me all the time.

   D. I have a lot of ideas to discuss with you.

3. Which correction should be made to sentence 6?
   A. Insert a comma after *next week*.

   B. Change I would to I'*d*.

   C. Capitalize internship program.

   D. Change partime to *part-time*.

University Entrance Exams

The Preliminary Scholastic Aptitude Test/National Merit Scholarship Qualifying Test (PSAT/NMSQT, 2003) has a math, a verbal, and a writing skills section. The 30-minute writing skills section has 39 multiple-choice questions on identifying sentence errors in usage, grammar, or diction (19), restructuring sentences (14), and improving paragraphs (6). Test takers must complete 39 questions in 30 minutes.

Beginning in 2005, the SAT (Scholastic Aptitude Test) will include a 25-minute essay to test organization, expression, and use of conventions of SWE (SAT, 2003). The scoring standards on grammar and usage for the essay range from "consistent facility in use of language, variety of sentence structures, and vocabulary" for the highest score to "usage and syntactical errors so severe that meaning is somewhat obscured" for the lowest score. There will also be a 25-minute multiple-choice test on improving sentences and identifying errors (diction, grammar, sentence construction, subject–verb agreement, proper word usage, and wordiness).

The English Placement Test (EPT) is a test designed to indicate which English course (or remediation) is appropriate for applicants to the California state university system, the largest university system in the United States (EPT, 2003). Students with a low score take remedial English or are encouraged to go to a community college for the first 2 years of higher education.

The EPT test has a composition that is evaluated for sentence and paragraph structure, usage, and grammar. The test also has a composing skills section of 45 multiple-choice questions. Among other things, test takers must read a statement and restructure it and then select which version of a sentence is worded clearly, logically, and correctly. The questions have to do with conversion of active verbs to passive verbs and vice versa, identification of the referent for an antecedent, parallel structure, and subject-verb interruption and agreement.

That is not the end of language arts testing in the California state university system. There is a systemwide upper-division writing requirement that students must pass in order to graduate (e.g., GWAR, 2003). Finally, potential teachers need to pass the CBEST (California Basic Educational Skills Test) in order to become a teacher (CBEST, 2003). This test has two essay questions evaluated on content, organization, coherence, style, word choice and usage, and syntactic complexity and variety.

LOOKING BACKWARD AND FORWARD

Many high-stakes tests have only a few questions on grammar, usage, and punctuation out of their total number of questions. However, in the course of a student's school career, these small percentages add up, and lack of success in written expression in SE or AE has important repercussions for school success, promotion from grade to grade, high school graduation, admission to college, scholarships, graduation from college, and career choice. Ultimately, language ideologies and attitudes affect us all as individuals and as a society; they have a huge impact on learners in the language arts or English classroom.

EXPLORING CHAPTER PERSPECTIVES

◆ *Discussion Questions*

1. Select several of the questions in this chapter's tables and contrast the various responses. What implications do they have for you personally?

2. Which language attitude do you think your language arts or English teachers had as you were growing up? Which attitude, if any, did your parents have? Which attitude do you hold?

3. Have you heard people make prejudicial comments about others' speech or writing? What did they say? Does this attitude appear in one of the tables? Did it refer to an individual's intelligence, morality, or productivity?

4. By what means do you think teachers communicate their positive and negative attitudes even if they do not say anything openly?

5. What overt and covert language policies were in effect at your high school? How did you feel about the standardized testing you went through?

6. How confident do you feel about teaching the items mentioned in the grade-level standards? Did you learn these in school? Discuss the terms you can define and make a list of the terms you cannot define.

◆ *Cooperative Exercise: An Opinion Piece*

A. **Homework.** Read the following guest opinion piece from a newspaper. While you are reading, underline all the insulting and negative words that the author uses and identify all the behaviors that are lumped together in her mind. What effect do these negative expressions have on you as a reader? What is the author saying about the behaviors she mentions? Write your answers in a notebook devoted to language, your Language Notebook.

B. **Pair Work.** Students who have prepared ahead of time form pairs to compare the insults and negative expressions you found. Then discuss the following questions, noting the main ideas from your discussion in your Language Notebook. Unprepared students begin at Step A and proceed to Step B in pairs.

   i. The author of this editorial says, "We have somehow, in the span of 40 years, developed a repugnance for the scholarly traditions that so many of our grandparents and great-grandparents championed and cherished." What were your parents or grandparents doing, watching, and reading 40 years ago? Where do you think this author got the idea that people were more scholarly 40 years ago? Do you think they were?

   ii. Should this person be a language arts teacher? Why or why not?

C. **Class Work.** Each pair presents several main points from their discussion and then reflects on the cooperative experience as a whole class. Use generalizations to report on answers to these questions. How did each pair work together? Did both people participate as much as they wanted to? Did all pairs participate in the class discussion?

HELLO? IS ANYONE OUT THERE SPEAKING PROPER ENGLISH?

by Margaret A. Boardman,
Fresno Bee, December 13, 1997

There is a story by Ray Bradbury about a man who is allowed to go back in time to kill a dinosaur. He is told to stay on a conveyor belt and shoot only the beast described because its death will not bring about any changes in the space-time continuum.

The man does not listen, steps off the belt and, in so doing, kills a butterfly under his boot. When he returns to his own time, things have changed. Signs are spelled with odd characters. More ominously, a demagogue, previously scoffed at, has been elected president.

I often wondered who killed the butterfly that changed America's history. What senseless boot stepped off the conveyor belt of time and mutated us into the land of the Philistines?

Strange Misspellings

The dead butterfly shows up in the strange misspellings that can be found all over town. "Congradulations!" reads a big sign in a large discount store touting a local team.

"We have moved those products to Isle 2A," broadcasts another. Alongside Gilligan's Isle, we presume. In grocery stores we are urged to buy "avacados," "cantalopes" and "tomatos." Shades of Dan Quayle. In addition, educated persons using what used to be fairly commonplace words find that many people have no idea what they're talking about. Recently a friend asked for the "gourmet" section of the grocery and was directed to Budget Gourmet frozen dinners, the only item within the clerk's ken containing that word.

"Have you rode the Ferris wheel?" inquires a lead anchor on the local news. Switching to another station, the very next line we hear from the reporter is, "Symbols are weaved into. . . ." On the radio a newsman tells us of something happening in Doddy County, Fla. It takes a moment to realize he is pronouncing the letters D-a-d-e as if they rhyme with body. King Ungrammatical, Queen Malaprop and Prince Mispronounce rule.

America seems to revel in its dim-witted behavior. Certainly it has raised the moronic to the level of godhead. One need only survey Jim Carey's tasteless, fatuous personifications and 90 percent of television sit-coms to see that this is true. . . .

Smartness has become equated with freakishness. Examine, if you doubt it, those who portray well-read, intellectually curious characters: the effete Crane brothers on "Frasier," Urkel the nerd on "Family Matters," the precociously prissy Gracie on "The Nanny," and the misfit Lisa on "The Simpsons."

We have somehow, in the span of 40 years, developed a repugnance for the scholarly traditions that so many of our grandparents and great-grandparents championed and cherished.

Do you think this "dumbing down" holds no consequences for you? Its effects, in fact, are sweeping. Whether it is in county offices where expensive, tax-funded computers sit idle on every desk because employees are given improper or no training, or in businesses where calls go unanswered because no one understands the new phone system, or in printed publications where grammatical errors abound because a spell-check program is the only thing standing between the reader and illiteracy, we are all affected.

(Continued)

Slovenly Brain Misuse

Worse still, this slovenly misuse of our brains leads to cruelty and stupidity of all sorts: addiction, racism, child abuse, street crime, and demagoguery.

Charles Dickens forewarned us in "A Christmas Carol:"

"This boy is Ignorance. This girl is Want," he has his ghost of Christmas present admonish Ebenezer Scrooge. "Beware them both . . . but most of all beware this boy." It is past time we took Mr. Dickens' warning to heart.

If not so frightening, it would be a fascinating phenomenon. After all, Americans are not stupid. Listening to fans discussing the plot turns and character motivations of their favorite soap operas make it clear that these are minds capable of fairly complex thought patterns.

Dim-Witted America

Yet hoping that such good minds might focus on literature, environmental concepts, political and historical influences, or community problem-solving appears a profitless wish indeed.

◆ *Writing Assignment*

Write a short essay in your Language Notebook in response to one or both of these prompts. Save your essay(s) for later use.

1. Write a letter to the author of this guest editorial expressing whether you agree or disagree with her and why.

2. Look up the language arts standards for your state on the Internet. Do you feel that your education in language arts will allow you to meet those standards? Will your background knowledge in grammar permit you to help your students meet the standards the way you would like to? Why or why not?

Introspection

Look at your essay(s) carefully and proofread for spelling, punctuation, and nonstandard or non-SWE usage.

◆ *Find Out More*

Language Attitudes

Andersson, L., & Trudgill, P. (1990). *Bad language*. Cambridge, MA: Blackwell.

Baron, D. (1994). *Guide to home language repair*. Champaign, IL: National Council of Teachers of English.

Cameron, D. (1995). *Verbal hygiene*. London: Routledge.

Daniels, H. (1983). *Famous last words: The American language crisis reconsidered*. Carbondale: Southern Illinois University Press.

Finegan, E. (1980). *Attitudes toward language usage*. New York: Teachers College Press.

Lippi-Green, R. (1997). *English with an accent: Language ideology and discrimination in the United States*. London: Routledge.

Milroy, J., & Milroy, L. (1991). *Authority in language* (2nd ed.). London: Routledge.

2

Grammar Learners and Learning

From the social and political context for grammar, our panoramic focus shifts to the individual human dimension of grammar. Like other types of human knowledge, grammatical knowledge increases and changes throughout the life span of an individual. Babies and toddlers acquire an unconscious knowledge of the grammar used in conversations in their community. However, when children go to preschool, kindergarten, elementary school, middle school, high school, and the university, the ways they need to express themselves change, and their knowledge expands to meet their different needs. This chapter focuses on who these learners are, how they learn, and what developmental stages they go through in acquiring grammatical knowledge and awareness.

THE VARIETY OF LEARNERS

Grammar learners come from diverse populations with different backgrounds, knowledge, and challenges. Although these learners are diverse, common goals cut across their diversity, and some of their needs intersect. For example, to succeed in middle school and high school, children need Standard Spoken English (SSE) and Standard Written English (SWE). Learners who share the ultimate goal of a university degree need to master Academic English (AE). The different challenges for learners and their teachers come about because each population starts in a different place.

Ingrid and Joel: Native Standard English Speakers

Ingrid and Joel have acquired their local SSE naturally, in their homes, without any direct instruction from their parents or other caregivers. However, in elementary school, they need explicit English instruction in usage to read and write SWE. SSE, for example, allows sentence fragments, but SWE does not. Expressions such as *Bob and me were late* are common in SSE but disallowed in SWE. In middle school and high school, Ingrid and Joel master AE for college. Any notions of grammatical terminology they have come from their foreign language study because their language arts teachers spend very little time talking about language.

Jennifer, Eustace, and Louis: Native Nonstandard Speakers

Jennifer, Eustace, and Louis have acquired a nonstandard variety of spoken English in their home and community. Jennifer speaks African American English, and Eustace speaks Cajun. (It should go without saying that not all minority group members can speak nonstandard varieties of English, and in fact some majority group members may also speak these varieties.) Louis is from a rural area where the normal speech has many nonstandard features, such as double negatives, different past tenses (*he done it, he seen it*), and different pronouns (*hisself,* not *himself*).

Jennifer, Eustace, and Louis understand SSE from their exposure to media, but the gap between their own typical spoken language and the standard usage in school makes speaking, reading, and writing more difficult for them. The needs of Jennifer, Eustace, and Louis must be addressed with sensitivity. If they want to learn the conventions of SAE, they can and will. However, if they do not want to use standard norms, their teachers face an uphill battle. Generally, teachers should offer the SAE expression as an alternative for learners to choose if they so desire. Above all, teachers need to be careful not to make learners such as Jennifer, Eustace, and Louis feel self-conscious or inferior because of the way that they or their family members speak or write.

Lorena and Mai: Nonnative Speakers

Lorena's and Mai's families mainly speak languages other than English in the home, so their schools have classified them as nonnative English speakers. Lorena is a foreign national, a citizen of Argentina, and Mai is a U.S. citizen by birth, the daughter of Hmong immigrants. (Nonnative speakers may also be naturalized U.S. citizens, resident aliens, or illegal immigrants.)

Lorena attends a regular classroom but has a pullout English-as-a-second-language (ESL) class for a few hours a day. An intermediate speaker and listener of English, Lorena reads and writes at a beginning level, so her ESL teacher focuses mainly on reading and writing, including grammar. Like other learners, if Lorena has the motivation to make changes in the way she speaks and writes English, she can learn a lot. However, if she lacks the motivation, it is very difficult for her teacher to influence her usage.

Mai has come up through a bilingual education program in her school district. Her proficiency level in English is very advanced in listening, speaking, reading, and writing. She is very fluent but has a few problems with grammatical accuracy. Mai is a successful bilingual and highly proficient in both of her languages. She has very good **metalinguistic awareness** (Tunmer & Myhill, 1984), meaning that her exposure to and facility with two languages have made her highly aware of language as an object to be noticed. She knows a lot about how language works even though she cannot always put her knowledge into words. Mai has been very successful with AE.

Hector and Li: Generation 1.5

A term for some native-born or immigrant learners who come from a bilingual background is **Generation 1.5,** meant to convey that these learners come after first-generation immigrants but are not quite second-generation bilinguals (like Mai) or

Figure 2.1 *Comparison of diverse learners and their common needs.*

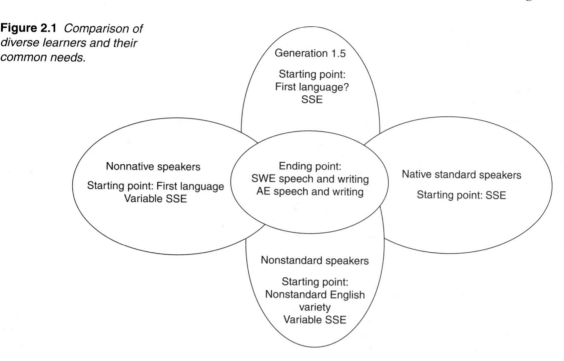

native speakers (Harklau, Siegal, Losey, 1999, pp. 4–5). Although Hector and Li are intelligent and get good grades, they lack metalinguistic awareness. They have never thought about language very much and have few intuitions about how language works. They know how to understand their first language, but they do not speak, read, or write it well. Their knowledge of their first language never developed fully because they stopped using it when they began going to school in English.

Hector and Li speak a local standard variety of English, with some nonnative errors, but Hector has also encountered strong peer influence toward a nonstandard variety of English. As children, they easily acquired basic English communication skills, that is, the common words and sentence patterns that allow them to interact in their schoolyard and neighborhood. However, they have not developed proficiency in academic vocabulary, reading, and writing. They have difficulty with higher-level academic work in English. There is a paradox here. Although English is the language that Li and Hector know best, they do not know it well enough to succeed at the university. And because they appear to speak fluently and well, their challenge with AE is invisible to their teachers (see Figure 2.1).

LANGUAGE ACQUISITION THEORIES

Language belongs to a community, but it is perpetuated in the mind of each individual within the community. How did Ingrid, Joel, Jennifer, Eustace, Louis, Lorena, Mai, Li, and Hector acquire their different ways of speaking? The acquisition of language remains one of the great mysteries of human psychology. Three complementary components lead to successful first- and early second-language acquisition: innate language acquisition principles, natural human interaction, and general learning processes.

Innate Language Acquisition Principles

Many researchers believe that humans have innate predispositions to learn grammar (Chomsky, 1965; Pinker, 1994). The structure of the human brain is universal among all humans, and grammar might be built into the brain as a set of principles about language. That explains why all children learn languages and why all languages have rather similar grammars. For instance, all languages have words for concepts, things, or beings, that is, **noun-like words.** All languages have words that express relationships between entities, or **verb-like words.** Sentences obey other abstract principles that do not seem to be accidental. The principles set children up to learn language quickly because they have expectations about what their native language structures are going to be.

Social Interaction

Humans naturally interact with each other in conversation, songs, speeches, story-telling, and the like. The interaction provides the data (sounds, words, phrases, sentences, meanings, and so on) for the baby linguist to work on (Clark, 2003; Harris, 1992; Ochs, Schlegoff, & Thompson, 1996). Interaction also gives the child direct feedback from being corrected and indirect feedback from being misunderstood. If a child mispronounces a word, uses a wrong word, or garbles his or her syntax, an adult sometimes tells him or her so but more often than not the adult overlooks the error and the child receives information only from the success or failure of his or her communication.

Of course, different cultures have different interactional styles. In some groups, parents interact directly with children; in other groups, children take a more observational stance while still being directly involved in how the adults interact (Ochs, 1988; Schieffelin & Ochs, 1986). In some groups, adults and children interact intensely; in some, adults and children interact much less; and in others, young children interact mainly with older children. In any case, children everywhere develop good language skills unless there is significant neglect and isolation (Clark, 2003, p. 396).

For the purposes of first- and early second-language acquisition, childhood neglect and isolation are often worse than child abuse. Children who are neglected and isolated do not receive enough interaction to promote good language acquisition, so by the time they begin school, they are already behind their nonneglected peers. Children who are abused but not neglected or isolated usually receive sufficient interaction to acquire language, although, of course, the nature of the interaction is usually detrimental to the child's social and personal development (see Figure 2.2).

General Learning Processes

Processes by which humans learn everything from playing tennis to chemical formulas are called *general learning processes.* Learning takes place consciously or unconsciously. In the area of language, the term **learning** usually refers to con-

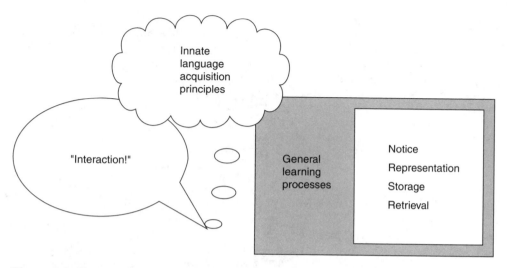

Figure 2.2 *Three complementary language acquisition/learning theories.*

scious language learning of grammar rules, vocabulary, and word meaning, such as what happens in school. The term **acquisition** refers to language learning in any setting that takes place beneath our awareness while interacting with others (Krashen, 2003, p. 1).

Declarative Knowledge

The result of learning is information stored in memory in the form of facts or generalizations that can be put into words, hence the name *declarative*. In cooking, the declarative knowledge is the recipe, the list of ingredients, and the list of steps to follow. Even people who know how to cook (procedural knowledge) can learn a new recipe or cooking method (declarative knowledge) to increase their versatility. In music, the declarative knowledge consists of what the musical notes and symbols mean, the musical scores, and how a musical instrument works. Some people play music by ear, that is, with procedural knowledge, but most accomplished musicians know that reading music symbols and new scores (declarative knowledge) frees them to learn something before hearing it performed.

Procedural Knowledge

Being the result of acquisition, procedural knowledge is often unarticulated information stored in memory that tells us how to do something. We can verbalize some of our procedural knowledge, but much of the time words do not do justice to procedural knowledge. Instead, we learn by doing. For example, in cooking, novice cooks gain procedural knowledge through experience with making a recipe. They learn how to make a dish better and better, but they cannot necessarily put their knowledge into words easily for someone else to reproduce. For others to learn, they need to practice

Figure 2.3 *Declarative and procedural knowledge. Learning to read, write, and type begins with declarative knowledge but becomes procedural as such tasks become automatic.*

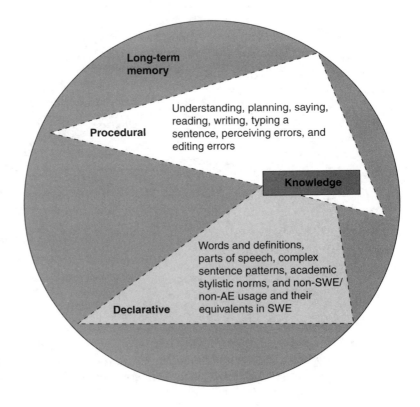

also. The same goes for people learning to play a musical instrument. Instructors can tell them how to play, but for procedural music knowledge, they need to play, practice, rehearse, and perform.

Both procedural and declarative knowledge have benefits: they strengthen and reinforce each other. Successful acquisition and learning over the long term result in a balance of both types of knowledge. If you try to do something with it, declarative knowledge can lead to procedural knowledge. If you try to put it into words, procedural knowledge can lead to declarative knowledge. This is true in the development of grammatical knowledge as well. Declarative knowledge ("all English sentences have both subjects and predicates") contributes to procedural knowledge, that is, the ability to find sentence fragments. Learning how to edit (procedural knowledge) and then reflecting on what editing entails contributes to more fine-grained declarative knowledge of SWE usage (see Figure 2.3).

It seems possible that both learning and acquisition proceed through the same general stages and by the same processes; they differ only in the amount of conscious awareness or attention involved (Cowan, 1995, p. 171). There are many theories of how learning takes place, but everyone seems to agree that certain stages, whether conscious or unconscious, are crucial: notice or attention, encoding or representation, storage in memory, and retrieval from memory.

Notice

The first step is realizing that there is information to acquire or learn. The words *notice* and *realizing* are not quite right, however, because they imply conscious awareness. Notice can take place beneath the level of awareness. It is easy to think of times when we notice something consciously before learning it. We might hear a new word that sparks our fancy, we might concentrate on a new aikido move, or we might carefully watch how an experienced driver changes gears. But certainly humans constantly acquire knowledge, especially procedural knowledge, while unaware of it as well. For instance, you might not be consciously aware of learning someone's name, but it comes out of your mouth later. You might not be aware of learning an advertising jingle, but it sticks in your mind. In fact, it is tempting to think that we gain most of our knowledge about language below the level of our conscious attention, as procedural knowledge, and that is why we do not necessarily know what we know.

Representation

Once we notice the information, we need to represent it in our minds. Procedural representations are probably not represented or encoded in words. They may be memories of motor commands or memories of doing something. Declarative representations are more verbal. For example, when we notice a new word that someone says, we form an auditory image of the word, that is, an image of the sound of a new word. When we first see a new word in print, we form a visual image of the word that encodes the appearance of the word. This is one reason why grammar presentation is crucial: using a graphic organizer, having multiple exposures, and putting information into your own words are good ways to improve representation.

Storage

Next, we store the representation in short- or long-term memory. If you form a mental image of a phone number, punch the numbers, and forget them, you have stored the image in short-term memory. If you read a new word and look it up in the dictionary but cannot remember it later, you stored the representation of the meaning in short-term memory. For acquisition or learning, information must be stored in long-term memory, often through multiple exposures, study, rehearsal, and reflection, to comprehend fully the information.

Retrieval

You need to recall the information stored in long-term memory. Maybe you have studied something for a test so that you feel you know it well, but during the test you are unable to retrieve the memory. If you go on to other parts of the test, some connected information you come across may trigger the memory. Maybe you have had the experience of forgetting someone's name, even someone you know quite well. The name hovers on the tip of your tongue. One way that people retrieve a name is to go through letters of the alphabet as a memory shortcut technique. A sound from the alphabet may remind you of the first sound of the name and therefore the whole sound of the name (see Figure 2.4).

Figure 2.4 *General learning/ acquisition stages.*

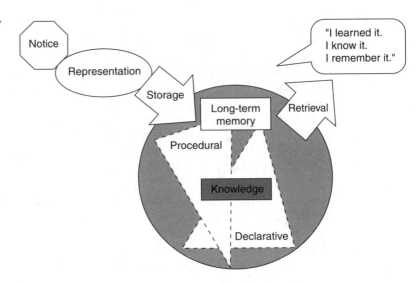

STAGES OF GRAMMAR LEARNING

Language learning goes on throughout our lives if we continue to have new experiences. We learn new words and expressions, such as *language ecology* or *prescriptivism*. Human resource professionals coach us in new and more sophisticated conversational strategies, such as conflict resolution or optimal sales routines. Although new words and conversational strategies start out as declarative knowledge, the more we use them, the more automatic and procedural they get. This is why the older we get, the more versatility we have in speaking and writing. Adults sometimes have the impression that children and teenagers have limited vocabulary or speak poorly. Language acquisition/learning is developmental, and teens need more time and experience for their language repertory to mature.

The Earliest Years

Babies acquire language procedurally, without understanding anything about it consciously. The innate language learning principles and the interaction with their environment allow babies to acquire a procedural knowledge of grammar quickly. If they are in a talkative home or day care environment and if their innate linguistic development is on schedule, children advance quickly in vocabulary and mastery of complex sentence patterns. The language that some SSE-speaking children use at home is different from the language of school. In addition, children who come from nonstandard dialect or other language backgrounds or children who have suffered significant neglect and isolation also find the gap between their home speech and the school language very large. Their procedural knowledge of grammar does not match that of the school, so it might take them some time to acquire the language that other children are already accustomed to. This puts some children at a distinct disadvantage from the start (Heath, 1986).

Many psycholinguists believe that innate language learning abilities operate only in childhood and no longer function as well after puberty (Clark, 2003, p. 392). If this is so, then the best time for developing excellent procedural knowledge of grammar is while children are in preschool and in kindergarten, through grade 8. Teachers can help by providing a rich language environment consisting of many types of literature and language-enhancing activities involving vocabulary and sentence patterns. The best time for children to become bidialectal or bilingual is in childhood, with a rich language environment in both dialects and languages. After puberty, acquiring procedural knowledge of grammar may be more complicated, hence the challenges faced by those who want to acquire a second language in adulthood.

Thus, children's early preschool, kindergarten, and elementary school experiences should be linguistically challenging and broad in scope to nurture procedural syntactic development. For example, Barnitz, Gipe, and Richards (1999) found that regular early exposure to children's literature enhanced syntactic knowledge. Barnitz (1997, 1998) argued for the use of authentic literary texts and a moderate amount of contextualized exercises with **sentence manipulations.**

Sentence manipulations are verbal or written practice exercises in which teachers model combining two short sentences into one more complex sentence with more sophisticated grammar. The complex sentences might have a conjunction, an adjective, or a relative pronoun, although teachers avoid these terms in the early grades and merely model the behavior. After sufficient modeling, learners begin to manipulate the sentences:

> The girl ate a bagel.
> The girl drank a glass of juice.
> Conjunction with *and* →
> *The girl ate a bagel and drank a glass of juice.*

> The girl ate a bagel
> The bagel was stale.
> Modification with an adjective →
> *The girl ate a stale bagel.*

> The girl ate a bagel.
> The girl was my best friend.
> Modification with a relative pronoun *who* →
> *The girl who was my best friend ate a bagel.*

Blackmore, Pratt, and Dewsbury (1995) suggested that the use of props to provide contextual support increased children's scores on a grammaticality judgment test. It makes sense to think that hands-on activities where language is paired with doing things probably enhances vocabulary and procedural grammar acquisition. In fact, this idea forms the basis for an ESL methodology called **Total Physical Response,** where learners learn language in the context of physical movements (Allen, 1995; Seeley, 1998).

The Development of Metalinguistic Awareness

However, declarative knowledge of grammar, or metalinguistic awareness, does not develop automatically. Metalinguistic awareness refers to the ability to stand outside of language and look at it as an entity separate from self, as an object of interest in its own right, and then to use language to think or talk about language. Children begin to acquire metalinguistic awareness through interaction *about* language.

Very young children know that a sentence such as *A boy ate a bagel* is a good sentence but that *Bagel a ate boy a* is not a good sentence in English. They know that *Jack and Jill went up the hill* means the same as *Up the hill Jack and Jill went.* They can repair syntactic mistakes that they make in speech, but they cannot articulate what they are doing and why (Gombert, 1992). In the earliest years, they may not be able to talk about these ideas on their own, but if they see someone model the behavior first, they can accept or reject sentences in grammaticality judgment tasks, match pictures with sentences, and make other comments that show that they are acquiring declarative knowledge of English grammar.

Nonnative and Generation 1.5 learners' proficiency with their first language often determines the amount of metalinguistic awareness they have in general. Bilingual people, such as Mai, whose natural knowledge of their first language is well developed and who have added a second language to their first language often have high metalinguistic awareness. Bilingual people, such as Hector and Li, whose first language is not well developed and has been largely replaced by the second language (which in turn may also lack development) may not have high metalinguistic awareness. Although this is not the learners' fault, it can affect their ability to succeed at advanced verbal academic tasks (see Figure 2.5).

Syntactic awareness, a subtype of metalinguistic awareness, is the knowledge of how words combine into phrases and sentences in a language. The development of syntactic awareness is dependent on the environment of the child. Some adults or older siblings read books and nursery rhymes, tell jokes and play word games, or point out interesting things about language in their conversations. Some parents comment on the sentences in the stories they read or, without obsessing, encourage children to speak in complete sentences sometimes. They nudge their children to express an idea more clearly. The more language explicit the environment is, the more explicitly declarative the child's knowledge of grammar is and therefore the easier he or she will find learning to read and write in school because it is usually at that point where the need to talk about language first arises.

Grammar and Early Literacy

The child's procedural and declarative knowledge facilitates very early the acquisition of literacy because knowledge of vocabulary, simple sentence patterns, meanings, and knowledge of the world transfer from listening and speaking to reading and writing.

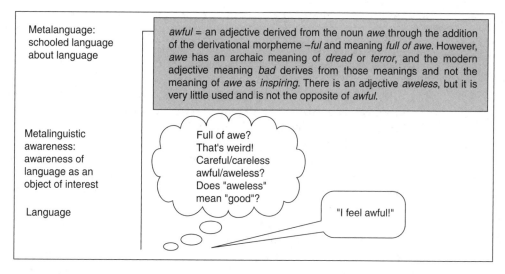

Figure 2.5 *Difference between language, metalinguistic awareness, and metalanguage.*

The transfer occurs because the words and sentences in early reading and writing correspond to speech patterns. For example, a preschool or kindergarten teacher often begins reading and writing instruction by having children talk about a picture they drew. The teacher writes the words and sentences below the picture so that the children begin to associate written words with the meanings they have drawn. Often the words and phrases are written down exactly as dictated, whether they form complete sentences or not. This method, an excellent one that can be used with older preliterate learners as well, is called the **Language Experience Approach** (Bertrand & Stice, 2002, p. 222). In any case, all prereading and prewriting activities work best if they approximate speech so that procedural grammar provides a bridge from listening and speech to reading and writing.

Researchers find that syntactic awareness has an impact on beginning reading stages (Tunmer et al., 1988) as well as later reading stages. For example, Nation and Snowling (2000) found that children who had difficulty comprehending what they read had poorer syntactic awareness than the good comprehenders, even though they were matched in age, decoding ability, and nonverbal ability. The syntactic complexity of the sentences they read affected their ability to read. Bowey (1986) found that fourth- and fifth-grade readers differed in their syntactic awareness as shown by their performance on an oral language task. Their performance correlated with their reading comprehension ability.

However, there are those who believe that syntactic awareness does not influence reading performance because the evidence, though persuasive, is not always conclusive. Part of the problem is that it is nearly impossible to separate procedural and declarative grammatical knowledge from each other. Children use declarative knowledge to learn and talk about reading, but they probably also rely on procedural knowledge of grammar to read. Someone might be an adequate reader using procedural knowledge of grammar but not have good syntactic awareness. For example, Gaux and Gombert (1999) found among sixth graders that the poor comprehenders of their reading had a syntactic deficit when compared to the good and average comprehenders. In addition, the average comprehenders performed worse than the good comprehenders in tasks assessing declarative knowledge of syntax but not in those assessing procedural knowledge of grammar.

If these results are valid, procedural knowledge of grammar is important for reading comprehension, and poor readers may have deficits in their procedural knowledge. Average readers have good procedural knowledge of grammar, and good readers seem to have good declarative knowledge of grammar, although it is unclear exactly what the causal relationship is between declarative grammar and good reading. The question is, Does declarative knowledge of grammar aid in reading, or does being a good reader aid in acquiring declarative knowledge of grammar? The direction of influence probably goes both ways. Possibly there is a third factor, such as language *aptitude,* that leads to metalinguistic awareness and to good reading as well.

The situation is probably similar in learning to write, although there is not as much research. Once someone knows the basics of writing, procedural knowledge of grammar allows him or her to write personal letters or lists because they are much like speech written down. However, many writing instructors probably agree that having some syntactic awareness assists in more advanced writing, even that done in the early grades, because writers need to be able to understand and think and talk about words, phrases, sentences, and paragraphs in order to learn to write better. They can do this better if they know some grammar terminology. They also need to examine their own writing for usage errors in SWE or AE and correct them.

Schooled Grammar

Schooled grammar is the declarative knowledge about English that children learn in school for their academic tasks. Schooled grammar is terminology (e.g., noun, verb, subject, and predicate) and usage rules (e.g., sentences need to have subjects and predicates, and verbs need to agree with their subjects). The terminology (also called **metalanguage,** or "language about language") and rules help a learner talk about grammar in the same way that knowing cooking terms helps someone cook or knowing how to read music helps someone play a new song. Usage rules help a writer produce academic writing. The language arts standards for each state and grade level dictate what the schooled grammar will be.

Noguchi (1991) and Weaver (1996) point out that schooled grammar instruction does not always improve writing ability. One problem with any study of this issue is that there are many variables in grammar instruction that make it hard to get a clear trend in results. For instance, if learners do not remember the usage rules they have been "taught," then one or more of these is true: learners did not notice, they did not represent the information, they did not store the information in long-term memory, or they cannot retrieve the information when they need it. Some other variables include number, age and motivation of learners, declarative knowledge and teaching ability of teachers, clarity of explanations, method of instruction, and amount and type of practice.

At any rate, because of the mixed research results, teachers generally form two camps: those who believe that knowledge of grammar metalanguage and rules improves writing and those who do not. The former have experienced success with grammar instruction and writing, but the latter have not seen any results. Those teachers who are successful are probably doing something else very well. Metalanguage and usage rules do not help writers unless they also acquire another type of procedural knowledge: how to edit their own writing. Editing involves the ability of writers to notice usage errors in their own writing and retrieve the correct form or apply rules to make a correction. If grammar instruction is not effective in improving writing, it may be because teachers and learners fail to learn how to apply it.

Academic Literacy

Academic literacy refers to the ability to perform the complex reading and writing tasks that learners need to do in later elementary school, secondary school, and the university. Although early reading and writing activities are similar to speech written down, certainly by third or fourth grade the demands of reading and the standards of writing differ quite a bit from ordinary speech. With each promotion to a higher grade, the reading and writing tasks become more complex until graduation from a university and even beyond for some people. Because of the characteristics of academic reading and writing, native, nonstandard, nonnative, and Generation 1.5 learners all face challenges.

Biber (1988) used a large database of spoken and written discourse to pinpoint how adult speech and writing differs in different formal and informal **registers** of language. Registers are varieties of language defined by the expressions and grammar used in certain domains of a culture. The registers he studied are telephone conversations, spontaneous speeches, personal letters, fiction, official documents, and academic prose. He found that speech and writing differed along a number of dimensions adapted here:

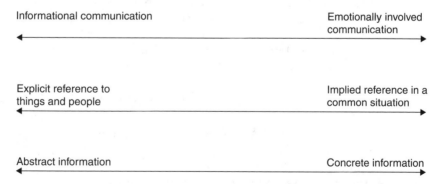

Informational communication ← → Emotionally involved communication

Explicit reference to things and people ← → Implied reference in a common situation

Abstract information ← → Concrete information

Each dimension correlated with different vocabulary and syntactic choices that the speakers/writers made. For example, more emotionally involved communication (phone conversations) had contractions, pronouns such as *you* and *it,* questions, few nouns, and few long words. On the other hand, communication designed to communicate information (official documents) had many nouns and long words and few questions and pronouns.

Communication with explicit reference to times, places, things, and individuals (official documents) had many complex multisyllabic nouns (*development* or *construction*) and few words such as *tomorrow, here,* and *now* (i.e., **adverbs**). Communication with implied reference to times, places, things, and individuals (phone conversations) had pronouns such as *he* or *she;* adverbs such as *today, tomorrow, now, here,* and *there;* and few multisyllabic nouns.

Abstract communication is about abstract subject matter, that is, concepts and ideas that have reality in people's minds. Abstract prose has many passive sentences, such as *It was observed that . . .* or *The findings were shown to . . . ,* because passive sentences do not state who did the observing or who interpreted the findings. Concrete communication is about things going on in the world at the present time. Telephone conversations have active sentences *(He goes . . . She walks . . .).*

In general, there is a continuum formed by the three dimensions:

Academic prose	Editorials	Personal letters	
Official documents	Prepared speeches	Spontaneous speeches	Face-to-face conversations
Professional letters	Simple fiction	Interviews	Telephone conversations

$\longleftarrow$ ────────────────────────────── $\longrightarrow$

Informational	Emotionally involved
Explicit reference	Implied reference
Abstract	Concrete

Learners acquire emotionally involved, concrete, implied referential language at home; in elementary grades, they learn the language of personal letters, spontaneous speeches, and interviews. As they go on in school, they learn to read and write SWE in the form of editorials, fiction, and prepared speeches. However, learners eventually need exposure to informational, abstract, explicitly referential AE, the language of academic prose, official documents, and professional letters.

Success in high school and later in college demands advanced academic listening, speaking, reading, and writing skills. Learners need to understand complex academic lectures and give coherent and appropriate public speeches in the classroom. They need to read and especially write academic essays, papers, and lab reports in their new dialect, AE, with few usage errors (see Figures 2.6 and 2.7).

LOOKING BACKWARD AND FORWARD

The human faces of English grammar are learners such as Ingrid, Joel, Jennifer, Eustace, Louis, Lorena, Mai, Li, and Hector in the K–12 classroom. Because of innate predispositions for language, the natural interaction they are involved in, and general learning processes, children are natural language learners. In school and outside of school, their language develops procedurally and declaratively throughout their childhood and, indeed, throughout their life span. However, it is in school, in the language arts or English classroom, where learners' advanced procedural and declarative knowledge of grammar must develop. To teach them, teachers need to have a clear idea of the language needs of their learners, beginning with the lexical and syntactic characteristics of AE. However, a couple of questions are raised at this point:

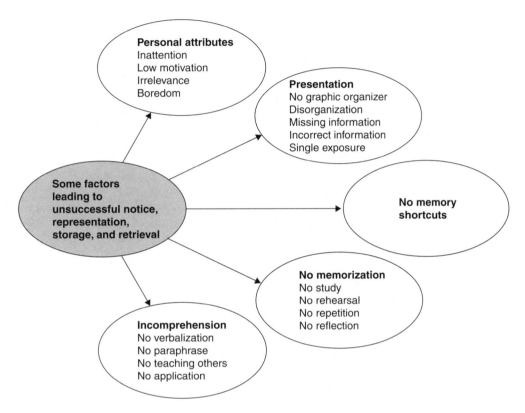

Figure 2.6 *Some factors leading to unsuccessful learning.*

If children are natural language learners, why are many so unsuccessful at learning SWE usage norms?

How can teachers best meet the needs of their learners?

EXPLORING CHAPTER PERSPECTIVES

◆ *Discussion Questions*

1. What type of learner do you identify with most closely? Describe your language background. What similarities and differences are there with the example learners in this chapter?

2. Do you remember becoming aware of language as a child through riddles, jokes, stories, games, or rhymes? For example, the ability to speak pig Latin (*Ig-pay Atin-lay*) relies on knowledge of English word structure—what is it? In order to initiate someone to the game, you needed to make this knowledge explicit. How did you do that? What other examples of word play indicate metalinguistic awareness?

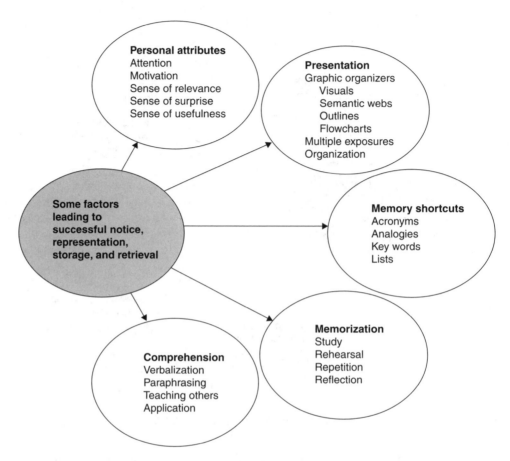

Figure 2.7 *Some factors leading to successful learning.*

3. Why would bilingual people who are highly proficient in both languages have good metalinguistic awareness? Why would it develop more fully in a bilingual setting?

4. Have you observed young children learning their first or second language? What can you say about their acquisition of grammar?

5. Do you speak or write AE well? If so, where did you learn it? If not, why not?

6. How do you go through the process of editing your academic writing? Do you ever consult a grammar book? Does your reading affect your writing positively? How?

◆ *Cooperative Exercise: Registers*

Biber (1988) cites Texts 1 to 5 as different registers of English. Some are examples from British English, but aside from the occasional spelling or different word, they are identical to American English. Can you tell which are British and which are American as you read them? What were the clues?

Then proceed to Part A.

1. (p. 130)

   B: anyway

      how did you get on *[pause]* skiing

   A: skiing *[pause]*

      skiing was good fun actually

   B: oh

   A: mm *[pause]*

      I I I enjoyed actually skiing and it was *[pause]*

      really quite funny

      being with *[short pause]* thrust together with

      sort of sixteen other people for a fortnight and *[pause]*

      and

   B: oh

      I'd love a fortnight's holiday where you can relax

   A: well it's it's fantastic

      because it's *[pause]*

      so completely different from anything

      that you *[short pause]* you know

      would ever get yourself to do otherwise

   B: yes

      yes

   A: I think

   B: yes

2. (p. 132) How you doing? I'm here at work waiting for my appointment to get here, it's Friday. Thank goodness, but I still have tomorrow, but this week has flown by, I guess because I've been staying busy, getting ready for Christmas and stuff. Have you done your Christmas shopping yet? I'm pretty proud of myself. I'm almost finished. Me and L went shopping at Sharpstown last Monday and I got a lot done, I just have a few little things to get. Thanks for the poster, I loved it, I hung it in my room last night, sometimes I feel like that's about right.

3. (p. 133) We felt that we needed a financial base on which to work, but the goals which we indicated for I are also included in the goals of L, including of course the occasional papers. . . . In the meantime, we are going ahead with plans to establish three language resource institutes resource centers in ESL, which will have three functions: (1) to be a resource center with a reading library of ESL materials and directors who are competent ESL professionals, (2) as a funnel for consultant activities both outward using local expertise needed in other areas

where we have L and inward bringing into the area needed expertise and including workshops, mini-conferences, and seminars, and finally (3) to offer educational programs.

4. (p. 131) The restoration of a further volume of the collection of Hunterian drawings has been completed at the British Museum. A selection from the collection of Pharmacy Jars was lent to The Times Book Shop in connexion with their Royal Society Tercentenary Exhibition. Two coloured engravings of the College in the early nineteenth century were presented to the Royal Australasian College of Surgeons by the President when he visited Melbourne.

5. (p. 137) It was difficult to tell whether he was unable to speak or whether he could see no point. Sometimes he started to say things in a hoarse whisper, looking ahead as if there might be people to either side who would stop him, but never got further than one or two words. Most of the time he lay on his back with his eyes open. After three days there seemed nothing Martin could do and he went to the office again.

They had given the speech to Burridge. They would be able, later, when time had become a little confused, to explain his failure by his father's illness, if they wanted to.

A. **Homework.**

i. Review the discussion in the chapter and draw these continua in your Language Notebook. Place each text (1–5) above along these continua in a subjective manner:

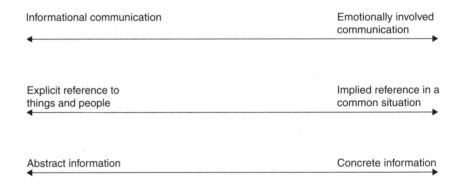

ii. For each text (1–5), count the number of instances of each syntactic factor in the following chart and enter it in the appropriate column on this chart, relying somewhat on your intuition about what each syntactic factor is. Write the number of instances under the number of the example.

Factor	Text	1	2	3	4	5
Contractions						
Pronouns						
Questions						
Verbs						
Words of two or more syllables						
Complex noun phrases (nouns that have many modifiers)						
Passive verb forms (be + past participle)						

B. **Group Work.** (Prepared students)

   i. In groups of five, discuss your answers. If there are any discrepancies, try to resolve them. Unprepared students should begin with Step A as individuals and then proceed to Step B in a group.

   ii. For each of the previous example texts, fill in the appropriate column on this chart with the average of the numbers found by individual students after discounting the highest and the lowest numbers. When your group is finished, hand in each individual student's chart to your teacher.

Example	1	2	3	4	5
Contractions					
Pronouns					
Questions					
Verbs					
Words of two or more syllables					
Complex noun phrases					
Passive verb forms					

iii. Reflect on the functioning of each cooperative group. You might answer these questions:

Did you complete your task within the time? If yes, what helped you do so? If no, what can you do better next time to complete the task?

Did everyone participate actively in the group work? If yes, to what do you attribute the active participation? If no, what can you do next time to make sure that everyone participates?

C. **Class Work.** Fill out the chart as a class by averaging the numbers from each group for each cell. Then, based on these averages, try to identify each example as academic prose, general fiction, professional letter, telephone conversation, or private letter. Place each example where it should be on the continua based on the responses. Would you revise your own or your group's subjective estimate?

◆ *Writing Assignment*

Write a short essay in your Language Notebook in response to one or both of these questions. Save your essay(s) for later use.

1. If these were language examples that nonnative speakers needed to read and understand, what would be easy and what would be difficult about each sample?

2. Do a search on a nonstandard variation of English (e.g., African American English or Ebonics, Cajun, Hawaiian, Creole or others). Summarize and evaluate the Web sites you find. What information did you find out about the speakers and the variant forms?

Introspection

Look at your essay(s) carefully and proofread for spelling, punctuation, and nonstandard or non-SWE usage.

◆ *Find Out More*

Aitchison, J. (1987). *Words in the mind: An introduction to the mental lexicon*. Oxford, UK: Basil Blackwell.

Baron, N. (1990). *Pigeon-birds and rhyming words: The role of parents in language learning*. Englewood Cliffs, NJ: Prentice Hall Regents.

Clark, E. (2003). *First language acquisition*. Cambridge, UK: Cambridge University Press.

Harklau, L., Siegal, M. and K. Losey (1999). "Linguistically Diverse Students and College Writing: What is Equitable and Appropriate?" in Harklau, L., Losey, K. and M. Siegal (1999). *Generation 1.5 Meets College Composition: Issues in the Teaching of Writing to U.S.-Educated Learners of ESL*. Mahwah, NJ: Lawrence Erlbaum Associates.

Peregoy, S., & Boyle, O. (1993). *Reading, writing, and learning ESL: A resource book for K–8 teachers*. White Plains, NY: Longman.

Wolfram, W.A., & Christian, D. (1999). *Dialects in schools and communities*. Mahwah, NJ: Lawrence Erlbaum Associates.

3

Grammatical Approaches and Curriculum

Our panoramic lens now focuses on another area surrounding the grammar teacher: curricular issues within the school setting. People in our society have the attitude that children should learn Standard Spoken English (SSE) and Standard Written English (SWE) in school and they hold their teachers accountable for their success.

The learning goals include both declarative and procedural knowledge of Standard English (SE). School districts and teachers develop curricula to meet the goals, trying to select the appropriate approach and materials. A survey of an on-line bookstore reveals that there are over 500 English grammar books on the market. How can teachers and school administrators choose the best textbooks to meet their learners' needs? They need to consider these issues:

What grammatical theory, if any, is the basis for the textbook?

What type of classroom is it appropriate for? A class in the structure of English, syntax, English as a second language, elementary language arts, or high school English?

What is the purpose for the textbook? Is it about describing language, imparting schooled grammatical information, increasing metalinguistic awareness, teaching standard academic usage, or correcting nonstandard usage errors?

What type of learner is it designed for? Are the learners SE speakers, nonstandard speakers, English learners, or Generation 1.5? Is the classroom composed of a variety of these types of learners?

How will the book fit into a language arts curriculum?

What "errors" does the book address, and how are they addressed?

APPROACHES TO GRAMMAR

The Descriptive Approach

Linguists look at the facts of a language objectively, and a grammar book written from this perspective is called a *descriptive grammar,* a work that lists the various words and structures of the language and shows their interrelationships (Greenbaum &

TABLE 3.1

Approaches to Grammar

Approaches	What Is Language?	What Is Grammar?	What Are Errors?
Descriptive			
Generative	The knowledge that an ideal native speaker/hearer has	A set of rules that generate a set of sentences in the language	Sentences not generated by the rules or slips of the tongue
Functional	The spoken/written discourse used in various natural settings	Recurrent syntactic patterns that achieve certain functions in discourse	Unlikely usages or slips of the tongue
Lexical	A set of meaningful chunks that, when combined, form continuous coherent text	Syntactic patterns that emerge from frequent collocations	Nonconventional or unlikely usages or slips of the tongue
Prescriptive	A normed system of communication that belongs to a culture	A conventional code of behavior to follow	Nonstandard usages or incorrect tranfers from another language
Pedagogical	Forms and functions used in a sociocultural setting	Second-language knowledge that serves four modes: listening, speaking, reading, and writing	A necessary part of the learning process as learners move from a first to a second language

Quirk, 1990). Descriptive grammars are specifically designed to increase the reader's schooled declarative knowledge of grammar (see Table 3.1).

For instance, descriptive grammarians would say that complete sentences in SWE have two constituent parts—a subject and a predicate—and that when there is no obvious subject in a sentence (i.e., no real doer of the action), English structure requires a **subject placeholder,** usually either *it* or *there.* For example, in the sentence *there are too many people in the room,* there is no real subject of the predicate *are too many people in the room,* so *there* appears as a placeholder. Other languages, such as Spanish, allow sentences without overt subjects.

Descriptive grammars differ in the perspectives they take on language. They take a formal rule-based perspective (generative), a perspective based on the way people use language to accomplish their purposes (functional), or a perspective that derives from words and the ways they most commonly combine with each other (lexicalist). For some grammarians, the three perspectives compete with each other, but to me, they complement one another. The different perspectives allow linguists to make different points about language and the way people use language.

Generative theory holds that a grammar is a set of rules or generalizations that the ideal native speakers/hearers of the language know in order to speak or understand their language (Radford, 1990). The term *generative* is used because of the idea that the rules generate or produce well-formed sentences (Newmeyer, 1998, pp. 9–13). An analogy can be made to a computer program that puts words together in a certain order to produce or generate a set of sentences. A generative grammar does more than merely describe the interactions of words and structures; it explains why a certain structure is the way it is. The explanations are often psychological, and thus generative grammars attempt to represent human knowledge.

Data for an explicit generative grammar often come from the linguist's own intuitions about language or from the grammaticality judgments of native speakers. For instance, linguists ask native speakers whether certain sentences are acceptable: *there are too many people in this room* versus *are too many people in this room.* (Ungrammatical sentences are marked with an asterisk. Some sentences are questionably acceptable and marked with a question mark.) Grammaticality judgments tap into the procedural but idealized knowledge that people have about their language even though people may not be able to explain why one sentence is good and another is bad.

Generativists would say that English belongs to a class of languages in the world that must have overt subjects. Therefore, the grammar of English could not generate *are too many people in the room.* Instead, the rules generate sentences with a subject placeholder, *there.* Errors are those sentences that could not be generated by the rules for SSE or SWE or are slips of the tongue, when people make mistakes accidentally.

Functional theory holds that grammar stems from the functions that speakers/ writers have to perform in language (Newmeyer, 1998, pp. 13–16). Grammar arises from the patterns that occur over and over again in many people's spoken and written communication in a natural setting. Functional grammars are also descriptive and explanatory, but the descriptions and explanations can be cognitive (from the mind of the speaker/writer), social (from the situation the discourse takes place in), and historical (from the grammatical changes that have taken place over time) (Cumming & Ono, 1997). The authority for the grammatical analysis is data gathered about the way that people naturally speak and write.

For instance, after looking at many sentences, a functionalist finds a tendency for new and unknown information to appear at the end of sentences and old and known information to appear at the beginning. The difference between *Too many people are in this room* and *There are too many people in the room* can be explained by a speaker's need to highlight the new information (*too many people*) by putting it at the end of the sentence. The *function* of the subject placeholder *there* is to allow the speaker/writer to highlight the new information. In this view, there is no right or wrong; instead, there is a continuum of correctness, depending on the formality of the setting the language is situated in. Any errors are structures that are highly unlikely to occur in natural speech or writing or are slips of the tongue.

Lexicalist theory rests on the idea that grammatical generalizations stem from patterns of common word combinations called **collocations** (Lewis, 1998; Willis, 1996; Willis & Willis, 1996).

COLLOCATIONS	GRAMMATICAL GENERALIZATION
distant relative, great pain→	Adjective + noun
community service, shopping bag→	Descriptive noun + noun
wait for, blame (something) on→	Verb + preposition
be careful, don't worry→	Imperative expression

Recently, innovative descriptive grammars are written on the basis of large databases of spoken and written text analyzed by means of a computer. The *Longman Grammar of Spoken and Written English* (Biber et al., 1999) is an example that is both lexicalist and functional. The lexicalist perspective on our sample sentence would focus on the frequent use of *there are* with any noun phrase as a collocation that children or English learners need.

The Prescriptive Approach

Prescriptive grammars are rule books that lay out the best **usages** of the most standard writers and speakers so that others whose language may be nonstandard or nonnative have access to them (Broadview Press Editorial Board, 1988). A prescriptive grammar includes the sentence *There <u>are</u> too many people in the room* as a remedy for people who say or write *There<u>'s</u> too many people in the room*.

A prescriptive grammar addresses questions of good speaking or writing **style** as well. A formal prescriptive grammar may instruct the writer not to end a sentence with a preposition (*He is the man I am speaking <u>to</u>*), not to use contracted forms (*did not* vs. *didn't*), or not to split an infinitive (*to speak <u>carefully</u>* vs. to <u>carefully</u> speak*), but these are stylistic questions, not grammatical ones. English allows these sentences, but some writers prefer to avoid them.

The data for prescriptive judgments come from a survey of the usage of the best writers and speakers or from the author's ideas of what sounds best or is more clear, but disagreements about prescriptive grammar and style are common. People have particular pet peeves about language, but the same usages go unnoticed by other people who have their own peeves. For example, some people cringe when others say *less people* or *less taxes* instead of *fewer people* and *fewer taxes*. Some people ignore that issue but make a judgmental remark when they hear people say *realetor* instead of *realtor* or *nuculer* instead of *nuclear*. Others dislike the use of *irregardless, hopefully,* or *these ones*. The prescriptive grammarian's errors are nonstandard or stigmatized words and grammar or expressions or style that the grammarian does not like.

The Pedagogical Approach

Pedagogical grammar books cover things that make English different from other languages, things that native speakers take for granted but that cause problems for nonnative speakers (Frank, 1993). After a statement that every English sentence has a subject or a subject placeholder, we might find these examples:

> <u>All the sales representatives</u> *pour into the reception after the meeting.*
> <u>The room</u> *is overcrowded.*
> <u>There</u> *are too many people in the room.*

An English grammar for Chinese speakers differs from one written for Spanish speakers because the learners need to focus on different aspects of English. For example, an English grammar book for Chinese learners stresses the articles *a* and *the*

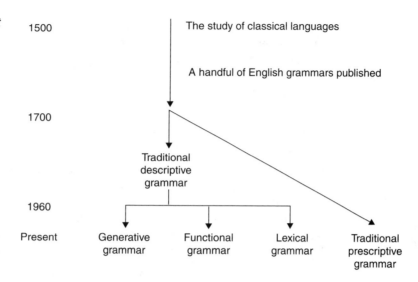

Figure 3.1 *The development of approaches to grammar.*

because that language does not have articles. A grammar for Spanish learners might also emphasize articles but explain how they are used differently.

Errors are an inevitable part of the transition from a first language to a second language. Nevertheless, some pedagogical grammars, especially advanced ones, have a strong prescriptive component as well. Nonnative speakers must often be conservative in choices of word and structure because they can face as much criticism or more than native speakers (see Figure 3.1).

TYPES OF GRAMMATICAL INSTRUCTION

Different grammatical approaches, curricular purposes, and learner needs result in a variety of grammar classrooms.

The Structure of English Class

The few children who went to school in the very old days (say, in the 1500s and afterward) studied Greek and Latin, classical languages used for advanced learning at the time. Children studied the structure of English phrases and sentences, but Latin provided the grammatical concepts and labels for English because grammarians thought that Latin had ideal grammar. Now we expect educated people to know math or science, but long ago an educated person knew grammar. With so much grammatical study going on, you can see why schools were called "grammar schools."

Today, the structure of English is an academic subject—a college-level class taken either as an elective for students interested in language or as a requirement for future teachers. The main purpose for the structure of English class is to increase the student's schooled knowledge of English. Although students sometimes take such a class to improve their reading and writing skills, in fact only an indirect connection between the traditional knowledge of the structure of English and good writing style exists. The indirect connection is that increased knowledge of English structure and word formation increases metalinguistic awareness and sensitivity to language, and this in turn improves reading abilities and writing style.

The Syntax Class

English or linguistics majors take a syntax class whose purpose is to describe how a small set of rules generates the infinite number of sentences of any language. More recently, some syntax classes have also incorporated a functionalist and/or a lexicalist perspective. Students gain deep insights into language, and their metalinguistic awareness surpasses the norm; however, like traditional descriptive grammar, the advanced study of syntax does not automatically lead to good writing style. Since it leads to metalinguistic awareness and sensitivity to language, however, there may be an indirect connection.

The Basic Skills Class

Until the 1600s, most English-speaking people were content with the way they spoke, even though there was considerable regional and social class variation. However, in the 1600s, because of social movements that shook up the status quo in England and because of increased interest in education, people moved to the cities and attempted to rise in social class. Prescriptive grammar arose from the need to know the "correct" way to speak so that people could minimize their country ways and move into the middle class. George Bernard Shaw's play *Pygmalion,* although it was written later, and the musical derived from it, *My Fair Lady,* reflect the lengths to which people would go to in order to speak with a high-class accent and grammar.

Thus, around the 1700s, we first see a bifurcation into descriptive and prescriptive grammar books and instruction. Although some grammarians believed that English could be described in its own terms, most grammarians still relied on concepts and categories from the study of Latin grammar to describe English (Barber, 1994, p. 204). Some grammarians also wanted to perfect English because they thought that it was less elegant and logical than Latin. The Bible had recently become available to read, and people thought that because God had given language to them, language must have been perfect at the beginning. Their idea was that classical languages were closer to the divinely inspired language; therefore, deviations from those norms could only have been degenerative (Millward, 1996, p. 242).

To clean up English, some grammarians proscribed (forbade) certain usages that they considered inferior. Many of the proscriptions written into prescriptive grammar books of the time were based on false notions, but they became codified as correct usage. For example, English had used double-negative expressions for centuries, but 17th- and 18th-century grammarians viewed them as illogical, so they tried to ban them. Of course, we know that many modern languages have double negatives as their norm; people do not seem to find them illogical at all. In addition, since Latin does not allow prepositions at the end of a sentence, these were forbidden in English. Barber (1994, p. 206) also suggests that these grammarians felt that linguistic distinctions reflected the reality of the world, so they carefully distinguished adjectives (*rapid*) from adverbs (*rapidly*) and past-tense forms (*spoke*) from past participles (*spoken*), hence some of the problems people have with these forms even today.

Many modern-day judgments about language began at that time. Barber (1994) says, "The prescriptive works had a quite overt class bias. . . . There are frequent references to the depraved language of common people, compared to the noble and refined expressions of the gentry. The language of tradespeople in particular comes in for condemnation, shopkeepers' cant being contrasted with the speech of persons of taste and refinement" (p. 205).

On the other hand, Millward (1996) is more forgiving: "The deeper, more pervasive, and more pernicious influence of the eighteenth century prescriptive grammarians lies in their having made 'correct' usage a moral rather than simply a practical matter. . . . Nonetheless, we should not overmalign the school grammarians. They were not deliberate linguistic tyrants, nor did they promote class warfare. They responded to a real demand on the part of people who wanted simple, clear-cut answers to usage questions, people who asked for concrete instruction and not abstract theory. We can fault the grammarians for the *false* information they gave, but not for the fact that they gave it" (p. 248) (see Table 3.2).

Today, to fix nonacademic, nonstandard, or nonnative "mistakes," people take a prescriptive grammar course in basic skills, mechanics, and writing style. They learn about **parallel structure,** that two parts of a conjoined sentence should be similar. That is, they learn to avoid writing sentences such as this: *To listen to bagpipe music and*

TABLE 3.2

Settings for Grammatical Instruction, Audience, and Type of Instruction

Grammatical Instruction Setting	Intended Audience	Approaches
Structure-of-English class	Future K–12 teachers and university students	Descriptive grammar
Syntax class	Linguistics and English majors	Advanced descriptive grammar and syntactic theories
Basic skills class	SSE speakers, nonstandard speakers, Generation 1.5, nonnative speakers	Prescriptive grammar
Grammar class	English learners	Pedagogical and prescriptive grammar
Language arts or English class	K–12 students: SSE speakers, nonstandard speakers, Generation 1.5, and nonnative speakers	Language awareness curriculum and descriptive, prescriptive, and pedagogical grammar

eating tofu burritos are the biggest pleasures in my life. This sentence is grammatical, and its form might even be common in ordinary speech, but the lack of parallelism in the underlined portions makes it awkward in formal SWE.

In this type of instruction, instructors often ignore metalinguistic awareness and minimize descriptive grammar (Noguchi, 1991). In fact, basic skills instruction is problematic because while some teachers are successful at getting students to apply what they learn to their own writing, other teachers experience only mixed success with it. Where does instruction go wrong?

First, learners need to learn the target forms as declarative knowledge, involving notice, representation, storage, and retrieval. Second, declarative knowledge must be converted to procedural knowledge. To edit a term paper, for example, learners need to notice that they have made a mistake, retrieve the target rule or fact, and make the correction correctly. Some composition teachers discover to their chagrin that students do not recognize the usage mistakes they are making and do not realize that a grammar rule will fix it (McQuade, 1980).

Because of mixed success, some teachers feel that basic skills instruction is a waste of precious class time. In addition, since it can be very dry and unmotivating, some teachers avoid such instruction in favor of more interesting activities. If teachers take this point of view, they will naturally not meet the language arts standards in their classrooms that mandate both declarative knowledge about language and procedural knowledge to notice and change usage errors. Therefore, their students might be linguistically handicapped when it comes to the assessments they face.

The Grammar Class

Nonnative speakers sometimes take a grammar class to make their speaking, listening, reading, and writing more accurate, but the attitude toward the usefulness of grammatical instruction is mixed. The **communicative method,** in which grammar is taught not by itself but only in service of real communication, has been in favor for quite a while (Larson-Freeman, 1986). The aim for beginning instruction is fluency and not accuracy. There is consensus that the formal presentation of grammatical description and feedback is best minimized in the beginning English as a second language (ESL) classroom because learning *about* the language does not necessarily translate into an ability to *use* the language.

If a Spanish speaker learns that the *third person singular of the present tense* takes an *-s* suffix (as in *He snores*), that declarative knowledge may not help the learner use the structure correctly in his normal communication. Likewise, negative feedback on grammar errors may actually discourage some beginning learners from developing fluency because they become self-conscious and self-critical. Instead, beginning and intermediate language instruction is communicative. Language is to be learned in the course of communicating with others in purposeful classroom tasks. Cooperative learning is often used to provide structures for purposeful communication. However, when learners get beyond the beginning stages of language fluency and into the later intermediate and advanced proficiency levels, the consensus about the role of grammatical instruction disappears.

The comprehensible input hypothesis (Krashen, 2003, p. 4) is that learners will improve their accuracy, given a high degree of motivation and exposure to correct comprehensible language, because people are innate language learners. Thus, there is little need to teach grammar in the classroom because learners acquire procedural grammar through exposure to language that is slightly beyond the learner's level of proficiency. Declarative or schooled grammar is not necessary because, in this view, it does not turn into procedural knowledge.

The **feedback hypothesis** holds that teachers should supplement the communicative method and the comprehensible input hypothesis with direct instruction in grammar and feedback to correct persistent errors (Ellis, 2002; Hinkel & Fotos, 2002; Lightbown & Spada, 1993, pp. 96–105). The rationale is that second-language learners, especially older ones, may not have access to natural language learning abilities for their second language. They may not have the motivation or attention for learning through comprehensible input. On the other hand, older learners have other academic abilities (e.g., focus, attention, and metalinguistic awareness) that help them learn through grammar instruction and feedback. In addition, if not corrected with direct feedback, nonnative usages become permanent, and the learner's language fails to develop accuracy even though it is fluent. When this happens, the learner's language is said to **fossilize** at a certain stage of development, after which little development in accuracy takes place. (Actually, there are a lot of social and psychological factors leading to fossilization. The presence or absence of grammatical feedback is only part of the picture.)

Some ESL researchers and practitioners argue that it takes overt declarative instruction and feedback in order to change fossilized language (Ellis, 1994, pp. 617–627). Like native speakers, if learners notice when their writing differs from SE writing and retrieve stored declarative knowledge, they can edit out nonnative usages. In addition, these researchers theorize that older learners benefit from a shortcut in learning because direct feedback is faster than "natural" trial and error.

But the feedback approach does not mean "drill and kill" methodology (Ellis, 1994, pp. 639–643). Within the context of the communicative classroom, if teachers notice that learners make an error repeatedly, they mention it overtly but without pointing out specific guilty parties. Instead, they give a very short explanation about a grammatical point in the form of a minilecture, use anonymous examples from classroom interaction or writing samples to model the correction, provide an exercise or two to do cooperatively, and watch for chances to review and remind learners while they are writing and editing. As intermediate learners become even more advanced, they too can learn Academic English (AE) norms and apply their knowledge to edit their own written work.

The Language Arts or English Class

The K–12 language arts or English class is the place where most children learn reading, writing, and speaking within the context of a well-rounded language arts curriculum. To meet the language arts standards in descriptive grammar and correct usage, these classes must also be a composite of the structure of English class, the basic skills class, and the ESL grammar class. Some English teachers teach descriptive grammar only because it is mandated; others teach it because they enjoy it and think that it helps increase their learners' metalinguistic awareness. Some teachers focus a lot of their attention on the elements of correct style, standard usage, and mechanics as applied to writing; others decide to spend less time. In addition, in many parts of the country, nonnative speakers are mainstreamed into all classrooms, so teachers must also teach English-versus-non-English usage.

The most effective teacher can move flexibly among these approaches easily, providing feedback, explanations, and practice on the spur of the moment or with little outside preparation. The most effective curriculum will increase the learner's identification, representation, storage, and retrieval of both declarative and procedural knowledge of grammar. The most effective instruction will increase metalinguistic awareness while improving the learner's abilities to use SE and AE.

Unfortunately, in traditional grammar instruction, teachers often provide confused and confusing explanations that are either too long or too brief, immediately followed by a battery of workbook exercises to practice the concepts. Learners do drills in which the specific grammatical form to be practiced is isolated from other forms and do worksheet exercises that ask them to fill in the blank with the correct pronoun form or textbook exercises that have them change a paragraph from present to past tense. Each exercise is repetitive and decontextualized, and each sentence has no relation to the previous or next one.

Such techniques have not always been effective because they do not lead to notice, representation, storage, and retrieval of declarative and procedural knowledge. Learners are overwhelmed with the minutiae of the grammatical exercises and get lost in the details. They do not see the relevance to their own language, and they get bored and tune out. Instead, if teachers create seminal, relevant learning experiences, both teachers and learners will be more successful.

One approach to grammar instruction goes in such a direction. The fundamental idea is to spark learners' interest in language in general, making language an interesting topic of discussion in the classroom, during which feedback on non-SWE and non-AE usages are just part of the big picture. Learners increase their metalinguistic awareness as well as their ability to notice their own language in particular and change it to match the target structures. They focus on the systems of language and how those systems create meaning. Through the study of social and regional dialects, they become language "consumers."

THE LANGUAGE AWARENESS CURRICULUM

Adopting the language awareness curriculum is mainly a matter of attitude change, although White (2000) has called it a "paradigm shift." Teachers move from a conventional point of view that language instruction is secondary to a perspective that language (in general and in particular) is as important a component in the language arts curriculum as any other (Andrews, 1993; White, Maylath, Adams, & Couzijn, 2000). In fact, the ability to use language effectively underlies success in other subject matter. The goal of the curriculum is to expand learners' metalinguistic awareness so that they take ownership of their dialect of English (or their native language) as well as SE norms (see Figure 3.2).

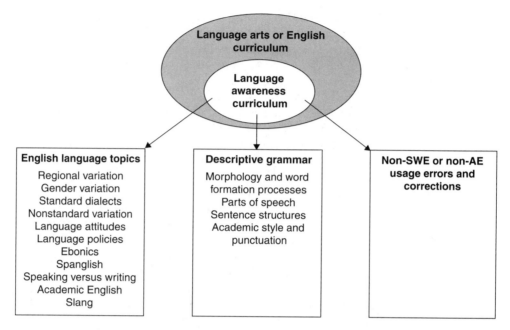

Figure 3.2 *Language awareness curriculum.*

Principles of the Language Awareness Curriculum

The language awareness curriculum focuses on three linguistic subject matters. The first subject matter is about English, especially sociolinguistic topics, such as the sociocultural history of English; its social class, age, gender, and regional variation (slang, dialects, register, jargon, formality, SSE, SWE, and AE); people's attitudes toward grammar; how English mixes with other languages (e.g., Spanglish, Ebonics, and Cajun); and the differences between speech and writing. These topics are designed to motivate, empower, and inform learners so that they own their language and value it while still understanding the need to make changes to accomplish a linguistic purpose.

The second subject matter is about the forms of English, their system, and how the system creates meaning. Included in this subject matter are interesting spellings, punctuation and capitalization, vocabulary, parts of speech, syntactic structures, and extensive word meanings. The focus is on appreciation of language, love of language, and, through it, access to academic language; teachers are not just trying to meet the language arts standards.

An appreciation for a language system empowers learners in a different way. For instance, Ferris (1999, p. 146) found that Generation 1.5 learners lack the metalanguage to make use of feedback from their writing instructors. This means that they do not understand terms such as *subject, verb,* and *agreement* and do not know how to fix these problems. This may be true of many native standard and nonstandard English speakers as well, so it is no wonder that they cannot edit their own work.

Finally, these two subject matters create a rich linguistic context to acquire the third subject matter: declarative knowledge about SWE and AE usage and procedural knowledge of personal editing procedures. Learners become actively involved as language observers because they keep a grammar notebook in which they document their own usage problems and solutions.

The language awareness curriculum recognizes that grammar learning is developmental and cumulative. Metalinguistic awareness and schooled knowledge of grammar accumulate over time. Children, teenagers, and adults need ample time to learn to recognize the typical nonstandard or nonacademic features that are common in their own writing so that they can edit their own work; to do so, they must know the correct forms and when to use them. This will not happen if basic skills instruction is limited to a 5-week crash course in freshman English. Instead, school districts and/or schools need a long-range broad-based language arts policy to enrich language awareness and language learning in every classroom, every year (Corson, 1999). Learners will get a sense of the accumulation of grammatical knowledge if they keep their Language Notebooks throughout the year or even over several years.

The language awareness curriculum is primarily interpretive and reflective (Ellis, 1994, pp. 643–647). At first, teachers invite learners to notice a grammatical pattern so that their awareness of the structure is activated. Learners develop a cognitive representation of it that they store in memory and begin to use the structure when they feel ready to do so. After some teacher prompting and modeling, learners begin to notice the presence of a grammatical feature in their text, such as a story or a textbook chapter. They discuss the form and comprehend the meaning of the feature and show an understanding of a passage that has been carefully constructed to contain examples of specific grammatical structures. Learners reflect on the language they observe around them, including their own dialect and usage, and they think about what dialect and style is appropriate for the speaking or writing task that they are doing.

This curriculum leads to notice, representation, and storage in memory because learners are active and because they receive multiple exposures to the same grammatical point. If learners notice a single grammatical feature on their own and find out about it, they will be more likely to internalize a representation of it, store the representation in long-term memory, and retrieve it easily when needed. Making a few personally relevant notations in a language notebook can be more useful in the long run than spending time doing exercises.

CASE HISTORY

Ms. Moreno Encourages Academic Writing Proficiency

Besides her other language arts goals, Ms. Moreno wants to make sure her ninth graders understand and write academic essays. Her specific focus on language for this lesson is complex noun phrases. After some introductory prereading activities, she has assigned her class to read an economic essay from the newspaper for homework. It had a few complex noun phrases in it.

The next day, she gives her class a few minutes to look over the article and ask questions. Then she begins her class with a short quiz to test for comprehension of the meaning of the article. She collects the quiz as an assessment, but she immediately goes over the quiz as a way of discussing the main points from the reading. Learners are motivated to listen because they want to know if they got the answers right or wrong. After 10 minutes, Ms. Moreno is confident that they have grasped the main ideas from the selection. She now turns to focusing on language issues.

She directs the learners' attention to the term *discount outlet merchandise* in the text. She asks them what it means, and they are able to give her an answer easily. She points out its structure of three nouns in a row and asks which noun is the most important and which nouns are descriptive. One young man is able to answer that the most important word is *merchandise* since that is what the article is about. Ms. Moreno then asks learners to find one other example that is like this one on the first page of the article. The other example also has three nouns in a row, and the last one is the most important. After some looking and a few mistaken guesses, a young woman comes up with *consumer power initiative*. They discuss what the complex noun phrase means.

Ms. Moreno invites her learners to come up with a generalization about the complex noun phrases. Some suggest that if there are three nouns in a row, the last one is the most important. Ms. Moreno asks class members to note the generalization in their Language Notebooks and to write down any similar constructions on page 2, which contains one example, "employee parking space." Everyone agreed that the example followed the generalization. A couple of learners find these also: *fast food franchise* and *major attraction*. They discuss these expressions, pointing out the similarities and differences between them and the others. These examples are also complex noun phrases, although their structure is different. The generalization evolved into the idea that in a complex noun phrase, there could be any number of nouns and adjectives, but the last and most important word was always a noun. Ms. Moreno called that noun the *head noun*. The learners made a list of the expressions in their Language Notebooks and made up some original ones.

Ms. Moreno has some Spanish speakers in her class, and she asked them, in a group, to translate their original expressions into Spanish because the grammar of Spanish complex noun phrases is very different from English. Once the phrases were in Spanish and written in their Language Notebooks, she asked them to translate them back to English without looking at the original expressions.

Ms. Moreno has prepared some follow-up exercises for tomorrow, so she leaves the topic for now and goes on to something else. However, at the end of the class period, she tells her class that they can leave as soon as they tell her the complex noun phrases they studied that day. When a couple of learners volunteer "consumer power initiative" and others say "discount outlet merchandise," they are allowed to leave.

USAGE ERRORS AND ERROR CORRECTION

One way to identify the major errors to address within the context of the language awareness curriculum is to look at the types of grammatical knowledge that young (and older) adults need for the business or professional world. Hairston (1981) surveyed a population of middle-class professionals to see which errors they were most critical of. These were usage errors typically made by native standard and nonstandard speakers and are categorized by their effect on the survey takers.

Non-SWE Errors

The "most serious" errors were nonstandard usages, such as *brung, had went, we was, he don't,* and double negatives. Incorrect subject pronouns, as in *him and Bill did it,* are quite standard in SSE even among some educated speakers, but such usage is not allowed in writing. Hairston (1981) found that "very serious" errors (excluding punctuation) were sentence fragments, run-on sentences, noncapitalization of proper names, *would of* instead of *would have,* incorrect subject–verb agreement, nonparallelism, faulty adverbs (*bad* instead of *badly*), and *set* used instead of *sit.* These are usage problems in making the transition from informal SSE to the more formal and rigid style acceptable in academic or professional writing. All learner populations might show these features in their writing.

The "serious" errors were wrong words, dangling modifiers, *I* as an object pronoun (as in *between you and I*), tense switching, and plural modifiers, such as *these* for singular words like *kind,* as in *these kind of errors.* The "minor" errors were the use of a qualifier before *unique* (*very unique*), the use of *different than* instead of *different from,* and the use of a singular verb with *data.* These are minor errors because they are already nearly standard for many people, even middle-aged professionals. These usages are common among native standard-speaking, native nonstandard-speaking, and ESL or Generation 1.5 learners.

It is possible that now, more than 20 years later, professional writers have different judgments about some of these grammatical breaches of etiquette, but this list is still useful. (Indeed, no one has done a more recent follow-up study as far as I know.) Hairston's research shows that the farther children advance in school, the more standard their language needs to be in academic and professional writing and speaking to be successful.

Teachers have the final word on which errors to select for feedback based on what they know about the amount of class time, the focus of the learning, the learners, and the error. It is more important to provide feedback on nonstandard usages in writing than in speech. Teachers need to be selective, working on a few specific usage problems at a time so that neither they nor their learners are drowned in a flood of red ink. Giving the right feedback at the right time and only in a positive, effective manner is crucial. Rather than disapproving of the learner or his or her language, a teacher simply offers the standard form with a neutral emotional tone. A teacher is always best off assuming the attitude of encourager and coach rather than judge, jury, and executioner.

Nonnative Errors

The question of what to correct for ESL or Generation 1.5 learners is a little different. Of immediate importance are **stigmatizing errors** that may cause the speaker or writer to be ridiculed or profiled. Usually, stigmatizing errors are caused by mispronunciation or inappropriate word choice. Two other types of ESL errors should receive feedback because of their effect on a listener or reader (Burt & Kiparsky, 1972, 1974). **Global errors** are sentence-level errors that result in erroneous comprehension of the message or in no comprehension at all. **Local errors** are smaller errors that affect one word or a constituent in the sentence and that do not impede comprehension but are noticed: a missing article, a wrong verb form, or a misplaced adjective. Furthermore, local errors are similar to Hairston's "most serious" category for native-speaking writers—those that stem from nonstandard usages. Teachers should deal with local errors if they are common among a number of learners in the class or occur over and over again in speech or writing and if they are errors that the teacher has focused some attention on in the past and wishes to reinforce (see Figure 3.3).

LOOKING BACKWARD AND FORWARD

Errors are not a sign of stupidity, lack of culture, or lack of trying. Our notion of what an "error" is arises simply from our expectations of how people "should" speak. In native speakers, any form that is not part of SWE or AE is a potential error. For nonnative speakers, any form that is not English, SWE, or AE is a potential error. Although teachers are usually content if learners have communicated successfully and have expressed interesting and thoughtful ideas, other people get hung up on the details. People hold strict expectations, especially for business or academic writing, and learners who do not meet them (and their teachers by association) are subject to criticism.

However, many teachers find that dealing with these details takes a lot of class time but does not lead to change. The class time devoted to decontextualized basic skills instruction and grammar worksheets can be better devoted to a language awareness curriculum that expands learners' metalinguistic awareness in three ways: knowledge about the English language; knowledge about English grammar, especially SWE/AE usage; and procedural skills, especially editing, to achieve SWE/AE usage. What teachers need to create, then, is a multidimensional classroom, stretching the traditional language arts or English subject-matter goals to include language.

EXPLORING CHAPTER PERSPECTIVES

◆ *Discussion Questions*

1. What kind of grammar class have you taken in school or college? Did you have a positive or negative experience with it? Why?

2. Do you think that learning about grammar helps you write better? Does it help you edit? Why or why not? Does it increase your metalinguistic awareness?

3. Go over what the various grammatical approaches had to say about sentences with *there is* or *there are*. Articulate in your own words how they exemplify the purpose or goal of the approach.

Figure 3.3
Examples of three categories of errors made by nonnative speakers of English.

Global errors	**= no comprehension or miscommunication** **Wrong word** I <u>have</u> twenty. Intended meaning: I <u>am</u> twenty. **Wrong pronoun** <u>She</u> brought his baby son. Intended meaning: <u>He</u> brought his baby son. **Missing words/wrong word** Heddy in the cook. Intended meaning: Heddy <u>is</u> in the <u>kitchen</u>. **Garbled word order** Saw the man the policeman. Intended meaning: The man saw the policeman.
Stigmatizing errors =	**ridicule or profiling (often pronunciation or lexical problems, not grammar)** **Wrong word** She is <u>embarrassed</u>. Intended meaning: She is <u>pregnant</u>. **Inappropriate slang** Please don't <u>knock</u> me up. Intended meaning: Please don't <u>wake</u> me up. **Formality** It's <u>a turn on</u>. Intended meaning: It's <u>very nice</u>.
Local errors	**= do not interfere with communication but may annoy readers** **Wrong word** She studies in the <u>bookstore</u>. **Missing article** She studies in library. **Missing subject** Studies in the library. **Wrong verb form** The student <u>study</u> every night.

4. What did your language arts or English teachers think about language as a part of language arts? Did they ever mention interesting things about language?

5. Brainstorm some topics that might be interesting to incorporate into a language awareness curriculum. Here are some to get you started:
   What is Spanglish?
   What is Ebonics?

How do you know people are from another part of the country as soon as they open their mouth?

What is your attitude toward various different regional dialects?

What are the features of the language of instant messaging?

What do you think about swearing?

◆ *Cooperative Exercise: A Plethora of Grammar Textbooks*

This assignment is designed to make you a better consumer of grammar books. When you are a teacher, you may or may not have a choice about which grammar materials are used, but it is always better to be a more educated textbook consumer. (This assignment can be done as homework using the textbooks listed in on-line bookstores.)

A. **Homework or Class Work.** As individuals, using a large number of grammar books from the library (or provided by your instructor), place each text into one of these categories: descriptive, prescriptive, or pedagogical. Write down one reason why you placed a certain book in a certain category. Fill out this form:

Type of grammar		
Descriptive		
Titles	Reason	Target readers
1.		
2.		
Prescriptive		
Titles	Reason	Target readers
1.		
2.		
Pedagogical		
Titles	Reason	Target readers
1.		
2.		
I am unsure about these books:		
Titles	Reason	
1.		
2.		

B. **Group Work.** Prepared students form groups of four. One student in each group is selected to be the Encourager. The Encourager makes sure that each student participates and that no one student dominates the discussion. The Encourager asks each student, "What do you think?" and is allowed to say "time out" if someone is talking too much. Discuss these questions:

   i. Did you have the books classified the same way? Were your reasons the same or were they different?

   ii. Can you make any generalizations about each type of grammar book?

   iii. Were there any books you were unable to classify into one category? Why was it difficult?

   iv. Take turns filling out this form, making sure that each student has a chance to write part of it. (Unprepared students work on Part A in class before going to Part B.)

Descriptive grammars have the following characteristics:

Their target readers tend to be

Prescriptive grammars have the following characteristics:

Their target readers tend to be

Pedagogical grammars have the following characteristics:

Their target readers tend to be

C. **Class Work.** Hand in all forms. Discuss the characteristics of each type of grammar book and their intended readers. Reflect on the cooperative process.

◆ *Writing Assignment*

Write a short essay in your Language Notebook in response to one or both of these questions. Save your essay(s) for later use.

1. Describe the ideal language arts or English teacher for the grade level you are interested in. Thinking about the language awareness curriculum, include a discussion of five characteristics of effective teachers based on your experience as a learner. Do you have these characteristics? Can anyone acquire these characteristics (and if so, how?), or are they innate?

2. Go to the Center for Applied Linguistics Web site *www.cal.org* and answer these questions in a short essay: What is the purpose of the Web site? Who is this organization intended for?

   One feature of this Web site is that you can ask a linguistics expert a question by e-mail. What question would you like to ask? Why? Find the list of topics. What topic interests you? Why?

   Click on the topic. What do you find there?

Introspection

Look at your essay(s) carefully and proofread for spelling, punctuation, and nonstandard or non-SWE usage.

◆ *Find Out More*

Language Awareness Curriculum

Andrews, L. (1993). *Language exploration and awareness: A resource book for teachers.* New York: Longman.

Eschholz, P., Rosa, A., & Clark, V. (1994). *Language awareness.* New York: St. Martin's Press.

Language Arts Curriculum

Tompkins, G. (2002). *Language arts: Content and teaching strategies.* Columbus, OH: Merrill Prentice Hall.

The History of English

Bryson, B. (1991). *The mother tongue: English and how it got that way.* New York: William Morrow.

4

Creating the Multidimensional Classroom

Many children, teenagers, and adults find learning grammar metalanguage painful, confusing, and meaningless. Let's analyze an instance of learning terms and concepts that was easy, clear, and meaningful to see how it happened. The following extract is from Rachel Carson's book *A Sense of Wonder,* in which she described how her grandnephew learned botanical terms. Learning botanical terms under some circumstances can be as painful, confusing, and meaningless as learning grammatical terms.

> When Roger has visited me in Maine and we have walked in these woods I have made no conscious effort to name plants or animals nor to explain to him, but have just expressed my own pleasure in what we see, calling his attention to this or that but only as I would share discoveries with an older person. Later I have been amazed at the way names stick in his mind, for when I show slides of my woods plants it is Roger who can identify them. "Oh, that's what Rachel likes—that's bunchberry!" Or, "That's Jumer [juniper] but you can't eat those green berries—they are for the squirrels." I am sure no amount of drill would have implanted the names so firmly as just going through the woods in the spirit of two friends on an expedition of exciting discovery.[*]

What are the characteristics that made this learning experience positive?

◆ Carson knew the subject matter well and loved it.

◆ Carson did not consciously teach; instead, she remarked on interesting things that attracted her attention.

◆ Carson commented on things matter-of-factly as she and her grandnephew were doing something else that was interesting and adventurous.

◆ Carson shared her personal response to the terms and concepts to be learned and the items they denoted.

◆ Carson and her grandnephew interacted positively. There were no pressures, tests, or drills.

◆ Carson repeated the terms as often as necessary and never focused directly on whether Roger remembered them.

This chapter shows how to re-create this learning experience as much as possible within the language arts or English classroom, incorporating the principles of the language awareness curriculum. Learners become aware of language in three ways. First, they learn about language, capitalizing on the interest that many people naturally have about the way people speak and write. Second, they learn descriptive or schooled English grammar as mandated by the language arts standards. Finally, they learn to recognize their own divergent usage and to correct it when they are trying to speak or write Standard Written English (SWE) and Academic English (AE). Including these three aspects means creating a curriculum in which language arts teachers do the following:

◆ Know about the English language (and its metalanguage) and love it.

◆ Remark on interesting aspects of language that attract their attention using metalanguage.

◆ Comment on language and metalanguage matter-of-factly as they and their learners go about other interesting activities.

◆ Share their personal experiences and responses to language, the metalanguage to be learned, and the words they denote.

◆ Interact positively with the learners. There is reduced emphasis on grammar tests and drills (except for the probably inevitable practice for standardized testing).

◆ Repeat the metalanguage terms as often as necessary and use a cyclical syllabus that reviews information frequently.

To incorporate the language awareness curriculum and the "Carson" method of instruction, teachers need to think about three other dimensions: classroom climate, methodology, and lesson planning. Teachers use relevant communicative and cooperative activities to create the classroom climate, follow guidelines for an effective instructional methodology, and plan their lessons to include multiple language goals and objectives.

THE COMMUNICATIVE, COOPERATIVE CLASSROOM CLIMATE

Relevance

Grammar exercises or worksheets with lists of random fill-in-the-blank sentences are generally not very significant. Instruction is not communicative when students sit in seats in separate rows and fill in grammar worksheets by themselves. On the other hand, when teachers embed grammar instruction in appropriate and motivating literature, student-generated compositions, persuasive speeches, controversial debates, or a study of local regional or ethnic varieties of English, instruction becomes significant to learners. Context is provided when the words, structures, and meanings of learning materials form the basis for explanations of grammar. When explanations rephrase expressions that the learners themselves wanted to say or write or clarify ideas that learners wanted to express, they are relevant. When

---

Box 4.1   Factors in Creating a Communicative Cooperative Classroom Climate

Classroom Climate
✓ Relevance
✓ Communication
    Information gap
    Choice
    Feedback
    Comprehension
✓ Cooperation
    Positive interdependence/individual accountability
    Negative interdependence/no accountability
    Learning to cooperate
    Grading
    Monitoring
    Group roles
    Reflecting on the experience
    Group size
    Group composition

---

grammatical feedback occurs within the context of listening, speaking, reading, or writing activities, that feedback is personalized. Teachers promote notice, representation, and storage in an informal natural way because the information is purposeful to learners (see Box 4.1).

Communication

Communicative grammar instruction leads to self-directed notice, representation, and storage of grammar points and to the retrieval of those points as needed. Retrieval is necessary for declarative knowledge to be applied to self-monitoring or self-editing tasks. In communicating about grammar, learners rehearse the knowledge, put it into words, teach others, and apply declarative knowledge to tasks.

Learners need the opportunity to communicate or negotiate with each other about usage errors or grammatical explanations. Negotiation is modeled on the characteristics of real communication (Taylor, 1987), which involves an information gap, a choice, feedback, and ultimately understanding.

Information Gap
In a negotiation task regarding grammar, the teacher constructs the task and the materials so that one learner has some information and another learner has other information. In order to accomplish the learning task, the learners share their information.

Choice

In communicative grammar tasks, learners have some choice about how they correct errors or explain the grammar rules.

Feedback

In communicative grammar instruction, learners get feedback from others and from the teacher about their errors and how well they correct those errors, and can explain them. The best feedback takes the form of gentle guidance so that learners can find the correct answers to their questions. Self-feedback is very effective; when learners correct their own errors, it is less threatening than being corrected by others, even the teacher. Self-correction also implies mastery of grammar rules and their applications.

Comprehension

In a communicative grammar activity, both speaker and listener comprehend each other and the topic of conversation. At the end of the learning experience, learners should reach a final comprehension of the usage problem, the explanation, the correct form, and how to edit.

Cooperation

Learning about grammar the traditional way with drills and worksheets can be dry, dull, unmotivating, and threatening. If used properly, cooperative learning methods are active, entertaining, and engaging (Jacobs, Power, & Inn, 2002; Johnson & Johnson, 1999). Such methods are empowering, not threatening, and they are motivating, not discouraging.

There are some additional benefits for learners. Learners who have different grammatical knowledge and abilities can pool what they know and what they can do as they work together on the cooperative task. As they work together, they must use language to talk about language; they explain grammar points to each other. Learners of different language backgrounds interact together, and the speakers of the standard language serve as models for the others, while all develop tolerance for the others' ways of speaking. In short, well-designed cooperative learning naturally involves communicative, meaningful interaction.

Positive Interdependence/Individual Accountability

Cooperative learning is not a matter of putting learners in groups and giving them something to work on together. On the contrary, cooperative learning must be planned and used properly in order for it to be a positive, productive experience for everyone. Well-planned cooperative learning leads to two characteristic outcomes: positive interdependence and individual autonomy. **Positive interdependence** refers to a relationship among the group members. It means that group members trust and depend on others to complete their tasks in a proper and timely fashion. **Individual accountability** refers to a characteristic of each individual group member. Each group member feels responsible for his or her preparation, group interaction, and ultimate learning. The two concepts are related in that if each group member feels individually accountable, positive interdependence for the group will result. Positive interdependence and individual accountability are more likely to result if teachers keep in mind the factors discussed in the following sections.

Negative Interdependence/No Accountability

Teachers need to avoid certain common situations that give cooperative learning a bad name. First, some learners may not complete their work, forcing others to do more of the work to finish the assignment. Second, some learners may take over and not allow others to participate, possibly because they are unwilling to let their grades depend on other learners. Negative interdependence is common in cooperative learning experiences that are poorly planned or unmonitored, but it is also true that some people need to learn to cooperate. You cannot assume that learners will come into your class knowing how to work well with others unless your school makes cooperative learning a whole-school objective.

Learning to Cooperate

Before their first cooperative experience, teachers should review the ideas of positive and negative interdependence and individual accountability and clarify their expectations. Teachers must be clear about how they will grade the assignment, how they will monitor the activity, what roles the learners will take, and how they will reflect on the experience after it is finished. It is in the spirit of cooperative learning for teachers to negotiate with their learners about grades, monitoring, and roles so that everyone feels ownership of the process.

Grading

Assigning grades to cooperative assignments is stressful because most learners do not mind working together but often want their own grades. At the beginning, teachers should experiment with grading individually while learners are becoming familiar with cooperative learning and increasing individual accountability and positive interdependence. However, as the cooperative experiences accumulate during the school year, learners will cooperate better so that they are more willing to let their grades reflect an interdependent effort. If they have worked well with the same group or with a number of classmates, there will be enough trust for them to rest their grades on. Learners who consistently slack off may be put into a group so that their lack of effort will not compromise groups that are working hard. If a few passive learners are placed together, they may feel some pressure to work more actively.

Monitoring

Teachers monitor the cooperative task at various stages to ensure that positive and not negative interdependence is taking place. For example, if teachers assign homework to be prepared before the cooperative classroom task, they monitor the individual preparation and use the information to split the learners into groups, doing this in a matter-of-fact way without humiliating those who have not prepared. Teachers simply place the unprepared learners together to do the homework task before starting the classroom task and give some words of encouragement to do the homework next time. Then all the groups are held accountable for finishing all the work. Teachers often reward groups that finish their task well and early because they were prepared. For example, they might be given some free time to read, do homework, work on computers, or talk quietly.

Such early monitoring has a number of benefits for positive interdependence and individual accountability. First, it ensures that group members are equally able to do the task and that no one will take advantage of others in the group. Second, it sends a clear message that you are expecting preparation and willing to reward it. Third, unprepared learners soon realize that the time they spend in class getting up to speed takes away from the time they can be discussing and interacting with others. Advance preparation should also have an impact on how well and how quickly they can do the cooperative task. (If this does not happen, you need to reevaluate the homework.) The early monitoring method is forgiving to those who are unprepared occasionally but minimizes the negative impact that unprepared students have on the cooperative group over time.

Group Roles

While the groups are at work on their assignments, teachers do not leave them to their own devices. Instead, they go from group to group, answering questions and checking on their progress. In addition, to increase the efficiency of the cooperative process and help groups monitor themselves, teachers assign each member a role to play. Typical roles are *encourager* (makes sure everyone contributes more or less equally by asking what each member thinks), *recorder* (takes notes and writes answers), *facilitator* (keeps the group on task, keeps track of time, and makes sure that one person does not dominate), and *observer* (notices positive interdependence and individual accountability). Good teachers notice when someone is doing well at a role and then comment on it. These methods could be called *monitoring-in-progress*.

Reflecting on the Experience

After each cooperative exercise, teachers ask learners to reflect on the experience, sometimes by asking them specific questions about their group's preparation, interaction, roles, and so on. Learners need some assistance to do this in an objective, impersonal way. (This feedback could be called *late monitoring*.) Reflection makes it clear to all that certain behaviors lead to positive interdependence and that certain behaviors prevent it. Teachers should always sum up the reflection period by making sure everyone knows that they have the opportunity to prepare better the next time, commenting on how well various people fulfilled their roles or acknowledging how groups succeeded at their task.

Group Size

The size of cooperative groups can range from the whole class to pairs. If teachers want to model or explain something, they should consider the whole class as one group. Otherwise, match the correct group size for each assignment or project. For example, if you have a lot of detailed work to do, the smaller the group, the faster they will work. Larger groups will tend to talk more and have more ideas, so they might be better for broader discussion questions or brainstorming.

For greater individual participation, smaller groups work better. In larger groups, a few people might dominate while the others stay more passive. For maximal understanding of material, smaller groups work better because some individuals get lost in larger groups and do not follow along. They are often embarrassed to ask questions if they think they are the only ones who do not understand.

Group Composition

Groups can be homogeneous or heterogeneous. Homogeneous groups have members with similar characteristics, such as gender, age, ethnicity, and language background. Heterogeneous groups, of course, are those in which members have a variety of backgrounds. The advantage of homogeneous groups is that group members are more likely to agree on the cultural or social interpretation of something; they can use their cultural, social, or language background to help each member understand or master some material. The main advantages of heterogeneous groups is that different perspectives are more likely, learners can help each other by offering diverse strengths and weaknesses, and individuals in the group may gain more appreciation for others from different backgrounds (if the cooperative experience is positive).

METHODOLOGY FOR GRAMMAR INSTRUCTION

Teachers use cooperative communicative activities within the three dimensions of the language awareness curriculum (language topics, descriptive grammar, and standard usage). However, learners sometimes require more direction to understand descriptive grammar and standard usage before doing cooperative work. The presentation of grammar is important because learners need to grasp, represent, and remember the point accurately (see Box 4.2).

Sequencing

Traditionally, teachers organize their grammar courses around discrete grammatical points in sequence and in isolation from other forms. For example, the first textbook

---

Box 4.2   Methodological Components

Grammar Instruction
- ✓ Sequencing
- ✓ Minilectures
     Inductive presentations
     Deductive presentations
     Exceptions to the rule
- ✓ Graphic organizers
- ✓ Practice

chapter (and the first lesson plan) is about the present tense, the second about the past tense, and so on. In each lesson, learners receive an explanation, apply the generalization in a series of exercises or drills, and then are tested on the given grammar point. After the test, the class moves on to the next point, and each learner is expected to use the grammatical structure as needed.

However, recall that Rachel Carson named and explained terminology to her grandnephew in response to something in the environment. Sequencing grammatical instruction should also be secondary to the subject matter of the language arts or English classroom. Grammatical terms and explanations occur in response to something in a reading or writing assignment or to meet the needs and questions of the learner.

Experienced teachers recognize two types of spontaneity: real and simulated. If the teacher has a wealth of declarative knowledge of grammar, grammatical instruction will occur in real, spontaneous encounters as teacher and learners roam through literature and academic prose together. However, sometimes grammar instruction has only the appearance of spontaneity. In fact, the teacher prepares a minilecture beforehand to have it ready for when a grammar point arises during a lesson. The teacher includes the grammar point as part of the lesson, although it may not be the main point of the lesson plan. The more teachers prepare minilectures, the more they are able to take advantage of real, spontaneous opportunities to work with grammar.

CASE HISTORY

Which of These Teachers Is the Star, and Which Is the Flop?

Mr. Green wants his students to write fluently. His long-term goal is to have the students write a research paper at the end of the term. Last week, he had learners practice writing direct quotes. Now he is having them learn how to paraphrase what different authors say. After looking at the first draft of their paraphrases, he notices that some students have problems with verb tenses. He decides that the typical verb forms for paraphrasing an author are the third-person singular present and past tense.

Smith says that . . .	Smith said that . . .
Garcia claims that . . .	Garcia claimed that . . .
Lew proves that . . .	Lew proved that . . .

Mr. Green prepares a minilecture about these verb forms and a set of examples for students to use as models as they are writing their paraphrases.

Mr. Brown wants his students to write fluently. He gives his students a variety of writing assignments that are coded to different grammar points that he follows in sequence throughout each school year. For example, in the first assignment, he asks the students to write about a city they know well in order to practice the present tense. The following week, he asks them to write about what they did over the weekend to practice the past tense. Each week he marks what they get wrong on their papers and hands them back.

Minilectures

Grammar presentations help learners notice and accurately represent in memory the target grammar point (Ellis, 1994, pp. 647–652). In an *inductive* presentation, the examples and applications precede the generalization. In a *deductive* presentation, the teacher gives the grammar generalization first, followed by examples and applications. Novice learners and older, academically oriented learners prefer deductive presentations, but others like the sense of personal discovery that an inductive presentation gives. These learners appreciate the opportunity to formulate the rule on the basis of what they observe about sentences. In their minilectures, teachers also need to incorporate clear information about common exceptions to the generalization or rule. What grammar learners do not like are random, disorganized, rambling presentations. An organized presentation helps the learner understand the material and represent it accurately and economically in memory. Teachers always begin by relating the grammar point to something that has been already learned or something relevant to the learner.

Inductive Presentation

In an inductive minilecture, the goal is to "induce" learning, that is, to motivate students to notice and represent a pattern themselves. Their sense of excitement at discovering a pattern themselves can lead to better recollection of the material. The steps in an inductive presentation are the following:

1. Draw learners' attention to the grammatical point and show its connection to already-learned material. Give at least one reason why this issue is important or relevant to them.
2. Give a series of examples taken from a reading or writing assignment and then invite learners to tell you what consistent patterns they notice. Always be encouraging, giving learners the benefit of the doubt for unclear answers.
3. Once learners have identified the patterns as well as they can, rephrase the generalization correctly and ask for other examples that follow the generalization. Have learners write the generalization in their Language Notebooks.
4. Discuss the most common exceptions to the generalization, if any.

Deductive Presentations

Many learners enjoy the inductive method teachers use to encourage them to notice things on their own about language, but this method can be more time consuming. When a grammar point comes up in class and you want to cover it quickly, it is often best to choose a deductive presentation. Deductive explanations begin with the generalization, then examples that fit the generalization follow. Finally, important exceptions are given, possibly in a garden path method.

Exceptions to the Rule

Teachers use the *garden path* method to discuss exceptions to grammar rules. In this method, the teacher causes learners to create errors and then correct them; teachers "lead learners down a garden path," so to speak. The garden path method is effective with English learners, but it can be effective with any learners because it helps them notice the exception and create a memory image to be represented and stored. Tomasello and Herron (1988, 1989) report on a study in which experimental subjects were led to make a specific error, at which point corrective feedback was given. For example, after learning a number of regular past-tense forms (*study/studied, want/wanted*) learners might induce the 'regular' past-tense form *digged*, at which point the correct irregular form, *dug,* is presented.

The experimenters hypothesize that this method is more effective than a more conventional method of correction by explanation and examples because it encourages learners to compare their own utterances and the correct target utterances actively. During the comparison, they mentally self-correct their original response. In other words, declarative knowledge becomes procedural knowledge, making it more memorable. The garden path method also increases motivation to learn because the learners become curious about rules and exceptions. Overall, the garden path method stimulates notice, representation, storage, and retrieval of grammar points and facilitates self-correction.

CASE HISTORY

Renata's Inductive Minilecture Script

1. The question is, When do we use *a* and when do we use *an*? This is important because some classmates are not using them correctly in their writing. They do not seem to know which is which. Let's help them put into words what the rule is so that they can write it in their Language Notebooks and refer to it when they are writing. Remember that *the* is the definite article. A/*an* are indefinite articles. We usually use them like this: <u>A</u> man walked into <u>a</u> church. <u>The</u> man said, "<u>This</u> church is cold."

2. What pattern do you see in these expressions? What determines the use of *a* or *an*?

A dog	An orangutan
A carrot	An apple
A pancake	An envelope
A number	An umbrella
A lily	An investigator

(A goes with a noun that starts with a consonant. <u>An</u> goes with a noun that starts with a vowel.)

Now look at these. Do these confirm or change your hypothesis?

An idle dog	A big orangutan
An old carrot	A green apple
An infinite number	A black umbrella

(A goes with any word that starts with a consonant. A*n* goes with any word that starts with a vowel.)

3. Can you give me more examples like these?
4. Without saying these, fill in the blanks based on the rules:

_____ university   _____ hour

_____ honor   _____ unicorn

Now say them out loud. Are these exceptions to the rule? What is the problem? The problem is that the choice of *a/an* depends on the sound of the word, not the spelling. These words are spelled with a consonant or vowel, but the pronunciation is the opposite. *University* and *unicorn* begin with a Y sound. *Honor* and *hour* actually begin with A.

5. Fill in the blank with the correct form of the indefinite article:

_____history of England

_____historical event

For no good reason in the present day, some people use *an* with the adjective *historical*, even though it does not follow the pattern. This usage should be abandoned, but for the moment, some people take this usage as a sign that someone is well spoken.

Graphic Organizers

Graphic organizers are visual representations of bits of information and the relationships among the pieces of information (Echevarria & Graves, 1998, pp. 131–135; Egan, 1999; Sorenson, 1991). They predigest the most important concepts in a graphic format so that they are easily read, understood, and learned. A graphic organizer that is simple and accurate is a wonderful thing, but one that is complex and misleading makes learning impossible. A poorly designed graphic organizer misrepresents the information, the relationships, and the organization so that learners are perplexed and unable to grasp the main ideas. Sometimes learners end up comprehending and learning something false. In addition, graphic organizers depend on cultural knowledge that we might take for granted in mainstream American society but that may not be common in other contexts. Therefore, sometimes learners need assistance in beginning to understand graphic organizers.

The form follows the function in the best graphic organizers. The first step in designing a graphic organizer is to consider carefully the content to present and to match it with a typical graphic structure, such as lines, charts, flowcharts, Venn diagrams, networks, pictures, maps, diagrams, outlines, or bulleted lists. Each graphic structure has specific uses, and graphic organizers that are well designed will be easy to work out and comprehensible for learners.

> **Lines** are a spacial representation of chronological events (time lines) or things ordered numerically or alphabetically. A line with an arrow on each side illustrates a continuum.

Charts have two dimensions with labels on the top (ABC) and on the side (YZ), creating pigeonholes or categories into which information can be stuffed.

	A	B	C
Y	Y + A	Y + B	Y + C
Z	Z + A	Z + B	Z + C

Flowcharts represent a process or procedure that has steps and a variety of outcomes. Dependencies between starting, intermediate, and ending points are important. Flowcharts are among the most difficult graphic organizers to get right—they are often incomprehensible unless well designed.

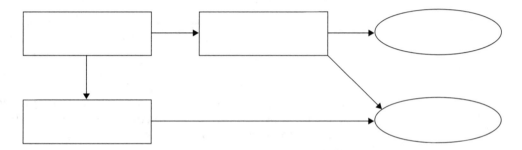

Venn diagrams show the overlap or intersection (or lack of such) between two concepts. The two concepts form two circles and the area that the two circles have in common includes the shared features.

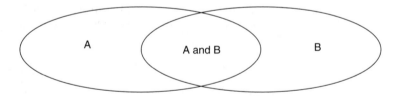

Networks can be ordered or not. Ordered networks, or **tree diagrams,** show a hierarchical organization from more general to more specific information.

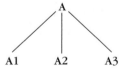

Semantic maps are unordered networks that show concepts and linked information in which the relationships are different or less clear. For that reason, they are often used for brainstorming ideas.

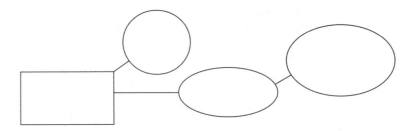

Visuals (pictures, maps, templates, or diagrams) illustrate relationships or display information related to a reading.

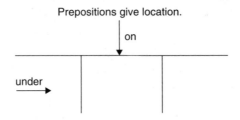

A **template** is either a pattern or a guide; it can have both a reproducing and a checking function, such as an equation or a rule. It often uses variables. If you insert numbers for the variables, you can reproduce the equation or check to see if the numbers work.

$$X + Y = Z$$
$$1 + 2 = 3$$
$$2 + 2 = 5$$

Outlines take the facts from a text and reduce them to an organized list of main concepts and subordinate concepts. The relationships are shown spatially through letters, numbers, and spacing. There are a variety of outline methods. Here is one.

Title

I. Point 1.
    A. Subpoint 1
        1. Secondary point 1
        2. Secondary point 2
    B. Subpoint 2
        1. Secondary point 1
        2. Secondary point 2
II. Point 2.
    A.
        1.
        2.
    B.
        1.
        2.

Bulleted lists are like outlines but the information is a series of concepts identical in importance. This graphic organizer is an example of a list.

- Lines
- Charts
- Flowcharts
- Networks
- Visuals
- Outlines
- Bulleted lists

CASE HISTORY

Rudy's Deductive Presentation with a Graphic Organizer

Rudy has noticed a few learners mixing up the order of adjectives in their descriptive writing. He wants to deal with it on the fly while they are on the subject because he knows that immediate feedback on writing is best. He thinks that it would take far too long to come up with the generalization about the order of adjectives inductively, so he decides to present it deductively using a graphic organizer. He already has a packet of material on this topic prepared from last year with a template and some example words, and he finds the file in his file cabinet. He puts an overhead transparency on the projector and says, "I noticed a few people were unclear about the order that adjectives need to have in English. Take out your Language Notebooks and write down what is helpful for you."

Order of Adjectives Modifying a Noun

1	2	3	4	
General	Physical State	Proper Adjectives General Adjectives	Descriptive Nouns	Head Noun
(blue)	(green)	(yellow)	(red)	(purple)

He has some words on pieces of paper that he has cut up into pieces. Each group gets a color-coded line of words to assemble into the correct order. Words in each column match the colors on the overhead.

excellent	old	Norwegian	peppermint	candies
beautiful	little old	Chinese	clay	figures
famous	tasty	Vietnamese	dessert	cakes
cheap	new	electric	string	trimmer
kindly	young	funny	woman	comedian
(blue)	(green)	(yellow)	(red)	(purple)

When each group has finished, they write down their phrase and pass the words to the next group. This way, each group does five phrases.

Rudy asks each group to find a sentence in their chapter book that could be modified with a set of adjectives. When they have found one, they begin working on sentence expansion. Sentence expansion means making the sentence longer and more detailed by adding modifiers and other words. Finally, Rudy presents the mistakes that learners made (anonymously on an overhead) and asks each group to correct them. They go over the correct answers as a whole class.

Practice

Once learners have noticed, represented, and stored and can retrieve an aspect of grammar through minilectures and meaningful communicative activities, practice helps learners generalize the representation that they have stored and retrieve it more quickly and automatically. Practice can turn declarative knowledge into procedural knowledge, but teachers always need to model the practice first.

Traditional methods of rote practice for descriptive grammar or usage problems include worksheets and exercises in grammar textbooks, and these can still be appropriate as long as they are individualized. **Individualization** means that each learner practices only what he or she needs to practice. It is not a good use of classroom time to have all the learners practicing the same grammar point unless all of them need assistance with it. Rather, teachers need to amass a file of worksheets or grammar exercises to hand out to learners as they need them and can benefit from them. However, even if teachers provide an answer key, individualized grammar practice takes a lot of monitoring.

That is the benefit of computer-assisted language learning (CALL) materials. CALL materials require less monitoring because learners get the right answers immediately and access a grammar tutor program to get immediate explanations of their errors. In some programs, learners cannot advance to later lessons until they have completed the earlier lessons. For some learners, working with a computer can make otherwise dull grammar exercises more interesting. A computer is infinitely patient (as opposed to teachers) and does not mind going over the same point again and again. Still, it is best not to overdo computerized grammar practice; it should be limited to the grammar points that the learner needs to practice.

MULTIDIMENSIONAL LESSON PLANS

One way for teachers to ensure that the multidimensional classroom becomes a reality every day is by writing multidimensional lesson plans, organized around at least four types of goals and objectives for each lesson. Typical language arts or English lesson plans include a subject area goal to meet the language arts content standards. The dimensions to be added are goals designed to meet language arts standards for descriptive grammar knowledge and usage and are drawn from the language awareness curriculum. These are English language awareness goals, descriptive grammar goals, and procedural goals that answer the question, What do learners need to know how to do with language in order to succeed with this lesson plan? (see Box 4.3). Of course, sometimes these goals overlap with each other.

Box 4.3 Four Types of Goals in the Multidimensional Lesson Plan	
Subject area goals	Shakespeare
English language awareness goals	Changes to English over time.
Descriptive grammar goals	Subject versus object pronouns
Procedural goals	Correcting subject pronoun forms-*me and him got
Subject area goals	*Pride and Prejudice*
English language awareness goals	British versus American English
Descriptive grammar goals	present perfect tense vs. past tense *have got/gotten* vs. *got*
Procedural goals	Correcting verb tenses and past participles- *do you got
Subject area goals	*Huckleberry Finn*
English language awareness goals	Social and ethnic variation
Descriptive grammar goals	Double negatives
Procedural goals	Editing double negatives - *don't got no

Goals and Objectives

Subject area goals come from broad curricular plans that carry over the semester or school year and meet the grade-level standards, the teacher's own interests, or the learners' specific needs or interests. For example, learners need to read certain types of fiction and nonfiction or specific books from a reading list; write in certain genres, such as business letters, poems, and myths; and accomplish speaking tasks, such as interviews, debates, and speeches.

English language awareness goals correspond to the subject area goals, but they focus on linguistic aspects of the content: language variation across <u>time</u> (e.g., the 17th-century English of Shakespeare vs. today's English), <u>space</u> (e.g., British vs. American English), and <u>social class</u> (e.g., the nonstandard dialects used in *Huckleberry Finn*). Other aspects are <u>age, regional variation, gender variation,</u> <u>formality</u> (e.g., slang, informal speech, and formal speech), <u>register</u> (e.g., sports, religion, politics, and academia), and <u>medium</u> (e.g., real conversations vs. movies and speech vs. writing).

Descriptive grammar goals, pulled from language in the materials meeting subject area goals and the English language awareness goals, also stem from the language arts grade-level standards or learner needs. Descriptive grammar goals include declarative knowledge: grammar terminology (e.g., noun, verb, subject, and direct object), usage norms for SWE and AE (e.g., *to, two,* and *too*), and stylistic preferences (e.g., dangling modifiers and parallel construction).

Procedural goals are derived from a comparison of the previous goals and the abilities and needs of learners. Teachers start with a list of the tasks that learners must do to complete a certain assignment or activity: reading, outlining, summarizing, brainstorming, writing, proofreading and editing, and using a dictionary. Then, working backward from the activity, the teacher breaks the task down to a set of objectives in response to the question, What do learners need to know *how to do* with language in order to succeed with this activity? For example, to be successful with a reading, all learners need to know the vocabulary and sentence structures contained in the reading. Thus, one clear objective is for teachers to prepare learners for success by going over new words or complex grammatical structures.

In order to be successful with proofreading and editing their own or another's writing assignment, learners need to notice the spelling, punctuation, or usage errors and know how to correct them or how to get the information needed to correct them. Therefore, the objectives for learners are to see someone model how to edit beforehand, create a checklist of usage problems to review and check for in the writing, and practice finding and correcting usage errors before they can do it on their own. In this way, teachers work backward from their ultimate goals to find the procedural objectives that help their learners achieve success.

Procedural goals also come from cooperative learning because learners need to learn the social and linguistic skills necessary to cooperate with others and develop individual accountability and positive interdependence. For one thing, they may need to acquire the language that allows them to perform certain roles. For example, if someone is playing the role of the encourager, he may need to know how to phrase a question such as "What's your opinion?" "Would you like to say anything?" or "I'd like to hear what you think." If someone is playing the role of the recorder, she may need to know these expressions: "Could you repeat that please?" "Could you spell that please?" or "I didn't catch what you said." She may need to know how to summarize or paraphrase what the group has said. Even with native-speaking children, it is important to model and practice polite requests, questions, and responses.

IMPLEMENTATION OF THE GOALS

Activities

To be truly "whole language," each lesson should include speaking, listening, reading, and writing of some kind (see Box 4.4). Effective grammar methodology requires con-

---

Box 4.4   Components of the Lesson Planning Process

Implementation
   Activities
   Sequencing of Activities
   Assessment
   Matrix

sideration of cooperative communicative activities, a minilecture, a graphic organizer, and practice, always in service of notice, representation, storage, and retrieval. Minilectures themselves have their own sequence.

Sequencing of Activities

Once teachers establish the goals, objectives, and activities to meet these goals and objectives, they turn their attention to planning the sequence of activities that will be most effective. The best sequence is one in which these activities build on each other; each one prepares the learner for the next until, at the end, the assessment takes place.

Assessment

Lesson plans include the assessment of cooperative learning and reflection, of the learners' effort and progress throughout the lesson, and of the learning outcomes. Teachers benefit from an assessment of their lesson plans as well.

Matrix

Matrices such as that shown in Table 4.1 can help teachers plan and evaluate a lesson. The goals, objectives, and other important components are listed down the left side of the matrix, and the activities, in sequence, are listed across the top. After deciding which activity meets which component, a check mark is placed at the intersection of the two. The more check marks, the better. Obviously, if an activity has no check mark, it needs to be removed or restructured. If a component on the left has no check mark, the lesson plan needs to be reworked.

LOOKING BACKWARD AND FORWARD

The matrix may seem excessively detailed and organized, but it is important to keep sight of the purpose of the language awareness curriculum, which is to emulate the learning experience that Rachel Carson created for her grandnephew, to the extent possible in the classroom. A related purpose for the language awareness curriculum is to expand learners' metalinguistic awareness in several dimensions.

Therefore, the metalinguistic awareness of teachers is crucial. To love the English language, teachers need to read about it. To teach descriptive grammar with excitement and spontaneity, they must store terms and structures in their memories. To help their learners learn and acquire declarative and procedural knowledge of SWE and AE, they must learn and acquire these variants themselves. To change learners, teachers must change first.

TABLE 4.1

Sample: For Ninth-Grade Class with 80% Nonnative Speakers

Goals and Objectives	Type of Activity / Description of Activity	Individual Activity / Reading/Research	Cooperative Activity / Brainstorm Questions and Write	Minilecture on Direct Questions	Individual Activity / Correct Questions	Cooperative Activity / Role-Play Interview
Subject area goal	Find out about professions	X	X			X
Language awareness curriculum goal	Interview a professional					X
Descriptive grammar goal	Structure of direct versus indirect questions		X	X	X	X
Usage goal	Word order in indirect questions					
Reading	Reading about a profession on the Internet	X				
Speaking	Conduct interview		X			X
Listening	Active listening to interviewee					X
Writing	Write list of questions Note taking during interview Summarize research and interview		X	X	X	

Individual Activity	Minilecture on Indirect Questions	Individual Activity	Minilecture	Individual Activity	Homework	Individual Assessment
Conduct Interview		Usage Problems Write Summary	Revise with Indirect Questions	Summary Draft	Edit Summary	Hand in Summary
X		X				X
X		X				X
X	X	X	X	X		
	X	X	X	X		X
		X				X
X						
X						
X		X	X	X		X

EXPLORING CHAPTER PERSPECTIVES ▨

◆ *Discussion Questions*

1. Have your experiences with cooperative learning been positive or negative? Describe what you have experienced using terms such as *positive interdependence, negative interdependence,* and *individual accountability.*

2. What did you learn about the English language (e.g., history of English or sociolinguistics) while you were in elementary, middle, or high school?

3. If you felt that you learned a lot about grammar, which instructional methods meant the most to you?

4. What are the chances of a paradigm shift in language arts or English instruction? What are the obstacles that must be overcome? Do you agree or disagree that such a paradigm shift is desirable?

5. Do you think that children, teens, or adults need to learn how to cooperate to learn? Do they need to learn certain language patterns to cooperate successfully? Make a list of the expressions that would be useful to know in order to cooperate.

◆ *Cooperative Exercise: Feedback on Non-SWE Usage*

A. **Homework.** These are most of the statements from Hairston's study of how serious some grammatical "errors" are. Do you know what is wrong with each one? Mark what you think is wrong individually as homework.

B. **Group Work.** Prepared students discuss their homework in groups of four. For each sentence, decide what the punctuation, capitalization, or usage error is and what the correction should be. Those students who have not completed the homework work in pairs together to decide on the error and the correction.

1. Tact not anger is the best tactic in this case.

2. He concentrated on his job he never took vacations.

3. Wellington said, Trains will just cause the lower classes to move about needlessly.

4. The three men talked between themselves and decided not to fire the auditor.

5. Never reveal your weaknesses to others, they will exploit them.

6. Everyone who attends will have to pay their own expenses.

7. Coventry is the most unique city in England.

8. People are always impressed by her smooth manner, elegant clothes, and being witty.

9. Almost everyone dislikes her; they say she is careless and insolent.

10. The state's hiring policies intimidate the applications of ambitious people.

11. The small towns are dying. One of the problems being that young people are leaving.

12. Having argued all morning, a decision was finally reached.

13. If the regulating agency sets down on the job, everyone will suffer.
14. The situation is quite different than that of previous years.
15. A person who knows French and german will get along well in Switzerland.
16. It is late in his term and inflation is worse and no one has a solution.
17. Out companys record is exceptional.
18. The President dismissed four cabinet members among them Joseph Califano.
19. When Mitchell moved, he brung his secretary with him.
20. Three causes of inflation are: easy credit, costly oil, and consumer demand.
21. When a person moves every year, one cannot expect them to develop civic pride.
22. We direct our advertising to the young prosperous and sports-minded reader.
23. The worst situation is when the patient ignores warning symptoms.
24. The army moved my husband and I to California last year.
25. He went through a long battle. A fight against unscrupulous opponents.
26. The lieutenant treated his men bad.
27. Sanford inquired whether the loan was overdue?
28. When the time came to pay the filing fee however the candidate withdrew.
29. The data supports her hypothesis.
30. Those are the employees that were honored.
31. Visitors find it difficult to locate the plant, which affects business.
32. Him and Richards were the last ones hired.
33. There has never been no one here like that woman.
34. These kind of errors would soon bankrupt a company.
35. My favorite quotation is, "Take what you want and pay for it.
36. The report paid attention to officers but ignores enlisted men.
37. If I was in charge of that campaign, I would be worried about opinion polls.
38. If Clemens had picked that option, his family would of been rich.
39. Its wonderful to have Graham back on the job.
40. Calhoun has went after every prize in the universe.
41. Next year we expect to send a representative to China (if Peking allows it.
42. Cheap labor and low costs. These are two benefits enjoyed by Taiwan-based firms.
43. The difficult part is if the client refuses to cooperate.
44. State employees can't hardly expect a raise this year.
45. The supervisor has no objections to us leaving.
46. Although the candidate is new to politics she has a good chance of winning.
47. A convicted felon no matter how good his record may not serve on a grand jury.

48. I was last employed by texas instruments company.

49. When leaving college, clothes suddenly become a major problem.

50. Enclosed in his personnel file is his discharge papers and job references.

51. The president or the vice-president are going to be at the opening ceremonies.

52. To me, every person is an individual, and they should be treated with respect.

53. Good policemen require three qualities: courage, tolerance, and dedicated.

54. The interruption will not effect my work.

55. I have always hoped to work in that field, now I will have the opportunity.

56. Senator javits comes from new york.

57. That is her across the street.

58. I believe that everyone of them are guilty.

59. Cox cannot predict, that street crime will diminish.

60. When we was in the planning stages of the project, we underestimated costs.

61. The union claims it's rights have been violated.

62. The company is prepared to raise prices. In spite of administrative warnings.

63. Jones don't think it is acceptable.

64. Man is not the only user of tools, apes can also learn to manipulate them.

C. **Group Work.** In your groups, once you have completed the test, find an example of each type of error in the following list. If there are terms you do not understand, make a note of them in your Language Notebook. This exercise is to help you learn the typology and terminology of common-non-SWE errors.

Nonstandard Form

Verb form

Negation

Other (try to label)

Wrong Word or Spelling

SSE Transfer to SWE

Pronoun form

Noun and pronoun agreement

Fragment

Run-on sentence

Wrong modifier (e.g., adjective instead of adverb or vice versa)

Subject–verb agreement

Punctuation

Apostrophe not necessary

Quotations

Comma not necessary

Comma splice

Word spacing problem

Capitalization

Missing parentheses

 Style

Parallel structure

Dangling modifer

Informal or awkward

Verb-tense switch

D. **Class Work.** As a whole class, go over your results from Part C. For the unknown terms that you noted in your Language Notebook, write a definition and add the examples from the class work.

◆ *Writing Assignment*

Write a short essay in your Language Notebook in response to one or both of these questions. Save your essay(s) for later use.

1. Select one of the grammar points from Hairston's survey. Decide if the presentation of that point is best done as an inductive or as a deductive minilecture. Write a script or case history that details how you might present it. Use this minilecture checklist: connection, relevance, organization (deductive/inductive), graphic organizer, exceptions, and practice.

2. Do a Web search on the words "Cooperative Learning." Select a few sites to read. Synthesize and summarize the most interesting points you find.

Introspection

Look at your essay(s) carefully and proofread for spelling, punctuation, and non-standard or non-SWE usage.

LEARNING TO TEACH

Characteristics of the Multidimensional Classroom

Put the letter of each of the following sentences under the correct category in the table that follows.

A. Teachers give very brief, accurate, and fairly spontaneous minilectures about a grammar point.

F. Grammar teachers organize their syllabus around specific grammatical problems, such as subject–verb agreement, the use of the apostrophe, or verb forms.

L. Accurate grammatical usage is the most important goal for the language arts or English classroom.

O. Teachers give detailed lectures about English grammar, followed by many workbook drills.

P. The syllabus or the textbook sequence determines the selection of which grammar point to cover.

R. Student interest and need determine the selection of what grammar points to cover.

S. Grammar teachers organize their syllabus and lesson plans around genres of literature, a composition topic, or a language subject area that learners are interested in.

T. Major goals of the language arts or English classroom are learning about language as well as learning to use SWE effectively.

	Traditional Grammar Classroom	Multidimensional Classroom
Syllabus Design Principle		
Learning Goal		
Method of Presentation		
Selection of Grammar Points		

Think about Mr. Green and Mr. Brown from earlier in this chapter. Which teacher creates which classroom?

◆ *Find Out More*

Interesting Books About English

Crystal, D. (1995). *The Cambridge encyclopedia of the English language.* Cambridge, UK: Cambridge University Press.

Fry, E., Fountoukidis, D., & Polk, J. (1985). *The New reading teacher's book of lists.* Englewood Cliffs, NJ: Prentice Hall.

Justice, P. (2001). *Relevant linguistics: An introduction to the structure and use of English for teachers.* Stanford, CA: CSLI Publications.

McArthur, T. (Ed.). (1992). *The Oxford companion to the English language.* Oxford, UK: Oxford University Press.

Computer-Assisted Language Learning

Maurer, J. (2000). *Focus on Grammar.* White Plains, NY: Addison-Wesley Longman. (Text with CD-ROM)

Noden, H. (1999). *Image grammar: Using grammatical structures to teach writing.* Portsmouth, NH: Heinemann. (Text with CD-ROM)

SECTION 2

The Microscopic Perspective

The multidimensional classroom with a language awareness curriculum requires instructional dialogue between teacher and learners and meaningful discussion in cooperative groups on descriptive grammar, usage norms for Standard Written English and Academic English, and editing skills. These requirements can be intimidating. If teachers are fearful that learners will ask questions to which they do not know the answers, they will be inhibited from encouraging free and easy talk. If teachers feel insecure about what they are teaching, they will unintentionally communicate this to learners. This section is an attempt to empower teachers in training by laying out the major and minor parts of speech and the challenges in their usage.

We can examine the English language like we examine a living creature through a microscope to see each of its tiny parts. We can describe the separate parts with their own characteristics, but we can also describe the systems of organs and tissues working together synergistically to achieve a function. The English language also has separate parts and systems that synergize to achieve a communicative function. These parts and systems are words and pieces of words, parts of speech, and phrases.

However, this section is somewhat of a paradox. It is an attempt to empower students, yet some students get lost in the details. To avoid feeling lost, students need to forget the old definitions they may have learned before. Then, by using any techniques for successful learning they can, they must develop their understanding of and memory for the descriptive facts, the forms, and the labels. This is declarative knowledge, or **metalanguage.** The chapters in this section also present **diagnostic tools** for determining parts of speech; if you learn to use the diagnostics, you can determine the part of speech of many of the words you see. That is procedural knowledge. The procedure is empowering because with just a little information, insight, and some metalinguistic awareness, anyone can feel confident enough to start teaching grammar.

Chapter 5 explains the important distinction between content words, which carry the meaning in a sentence, and function words, which create a grammatical frame to help one comprehend the meaning. The chapter introduces the **discovery procedure,** in which students learn how to use the characteristics of a word in context as diagnostics to determine what part of speech it has. The distinction between content and function and the discovery procedure also extend to the smallest building blocks of words—derivational and inflectional morphemes—the topic of Chapter 6. If you can look into the structure of a word, you can gain more information about its part of speech.

The remaining chapters in this section present declarative and procedural knowledge about the other parts of speech. Chapter 7 is about nouns, Chapter 8 is about determiners and pronouns, Chapter 9 is about adjectives and adverbs, and Chapter 10 is about verbals, a term that includes verbs and other verblike words. The final chapter of this section, Chapter 11, is about prepositions and particles.

5

Word Categories and Words

A logical place to begin to look at parts of speech is at the basic level of the word. Words are composed of smaller components, such as *suffixes* and *prefixes,* at the same time that they themselves are components of larger pieces of language called *phrases.* Words are divided into different parts of speech, or different *syntactic categories.* The linguist's task is to determine what the categories are, how the categories relate to each other, and what specific words belong to which categories. How do they do that?

SYNTACTIC CATEGORIES: CRISP OR FUZZY?

Traditional Categories

Some people think that parts of speech are separate and distinct grammatical categories into which words are placed according to their semantic definitions, as shown in Table 5.1. These are called *traditional parts of speech* (or "classical" categories; Newmeyer, 1998).

Semantic Definitions

Some people think that each word has one and only one part of speech and that if a word meets the semantic definition of a certain category, then it belongs in that category. The semantic definition of *noun* is "person, place, or thing"; therefore *apple* is a noun because it is a thing, *baby* is a noun because it is a person, and *chair* is a noun because it is a thing. If a word is in one category, it cannot be in another.

Crisp Categories

These syntactic categories have precise boundaries between them; they are **crisp categories.** *Noun* includes all words that have "person," "place," or "thing" in their definitions. *Verb* includes all words that have "action" or "state of being" in their definitions. However, crisp categories based on semantic definitions create some problems for teachers and learners.

TABLE 5.1 ▨▨▨▨▨▨▨▨▨▨▨▨▨▨▨▨▨▨▨▨▨▨▨▨▨▨▨▨

Traditional Parts of Speech

Nouns	Verbs	Adjectives
apple	amble	active
baby	be	bellicose
chair	call	captivating
dog	deal	dead
explosion	explode	evasive
fun	fill	fair

Problems

In a typical classroom scenario, teachers introduce parts of speech with their semantic definitions beginning in about fourth grade. Children practice identifying parts of speech with "sanitized" grammar, that is, exercises carefully constructed to have only examples that fit the definitions. In this case, learners do not come across any perplexing words, and they do not ask questions that teachers cannot answer. In the real world, however, grammatical analysis is messy, and words are perplexing. Semantic definitions and crisp categories do not give teachers or learners any <u>strategies</u> to resolve grammatical dilemmas, so they may feel stupid and powerless.

In another scenario—a classroom with many English learners—teachers talk of traditional notions such as "adjectives modify nouns." Later, the learners find out that comparative adjectives take the suffix *-er,* as in *taller, shorter,* or *fatter.* A few enterprising English learners sometimes begin producing expressions like this: **the stoner wall* or **the milker glass.* The teacher cannot give a coherent <u>explanation</u> to learners for why those expressions are wrong even though he or she knows that they are wrong. The modifier seems to be an adjective, so why can it not take *-er?*

Prototypes

Part of the problem is that semantic definitions work best for prototypical examples of each part of speech but do not work for nonprototypical examples. Prototypical nouns are names for persons, places, and things. Prototypical verbs are actions and states of being. But in real language, only some nouns are persons, places, and things. Others—**abstract nouns,** such as *happiness,* or **activity nouns,** such as *swimming*—do not match the semantic definition well. Many verbs refer to actions or states of being, but many others do not (e.g., *elapse*). These nonprototypical words can confuse learners.

Another complication is that words can act like they belong in two categories. Nouns such as *explosion* and *hibernation* refer to both actions and states of being as much as their corresponding verbs do. The word *painting* illustrates a range of nouniness and verbiness in each of these sentences:

The painting is beautiful.
Painting is relaxing.

> *I love painting.*
> *I am painting right now.*

Rigid, crisp categories cannot represent nonprototypical words easily because some words are not either/or but rather both.

Functional Shift

These examples, collected from real speech, show that there is another problem. English words switch their syntactic category; for example, nouns easily become verbs:

> *The dictator has <u>hitlered</u> his country for a long time.*
> *Who is going to <u>person</u> the booth at the craft fair?*
> *Let's hope they don't get <u>Waco'd</u>.*
> *The unruly students <u>egged</u> the principal. (threw eggs at)*
> *You just <u>glue-gun</u> the fabric to the wood.*

Functional shift is a normal and very productive word formation process in English. If English speakers need a verb, they simply use a noun as a verb.

A Vicious Cycle

The most serious problem is that traditional notions of parts of speech create a vicious cycle for learners and teachers. Many children do not find such parts of speech helpful, and they get frustrated. Children who do succeed in learning grammatical terms—children with a high metalinguistic awareness or an aptitude for language—seem to learn the parts of speech intuitively despite the way they are taught. Teachers do not have much motivation to spend precious classroom time teaching metalanguage if it is frustrating for some learners and repetitive for others who may grasp it quickly. In addition, many teachers are themselves the product of traditional grammar instruction and do not feel very confident about their own knowledge of metalanguage. The less confident teachers are, the less willing they are to teach the subject matter. If they do teach it, they fall back on the traditional notions because they do not know any alternative that works better. The cycle is complete.

To break out of the vicious cycle, we need a notion of part of speech that comes from the ways in which words function in English. First, the categories must be based on something more concrete than semantics. Second, it has to give learners and teachers a strategy to determine the part of speech of any word they come across. Finally, it must offer consistent explanations for linguistic data.

Functional Parts of Speech

A new way of looking at parts of speech has emerged from functional studies of language, from psycholinguistics, and from cognitive science (Croft, 1991; Cumming & Ono, 1997; Heine, 1993; Hopper & Thompson, 1984, 1985; Langacker, 1987, 1991; for a good summary but an opposing view, see Newmeyer, 1998). The new perspective is that words in isolation are not assigned to grammatical categories. We cannot say, for example, that *love* is a noun or that *old* is an adjective unless we see the word used in a context.

Weighted Preferences

However, words do have preferences (or **weights**) for certain uses, and these weights can be very strong. For example, the words *apple* or *boy* are strongly weighted toward use as nouns, but they appear as verbs in innovative uses such as *The students appled the teacher* or *The scouts didn't man the booth; they boyed the booth.* The word *run* is strongly weighted toward being a verb, yet it has weights for noun as well: *The run was tiring and long.* We must examine the context and the function of the word in context to determine what part of speech it has.

Fuzzy Categories

In contrast to crisp categories, functional grammatical categories are **fuzzy.** Fuzzy categories have a more complex structure in that they include both prototypical members and outlying members. Outlying members fit into the category partially, and they may fit into other categories as well. *Red,* for example, can be a noun, but it is not the name of a person, place, or thing. Similarly, the word *painting* can be used as a noun, but it is also an action and therefore meets the criteria for verbs. The word *bored* as an adjective can describe a noun, but it also can be an action (*The meeting bored him*) or a state of being (*He was bored by the meeting*), so it is also very verblike. Therefore, parts of speech have imprecise, permeable boundaries; they are fuzzy, not crisp (see Figure 5.1).

Category Definitions

The characteristics of prototypical members of each category define the category, and nonprototypical members fit in more or less. The characteristics of prototypical members come from meaning, function, syntax, and word formation. These characteristics also serve as diagnostic tools to determine category membership of candidate words and offer explanations for linguistic data.

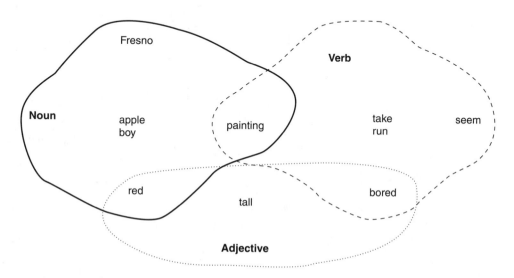

Figure 5.1 *Fuzzy parts of speech.*

CONTRASTING TWO GRAMMATICAL PROCEDURES ▬▬▬▬

Knowledge of the English parts of speech is declarative knowledge. When we use that knowledge to determine the part of speech of any given word, we are using procedural knowledge. We can contrast two procedures: a traditional one that does not work very well and a discovery procedure that offers learners some strategies to discover a word's part of speech.

The Traditional Procedure

The traditional procedure relies on a semantic definition, such as "an adjective is any word that modifies a noun." Within the category of adjectives, there is a subcategory of *determiner* (e.g., *the, that, his*) because those words modify nouns (see Figure 5.2).

Procedural Problems

Applying this procedure is simple. Learners memorize the simple definition and consider anything that modifies a noun an adjective. Determining a word's part of speech is superficially easy, but unfortunately the results are often incorrect. For one thing, even beginning grammar learners might find it counterintuitive to treat two different types of words as if they were the same:

◆ Determiners constitute a small group of unchanging words that occur over and over again. Their meanings are grammatical and are unlikely to be found in a dictionary for a native speaker.

◆ Descriptive adjectives constitute a huge class of words that are susceptible to borrowing from other languages and innovation. They are found in all dictionaries.

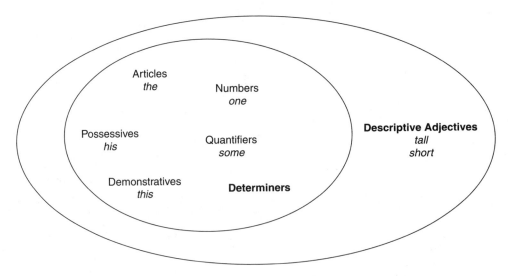

Figure 5.2 *A semantic theory of adjectives.*

These other differences between determiners and adjectives are not explained by a procedure based on semantics:

◆ Syntax:

Determiners occur at the beginning of a noun phrase, such as *this red book, his intelligent professor,* or *some enchanted evening.* Adjectives must occur right before the noun.

Adjectives can also occur after the verb *to be,* but determiners cannot: *is red, are intelligent,* or *will be enchanted.*

Adjectives can take the word *very,* but determiners cannot.

◆ Function:

While both determiners and adjectives modify the noun (roughly speaking), the determiner gives mainly grammatical information, while the descriptive adjective characterizes or attributes some meaningful property to the noun.

◆ Suffixes:

Determiners do not usually take endings such as *-er* or *-est,* with only one prominent exception *(few, fewer, fewest).*

Descriptive adjectives take the suffixes *-er* and *-est* (or the words *more/most*) and can also take other suffixes, such as *-ful* or *-less.*

Because the traditional procedure overlooks very basic differences when determining parts of speech, it does not work very well. It offers confusion, not explanation. Even worse, this procedure does not offer the learner tools or strategies to figure things out if the definition does not work.

The Discovery Procedure

The discovery procedure stems from a careful study of the characteristics of words in contexts to determine the defining properties of the grammatical category as a whole:

CATEGORY 1	CATEGORY 2	CATEGORY 3
his	*active*	*imagination*
the	*bellicose*	*statement*
their	*captivating*	*smiles*
two	*dead*	*birds*
this	*evasive*	*tactic*
some	*fair*	*consequences*

Fuzzy Reasoning

Because syntactic categories are fuzzy and defined by a series of properties, **fuzzy reasoning** is the basis for the discovery procedure. Fuzzy reasoning is based on uncertain, conflicting information of different weights and importance. Fuzzy reasoning is common in our daily lives (see Figure 5.3); we use it whenever our decisions operate within the gray areas of competing information. In fuzzy decision-making, we come up with a reasonable hypothesis, or a **best guess,** by allowing some information to carry

Let's say you're driving in the country. You come up behind a slow-moving vehicle on the road, and you must decide if you should pass it or not. There are a lot of uncertainties here. There is a lot of competing information of different importance and weight. Some issues are the following: Is there an oncoming car in the other lane? (If yes, it is very heavily weighted against passing.) Is there a broken yellow line or a solid yellow line? (If the latter, it is heavily weighted against passing.) Is there road work ahead? (If yes, don't pass.) Is the slow-moving car a police car? (If yes—well, you get the picture.)

Figure 5.3 *Fuzzy reasoning in daily life.*

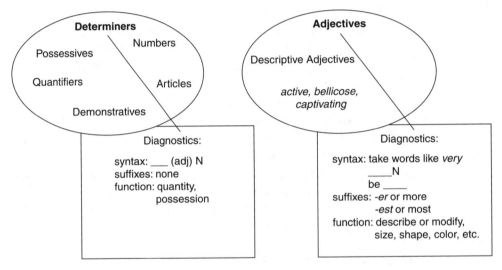

Figure 5.4 *Discovery procedure using diagnostics for adjectives and determiners.*

more weight than other information. Weights are increased or decreased on the basis of other knowledge. The most heavily weighted information forms the solution or leads to a decision. Some of this information is syntactic, but other information involves meaning, context, and word formation.

The human brain can apply fuzzy decision-making procedures quickly and, for the most part, accurately, but it must have declarative knowledge and experience in order to do it. So it is with determining a word's part of speech. Learners need to have information about the word, candidate parts of speech, experience with weighted information, and practice with the procedure.

Determining a Word's Part of Speech

To determine whether a word is a determiner or an adjective, you need to examine the properties of the word in context and use the diagnostics for each part of speech (see Figure 5.4).

At first, applying diagnostics can be clumsy because students do not remember what the diagnostics are. However, diagnostics such as those exemplified in Box 5.1

Box 5.1   Sample Discovery Procedure for *Every* and *Black*

Every black cat caught a mouse.

Is *every* an adjective?
 Diagnostics:
  Very: *very every (ungrammatical expressions marked with an
                     asterisk)
  be _____: *be every
  more/-er: *more every, *everier
 Decision: Based on this negative evidence, *every* is not an adjective.

Is *every* a determiner?
 Context: determiner (adjective) noun

                   every (black) cat

 Suffix: None
 Function: Quantity
 Decision: Based on this positive evidence, *every* is a determiner.

Is *black* an adjective?
 Diagnostics:
  Very: *very black*
  be _____: *be black*
  more/-er: *blacker*
 Decision: Based on this positive evidence, *black* is an adjective.

---

are the same from each instance to another, so declarative knowledge grows from practice. As students gain knowledge and experience with the procedure, they see it as a tool—a strategy to follow when they are perplexed about a word. And as they apply the procedure, they find explanations easier to understand. Most of all, as they apply the procedure actively, they acquire syntactic awareness.

CONTENT AND FUNCTION WORDS

Languages have a primary distinction between two types of words: **content words** and **function words.** In the sentence *The girl planted the small tree carefully,* the content words are *girl, planted, small, tree,* and *carefully.* The function words are *the* and *the* as shown in Figure 5.5. The determiner *the* tells us that the word *girl* and the word *tree* refer to a specific girl and tree that hearers or readers have already identified in their minds. Adjectives such as *small* are content words, and determiners such as *the* are function words. A procedure to determine parts of speech that treats both of these as the same (i.e., adjectives) misses this important and fundamental point.

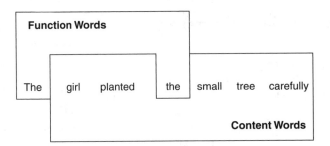

Figure 5.5 *Content and function words.*

CONTENT WORDS = THE *OPEN* CLASS

◆ Carry the weight of meaning

◆ Allow for invention or borrowing from another language

◆ Are nouns, verbs, adjectives, and adverbs

FUNCTION WORDS = THE *CLOSED* CLASS

◆ Supply grammatical details about words and meaning

◆ Form a syntactic frame for content words

◆ Are resistant to invention or borrowing

◆ Are prepositions, pronouns, conjunctions, determiners, etc.

There are other differences between content words and function words. Content words (e.g., *man, teacher, eat, happy, rapidly*) occur relatively infrequently, but function words (e.g., *the, in, be, and*) occur very frequently. Content words tend to be longer than function words. The number of content words is very large and always grows, but the number of function words is smaller and static. Content words receive more stress in spoken sentences than function words, which are usually unstressed, sometimes to the point of inaudibility. For example, the question *Did you eat yet?* is often reduced to *Jeat yet?*

Content Words and Meaning

Grammar exists to convey meaning. Meaning starts in our heads because it stems from our perceptions and imagination, but it is about things in the world or things we think are in the world. For example, our sentence *The girl planted the small tree carefully* could be about a real girl, a real tree, and a real planting incident in perceptions or stored in long-term memory. Alternatively, it could be about an imaginary girl, an imaginary tree, and an imaginary planting incident in working memory. In either case, the words refer to entities and relationships in a *mental* situation that may or may not accurately reflect what is in the world. The sentence communicates either mental reality equally well.

Spoken and written sentences refer to mental situations. Nouns refer to mental entities, adjectives tell us information about the entities, verbs refer to the relationships between the entities, and adverbs (prototypically) inform about the relationships or the situations themselves.

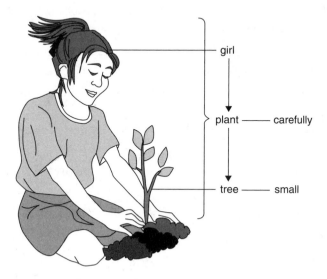

Based on the mental entities, relationships, and situations, content and function words arrange themselves into typical **syntactic templates,** or frames made of parts of speech that commonly go together. Syntactic templates are few in number. The following template, called a **noun phrase (NP),** is determiner (adjective)

noun, where the adjective is optional. Categories that are optional are marked by parentheses:

$$
\begin{bmatrix}
\text{(Det)} & \text{(Adj)} & \text{N} \\
\text{The} & & \text{girl} \\
\text{The} & \text{small} & \text{tree}
\end{bmatrix}
$$

Function Words and the Meaning of Discourse

We understand the meaning of the sentence *The girl planted the small tree carefully* from the content words alone. Because the function words are not essential to the meaning of a single sentence, some people fail to appreciate the importance of function words in our comprehension of **discourse,** or texts that are longer than one sentence. In long discourse, we comprehend the meaning of each sentence and the overall meaning more easily and rapidly if there are typical syntactic templates made up of content and function words that we can recognize (see Figure 5.6).

Contrast your experience reading the first paragraph and your experience reading the second:

1. newspaper carry big story man bit dog false people believe illogical silly people believe call talk show radio discuss host egg make fool when find out story untrue want sue talk show host.
2. The newspaper carried a big story about a man who bit a dog. It was false, but many people believed it even though it was illogical and silly. The people who

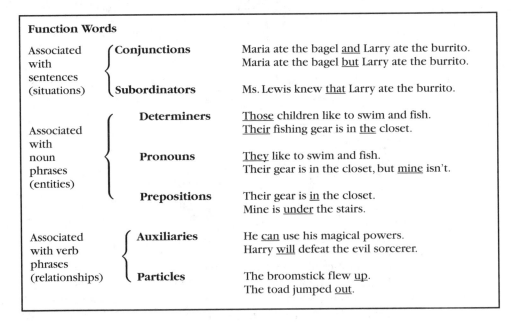

Function Words

Associated with sentences (situations)	Conjunctions	Maria ate the bagel <u>and</u> Larry ate the burrito. Maria ate the bagel <u>but</u> Larry ate the burrito.
	Subordinators	Ms. Lewis knew <u>that</u> Larry ate the burrito.
Associated with noun phrases (entities)	Determiners	<u>Those</u> children like to swim and fish. <u>Their</u> fishing gear is in <u>the</u> closet.
	Pronouns	<u>They</u> like to swim and fish. Their gear is in the closet, but <u>mine</u> isn't.
	Prepositions	Their gear is <u>in</u> the closet. Mine is <u>under</u> the stairs.
Associated with verb phrases (relationships)	Auxiliaries	He <u>can</u> use his magical powers. Harry <u>will</u> defeat the evil sorcerer.
	Particles	The broomstick flew <u>up</u>. The toad jumped <u>out</u>.

Figure 5.6 *List of function words.*

believed it called into a talk show on the radio to discuss it and the host egged them on to make fools of themselves. When they found out that the story was untrue, they wanted to sue the talk show host.

In the first, the reader encounters a list of random words and infers the relationships among the content words on the basis of her experience with the world. The reader juggles the word meanings and relationships while making other inferences that are also uncertain. Holding all this uncertainty in working memory causes the reader to find this text difficult to understand and remember.

In the second paragraph, the function words and the syntactic templates clarify the entities and their relationships, so that they can be stored in memory easily. The reader makes fewer inferences, there is very little uncertainty, there is less cognitive work, and the paragraph is easier to understand and remember.

If readers cannot use function words and templates as cues to discourse meaning, everything they read would be like the first paragraph. This may be the case with readers who lack syntactic awareness or learners with low proficiency in English.

More Fuzzy Distinctions

Content Versus Function

The distinction between content and function is an important and basic one, but like most distinctions in language, it is a continuum and not a hard-and-fast separation, as shown in Figure 5.7. For example, we include prepositions as function words, and some prepositions, such as *of* or *to,* do seem to mark grammatical relationships in this sentence: *The retiring professor of English gave the old books to the students.* However, other prepositions make an important contribution to overall meaning, as in the sentence *He donated the books after his last class and before his last department meeting.*

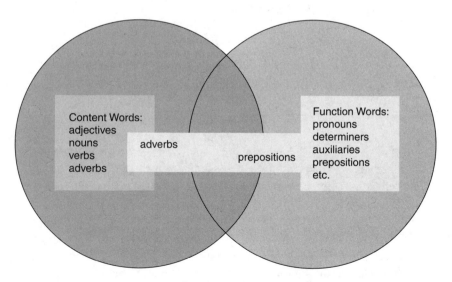

Figure 5.7 *Fuzzy boundary between content and function.*

A TEACHING MOMENT

One Word or Two?

These are one word in SWE and should always be written as such: *already* (*They were already singing*); *altogether, anymore, another, anyone, anybody, nobody, everyone, everybody, cannot,* and *maybe* (to mean *perhaps*); *ourselves;* and *whatever.*

These are two separate words in SWE: *a lot, all ready* (*The children were all ready to sing*), *all right, every time, in spite of, may be* (*He may be here*), and *no one.*

Similarly, we consider adverbs content words, but some of them only add a small grammatical nuance to the meaning of the sentence and would be unusual for a native speaker to look up in the dictionary. In this sentence, *very* and *too* are adverbs, more specifically, **intensifiers:** *The <u>very</u> ancient professor was <u>too</u> kind to ask for money.* It would be hard to imagine borrowing a new intensifier, such as *very* or *too,* from another language or coining a new one out of the blue.

In addition, function words can be used as content words. For example, prepositions have been converted into verb or noun forms along the lines of *They outed their friend at his birthday party* or *They went along on the class outing.* Thus, it seems that even the fundamental distinction between content and function words is fuzzy and not crisp. As always, we must consider the context of the word to make a determination.

Languages use another type of word, called **inserts,** in addition to content and function words. Inserts, such as *yeah, huh, bye,* and *uh-oh* are especially common in

---

A QUESTION OF STYLE

Content words and function words differ from informal style in conversation and fiction to formal style in news and especially academic writing. Here are some differences:

	Conversation	Academic Prose
Nouns	man, woman, day	proof, evidence, tests
	supper, breakfast	author, premise
Verbs	have, do, get	claim, prove, establish
Adjectives	happy, depressed	former, obvious, clear
Adverbs	very, too,	absolutely, unmistakably
Prepositions	in, to, over	throughout, despite
Pronouns	I, you	he
Conjunctions	and, or	neither/nor

Learners need to learn to avoid certain informal phrases in writing, such as *a bunch of* and *kind of,* and begin to use vocabulary more appropriate to formal style.

conversation (Biber, Johansson, Leech, Conrad & Finegan, 1999, p. 56) but are rare in writing, except in written conversations in fiction. Inserts are neither content nor function words.

There are also **multiword lexical units** (Biber et al., 1999, p. 58), such as *sort of* (or *sorta*) or *going to* (or *gonna*) that function as one word in Standard Spoken English (SSE) but are more than one word in Standard Written English (SWE), with resultant spelling errors. Multiword lexical units can be combinations of function and content words.

EXPLORING CHAPTER PERSPECTIVES

◆ *Discussion Questions*

1. What are some examples of fuzzy reasoning you use in your daily life?

2. With your writing assignment from Chapter 1 in your Language Notebook, rewrite a paragraph with only content words to the best of your ability. Give it to your partner to read. How easy or hard is it for your partner to understand your meaning? Then rewrite another paragraph from your essay with only function words as best as you can. How easy or hard is it for your partner to understand?

3. What were your experiences with traditional parts of speech and traditional ways of distinguishing parts of speech? How did you learn declarative knowledge about the parts of speech in English? What procedural knowledge did you acquire to help you determine the part of speech of a word?

4. In the past 25 years or so, people occasionally have (sometimes partly in jest) called for a pronoun of inderterminate gender similar to *he* and *she.* Suggested pronouns have been *hesh, shehe,* and even *shesh.* Do you think this suggestion will ever be successful? Why or why not?

◆ *Cooperative Exercise: Spanglish*

A. **Homework.** Read the newspaper article by Deborah Kong titled "Spanish-English Blend Talks Its Way into TV and Academia" and write notes to answer the following questions in your Language Notebook.

1. Is Spanglish a real language? What do critics of Spanglish think of it? What does it mean to some Spanglish speakers?

2. What is the origin of Spanglish? Will Spanglish replace English? What is the future of Spanglish?

3. What is your opinion of the translation of Don Quixote into Spanglish? Who do you agree with?

4. The word *violadores* is a mistranslation of the word *violators.* Look up the word *violator* in a good dictionary. Where did it come from? Are the two words historically related to each other? Why does *violator* mean one thing and *violador* mean another?

5. What part of speech are most of the Spanglish words in the article? How can you tell what part of speech they are if you do not know what the word is? There are a few examples of another part of speech. What is it?

B. **Pair Work.**

1. Compare your answers to the questions in Part A and supplement your own notes with what your partner adds to your ideas.

2. Draw the chart below in your Language Notebook. Take one or two of the numbered sections of the text, discuss each word, and divide them into four categories. In each case, be ready to explain your answer.

Content Words	Function Words	Inserts	Not Sure

C. **Class Work.**

1. Spot-check answers from columns 1 to 3. Go over any words in column 4 and assign them to one of the other categories.

2. Hand in your chart from Part B.

◆ *Writing Assignment*

Write a short essay in your Language Notebook in response to one or both of these prompts. Save your essay(s) for later use.

1. Write about your experiences with learning traditional parts of speech and traditional ways of distinguishing parts of speech. Do you think that fuzzy parts of speech and the discovery procedures will help you? Why or why not?

2. What is your opinion of Spanglish and the article we read? When you are finished, place your ideas and opinions in the continum of language attitudes from Chapter 1.

Introspection

Look at your essay(s) carefully and proofread for spelling, punctuation, and nonstandard or non-SWE usage. When you are finished with your essay(s), underline all the content words. Circle all the function words. What words were you unsure of?

SPANISH-ENGLISH BLEND TALKS ITS WAY INTO TV AND ACADEMIA

By Deborah Kong

Reprinted by permission of *The Associated Press*

(1) In the wacky cartoon world of the "Mucha Lucha" wrestling school, Buena Girl is trying
(2) to help her friend gain weight in preparation for his match with three big "brutos."
(3) "And now for the ultimate in buena eats! El Masked Montana's mega torta!" she says,
(4) stuffing an enormous sandwich into his mouth.
(5) The WB network's new show is peppered with a blend of Spanish and English dialogue
(6) often called Spanglish. And TV isn't the only place you'll find it.
(7) An Amherst College professor recently completed a Spanglish translation of the first
(8) chapter of "Don Quixote," and Hallmark is expanding its line of cards that mix
(9) America's most commonly spoken languages.
(10) Not everyone is happy to see Spanglish creep into the mainstream. Critics see it as a
(11) danger to Hispanic culture and advancement. But Spanglish speakers, who often move
(12) nimbly between the two languages and cultures, say it is an expression of ethnic pride.
(13) "Spanglish is proof that Latinos have a culture that is made up of two parts. It's not that
(14) you are Latino or American," said Ilan Stavans, the professor of Latin American and
(15) Latino culture who translated Miguel de Cervantes' masterpiece. "You live on the
(16) hyphen, in between. That's what Spanglish is all about, a middle ground."
(17) Spanglish speakers span generations, classes and nationalities. Immigrants still
(18) learning English may turn to Spanglish out of necessity, bilingual speakers may dip into
(19) one language, then weave in another because it's more convenient.
(20) "There are certain words or sayings that are just better in Spanish," said Danny Lopez,
(21) 28, who speaks Spanglish with friends and family, though seldom at work.
(22) "When I talk to my dad, I'll say, "Hey Dad, I remember sitting in abuelita's cocina when
(23) we were little, and we were drinking a taza of café," said Lopez, describing memories of
(24) his grandmother's kitchen. His family has lived in the United States for four generations.
(25) Stavans traces Spanglish's origins back to 1848, when the treaty that ended the
(26) U.S.-Mexican War signed over much of the Southwest to the United States, abruptly
(27) transforming Spanish-speaking Mexicans into Americans.
(28) But the modern phenomenon has plenty of pop culture examples, from Ricky Martin
(29) scoring a big hit with "Livin' la Vida Loca" to top-selling Mexican singer Paulina Rubio
(30) doing all of her songs in Spanglish as she opens for Enrique Iglesias.
(31) At mun2, a cable network that shows music videos, comedies, game shows, extreme
(32) sports and other programming targeted at 14- to 34-year-old Hispanics, language has
(33) evolved in the last year. When it launched, most of the programs were in Spanish. But
(34) the network, a division of NBC-owned Telemundo, will soon be mostly English and
(35) Spanglish, in response to viewer preferences, said spokeswoman Claudia Santa Cruz.
(36) Stavans translated Cervantes into Spanglish this summer in response to a
(37) Spanish-language purist who asserted the linguistic mix would never be taken seriously
(38) until it produced a classic like "Don Quixote."

(Continued)

(39) "In un placete de La Mancha of which nombre no quiero remembrearme, vivia, not so
(40) long ago, uno de esos gentlemen who always tienened una lanza in the rack, una
(41) buckler Antigua, a skinny caballo y un greyhound para el chase," his translation begins.
(42) Stavans' work signals Spanglish's move into academe: He also teaches a class on
(43) Spanglish and is working on a Spanglish dictionary, to be published next year.
(44) But Antonio Garrido of the Institute Cervantes in New York, said a Spanglish "Don
(45) Quixote" is a joke.
(46) "The idea is good English and good Spanish. Spanglish has no future," said Garrido,
(47) director of the institute created by the Spanish government to promote Spanish and
(48) Hispanic-American language and culture. "A person who doesn't speak English well in
(49) the United States doesn't have a future."
(50) Roberto Gonzalez Echevarria, a professor of Hispanic and comparative literature at Yale
(51) university, agreed, saying Hispanics should learn to speak both English and Spanish
(52) well. He fears "we're going to end up speaking McSpanish, a sort of anglicized Spanish.
(53) I find it offensive that United States' values and cultural mores, all that, are
(54) transmitted through the language filter into Spanish culture."
(55) He cited one example of a Spanglish pitfall: In a deli in Puerto Rico, he saw a sign that
(56) warned parking was for customers only.
(57) "Violadores" will be prosecuted, it said. The word was used because it sounds like the
(58) English word for violators, but the problem is that "violador" primarily means "rapist"
(59) in Spanish, he said.
(60) Stavans, who said he speaks Spanglish with his children, doesn't advocate replacing
(61) English with Spanglish. But he says it should be recognized as a valid form of
(62) communication.
(63) "Language is not controlled by a small group of academics that decide what the words
(64) are that we should use. Language is created by people and it is the job of academics to
(65) record those changes," he said.
(66) A recent survey by the Los Angeles-based Cultural Access Group found 74% of
(67) 250 Hispanic youths surveyed in Los Angeles spoke Spanglish, most often with friends,
(68) other young people, and at home.
(69) The WB network says "Much Lucha"—"lucha" means wrestling—reflects that reality. The
(70) zippy cartoon doesn't pause to translate Spanish phrases, but sprinkles them throughout
(71) to spice up dialogue.
(72) "This is the way that young Latino kids speak," said Donna Friedman, the Kids
(73) WB executive vice president.
(74) Hallmark says its cards also echo how people speak, "Que beautiful it is to do nada, and
(75) then descansar despues," reads one, which translates to, "How beautiful it is to do
(76) nothing, and then rest afterward."
(77) The greeting card company is expanding its line of Spanish-language cards, which
(78) includes Spanglish ones. They're aimed at younger recipients rather than mothers,
(79) aunts, or grandmothers, "who may not approve of mixing languages," according to the
(80) company. In Los Angeles, Lalo Alcaraz and Esteban Zul run a Web site, pocho.com,
(81) which offers "satire, news y chat for the Spanglish generation."

(82) "We don't live neatly in two worlds. I teach my kids Spanish, yet my wife and I speak
(83) English to each other," said Alcaraz, whose new Spanglish comic strip, "La Cucuracha,"
(84) will appear in newspapers next month. Spanglish is "its own unique point of view. It's
(85) more of an empowering thing to us, to say we have a legitimate culture."

Note: Language Lessons

Spanglish, a combination of Spanish and English, is spoken throughout the United States by many of the nation's more than 35 million Hispanics. It varies by region and nationality, such as with Puerto Ricans and Dominicans in New York, Mexican Americans in the Southwest, and Cuban Americans in Florida.

TEACHING TO LEARN

Distinguishing Content from Function

Taking turns with a partner and for each pair of sentences with homonyms, label the underlined form as content or function in the context of the sentence (declarative knowledge).

1. Yeng <u>will</u> study very hard for the English Placement Test.
2. Where there's a <u>will</u>, there's a way.
3. Sue hid the money in an coffee <u>can</u> in her freezer.
4. Do you think anyone <u>can</u> find it?
5. Those tomatoes don't taste <u>like</u> these.
6. I <u>like</u> food diversity.
7. <u>May</u> Lee enjoys reading the dictionary.
8. She <u>may</u> have the biggest vocabulary of anyone I know.

Then verbalize how you identified the word as such (procedural knowledge) as best you can.

LEARNING TO TEACH

Grammar Logs (VanDeWeghe, 1993)

Description: When teachers individualize their curriculum, it is more relevant to the learner. The best way to individualize learning and increase individual autonomy is to put the learner in charge of his own learning. In this activity, teachers and learners place the same value on speech and writing; learners verbalize the difference between them. Although teachers and learners need to spend time on the grammar log to learn from the activity, it should not detract from writing itself.

Goals

Subject area goal: acquisition of SWE writing conventions

English language awareness goal: contrastive analysis of learner's speech and Standard Written English

Descriptive grammar goal: metalanguage to explain or comment on differences

Procedural goals: proofreading and self-editing

Assessment: Teachers collect grammar logs and make comments on them. They can be interactive journals with minimal grading.

Methodology: Begin keeping a grammar log. Make a note of non-SWE or non-AE usages that your instructors mark in your writing, that you find yourself in any writing you do, or that you know are a common problem for you.

Take a section of your Language Notebook and make three columns. Label the first column "My Speech," the second "SWE and AE," and the third "Explanation." Go through the essays you wrote in previous chapters or other written work you have done. Make additions to your grammar log throughout the semester.

My Speech	SWE and AE	Explanation
kinda	kind of or very	2 words,
gonna	going to	informal usage

6

Words and Word Formation Procedures

Lexical awareness—awareness of words and word formation—grows like a mushroom; the more you know about words, the more you see in the words you come across. The more you see, the more intrigued you become, and the more you learn. Lexical awareness expands exponentially. (Watch out, though, you might find yourself reading the dictionary for fun!)

Lexical awareness is not separate from syntactic awareness because words carry important clues about their part of speech that we exploit in the discovery procedure. We need to focus on words with a finer setting on our microscope to see their smallest meaningful components: morphemes.

Morphemes are the bits and pieces from which words are formed (see Box 6.1). A morpheme is a minimal language form with its own meaning. This definition has three conditions. First, there must be a **form,** a unit of language that usually consists of a sequence of sounds in speech and in letters in writing. Second, the form must be associated with a **meaning,** either a grammatical meaning or a meaning with real content. Third, the form must be **minimal** in that it cannot be broken down into any smaller meaningful units.

FREE MORPHEMES AND COMPOUNDING

Free Morphemes

Single-morpheme content or function words (or inserts) used independently are called **free morphemes.** The word *sun* is a free morpheme because it has a form consisting of three sounds, and its meaning can be found in any dictionary. Its form cannot be broken down into smaller meaningful units. None of the letters or sounds by themselves have inherent meaning. Other free morphemes are *star, eat, blue, Illinois, to, of, you*, and *whom*.

Compounding

When people form new English words by juxtaposing two or more free morphemes, it is called **compounding.** Typical examples are *bookshelf, cowboy,* and *watchdog*.

Box 6.1   Three-Part Definition of a Morpheme

1. a *minimal*
2. *form*
3. with a *meaning*

Compounds are typically stressed more heavily on the first word than on the second. In fact, the stress pattern is usually taken as a defining characteristic of a compound because our writing system does not treat compounds uniformly. Sometimes they are written as one word, but sometimes they are written with hyphens: *well-known, five-year-old,* or *sister-in-law*. Sometimes compound words are written with no obvious marking at all: *wine glass* (a glass for wine, not a glass of wine or a glass made of wine), *candy dish* (a dish for candy, not a dish of candy or made of candy), and *shopping bag* (a bag for shopping, not a bag that is shopping). Examples such as these are considered compounds mainly because of their stress pattern and the fact that they can be paraphrased with the word *for*.

Compounds are made up of a variety of different parts of speech. Compounds that are nouns can be noun–noun combinations such as *bookshelf* or *candy dish* or adjective–noun combinations such as *blackberry* or *green waste*. Some noun compounds have a more complex syntactic structure involving two nouns and a preposition: *commander-in-chief* or *attorney-at-law*. Some noun compounds are formed by functional shift from phrasal verbs: *pickup* and *layoffs*. Compound adjectives are also possible: *redhot* and *gray-haired*. Compounding has affected function words historically, but it does not seem to be very productive at present.

prepositions:	*out of, into, within*
pronouns:	*something, everyone, himself*
determiners:	*another*
auxiliaries:	*cannot, might could* (in some dialects)

A TEACHING MOMENT

Compounding

Not all languages allow compounding. Spanish, for example, is quite resistant to compounding. Therefore, Spanish speakers often prefer to use the paraphrase *the glass for wine* (or the possessive *the wine's glass*) instead of the compound *the wine glass*. It is surprising how much this simple difference can interfere with speaking and writing in English.

BOUND MORPHEMES

If a morpheme must be attached to another morpheme or word to make sense, it is called a **bound morpheme.** Bound morphemes are either derivational or inflectional.

Derivational Morphemes

The three types of derivational morphemes—**prefixes, suffixes,** and **bound roots**—create new words.

Bound Roots

Usually of Latin or Greek origin and quite common in Academic English (AE), bound roots require a prefix or a suffix to form a word. The underlined part of *prescriptive* and *projection* are bound roots.

Prefixes

The prefixes *pre-, pro-,* and *sub-* are morphemes that must be attached in front of another free or bound morpheme to be meaningful, as in the words *prescriptive* and *projection*.

Suffixes

Suffixes are bound morphemes added after other free or bound morphemes. Examples are *prescriptive* and *projection*. English derivational morphemes are characterized by the following:

◆ They are bound roots, prefixes, or suffixes.

◆ They often result in a change in the part of speech when a suffix is added. Some suffixes (e.g., *-hood, -ship*), all prefixes, and bound roots do not affect the part of speech.

◆ They vary in productivity. In other words, some derivational morphemes (*-tion*) occur in many words, some (*-ling*) in few.

◆ They make a substantial and sometimes unpredictable change in the meaning of the word (*scholarship, friendship*).

◆ They result in what we would think of as a new and different word.

Derivation

Deviation is a word formation procedure in which a new word is formed from combining free morphemes, bound roots, and/or derivational morphemes. Examples of derivation are shown in Figure 6.1. From the noun *clue* (not a bound root but a free

List of Some Derivational Morphemes

Prefixes:

a-	on	afoot, aboard
ambi-	both	ambiguous, ambivalent
anti-	against	antiwar, antisocial
auto-	self	automatic, automobile
bi-, bin-	two	biweekly, binary
cent-	hundred	centennial, century
de-	from/down	degenerate, declaim
inter-	between	intersect, interdependence
micro-	small	micromanage, microscope
neo-	new	neonate, neoclassical
poly-	many	polyglot, polychrome
post-	after	postdate, postpone
pre-	before	predate, prefix
prot-/proto-	first	prototype, protein
re-	again	reexamine, rethink
semi-	half	semicircle, semiconscious
sub-	under	subordinate, subdivision
tele-	far	television, telephone
trans-	across	translate, transport
un-	not	unkind, unpleasant
un-	reverse	undo, unzip
under-	below	underfund, underestimate

Classical Suffixes

-arian	one who	librarian, humanitarian, agrarian
-ate	state/quality	desperate, candidate
-ation	action/process	refrigeration, electrification,
-cy	state/quality	diplomacy, accuracy
-ian	relating to	simian, authoritarian
-ism	doctrine of	socialism, anarchism
-ist	one who	artist, linguist
-ize	make	standardize, euthanize
-ment	action/process	judgment, development
-mony	product	hegemony, matrimony
-oid	relating to	paranoid, humanoid
-ology	study of	biology, chronology, morphology
-ous	full of	nebulous, nervous
-tion	state/quality	intention, attraction
-tude	state/quality	certitude, attitude
-ure	action/process	nurture, nature

Figure 6.1 *Examples of derivational morphemes and bound roots.*

Native Suffixes

-er/-ar/-or	one who	baker, beggar, actor
-en	made of	golden, wooden
-en	make	whiten, blacken
-dom	state of	kingdom, wisdom
-ful	full of	careful, colorful
-hood	state of	womanhood, boyhood
-ish	like/from	childish, Spanish
-less	without	childless, careless
-like	like	childlike, houselike
-ling	small	inkling, duckling
-ly	manner	happily, clearly
-ship	quality of	friendship, penmanship
-some	quality of	handsome, awesome
-th	order	fourth, thirtieth
-ward	direction	toward, homeward
-y	quality of	salty, cloudy

Greek and Latin Bound Roots

form	*meaning*	*Use*
-andr-/-anthr-	man	polyandry, anthropology
-ang-	bend	angle, triangle, angular
-arch-	chief	archcriminal, patriarch
-ast-	star	astronomy, asterisk, disaster
-chron-	time	synchronize, chronic, chronology
-cycl-	circle/ring	cycle, Cyclops, encyclopedia
-crat-	rule	aristocrat, autocratic, democracy
-dict-	speak	dictate, prediction, interdict
-doc/dox-	belief	doctrine, orthodox, heterodox
-log-	word	apology, monologue, catalogue
-mit/miss-	send	mission, permit, remit
-morph-	shape/form	morphology, metamorphosis
-path-	feeling	empathy, sympathy, pathology
-poli-	city	police, metropolis, policy
-pop-	people	populate, popular, repopulate
-the-	god	theology, atheist, theosophy
-tract-	pull/drag	tractable, attractive, tractor
-volv-	roll	involve, revolve, evolve

Figure 6.1 *Examples of prefixes, suffixes and bound roots.*

root), we form the adjective *clueless*, which has a different part of speech and a different meaning. We can continue to apply the procedure to form new words almost indefinitely. For example, to *clueless* we can add another suffix to form an abstract noun: *cluelessness*. Note, however, that we do not have the word *clueful* yet even though it might be a very useful word. This demonstrates the quirky nature of derivational morphemes (some other word formation procedures besides compounding and derivation are described in Figure 6.2).

**Derivation and
Academic Vocabulary**

A nonnative learner may have problems with derivational morphology because derivation may not be an important process in the learner's first language. Languages with little derivation are Chinese or Hmong. If students of English as a second language are unfamiliar with English derivational morphemes and how they function, they cannot use them to form words or even to understand unfamiliar words they come across in their reading or on tests. This is a disadvantage because academic language is often made up of Greek- or Latin-derived words.

Most learners, nonnative or native speaking, need to increase their academic vocabulary. They need to become familiar with common derivational prefixes, suffixes, and bound roots that are used in academic prose so that they can use morphological clues to guess a word meaning while reading. Instruction is often based on word families—sets of words with common roots and different prefixes or suffixes. Note that sometimes the prefixes have different forms. Subport→<u>sup</u>port or inport→<u>im</u>port in different words:

subject	reject	inject	
subvert	revert	invert	} Word Families
support	report	import	

INFLECTIONAL MORPHEMES

The concept of content and function is as relevant to morphemes as it is to words. Corresponding to content words are the derivational morphemes; corresponding to function words are the inflectional morphemes:

Derivational morphemes ◄─────────────────────► Inflectional morphemes
Content   Function

Derivational morphemes make a significant contribution to the meaning of the derived word and the sentence it appears in. In contrast, inflectional morphemes supply grammatical nuances that are important for understanding the meaning of the word or sentence. Like function words, they are part of the syntactic frame or template, and also like function words, inflectional morphemes are fewer in number, but each one occurs frequently.

The underlined bound morphemes in the sentence *He donate<u>s</u> the book<u>s</u>* are inflectional. The noun *books* is made up of the free morpheme *book* plus the **plural** inflectional morpheme -*s*. The verb form *donates* is made up of the word *donate* plus the **third-person singular present tense** inflectional ending -*s*. The expression **third-person singular** comes from the traditional verbal paradigms in the study of

Besides **derivation** and **compounding,** we have seen a third word formation procedure, **functional shift,** in which a word with one part of speech is derived from a word with a different part of speech simply by changing its function. Noun-to-verb conversions are common, sometimes despite obvious noun morphology: *to author a book, to conference with a student,* or *to transition to another phase.* Here is a list of some other common English word formation procedures.

Coinage: New words or names can be invented out of the blue for new products or concepts: *xerox, kleenex,* or *googol.* Coined brand names are then often generalized as common nouns, a word formation procedure called **generalization.**

Blending: New words can be formed by taking part of one word and blending it seamlessly with another word: *chocoholic, reaganomics, brunch,* or *prideandjoyography.*

Acronym: New words can be formed by taking the initials of a longer phrase and pronouncing them as a word. At first, the words are often written in all capital letters, but that can change: *AIDS, SIDS, NATO,* or radar. Acronyms are distinguished from abbreviations, in which the initials are pronounced as letters: *FBI, CIA,* or *UN.*

Back-Formation: New words are formed by subtracting derivational morphemes or what appear to be derivational morphemes. Examples are *enthuse* (from *enthusiasm*), *laze* (from *lazy*), and *couth* (from *uncouth*). Back-formations vary in acceptability and formality and differ from clipping, a very common procedure in which a word is simply shortened, often informally or as slang: *pro* (from *professional*), *math* (from *mathematics*), or *prez* (from *president*). Back formation results in a new word often with a different part of speech, but clipping does not.

Figure 6.2 *Other word formation procedures.*

Latin, which were drawn in two dimensions based on **person** and **number** (singular and plural), creating six cells in a table:

PERSON	SINGULAR	PLURAL
First	*I walk*	*we walk*
Second	*you walk*	*you walk*
Third	*he/she/it walks*	*they walk*

In Latin (and its daughters, the Romance languages), each of the cells has a verb with a different inflectional ending, but in English the only inflectional ending in the present tense is the third-person singular. In English, there are eight inflectional morphemes, shown in Box 6.2.

ENGLISH INFLECTIONAL MORPHEMES ARE CHARACTERIZED BY THE FOLLOWING:

◆ They are always suffixes and never roots or prefixes.
◆ They do not change the part of speech when the inflected word is compared to the base they are added to.
◆ They are very productive; they can be added to almost any word of a certain part of speech.
◆ They cause a predictable change in meaning.
◆ They do not result in a new and different word, just a different form of the same word.

Box 6.2   List of Inflectional Morphemes in English

Nouns:
Regular plural -s: He needed two book<u>s</u>.
Possessive -s: The professor'<u>s</u> books are old.

Verbs:
Third-person singular present tense: -s He donate<u>s</u> the books.
Regular Past tense -ed: He dona<u>ted</u> the books.
Regular past participle -ed: The books were dona<u>ted</u>.
Present participle -ing: He is giv<u>ing</u> away his books.

Adjectives and Adverbs:
Comparative -er: His books are old<u>er</u> than mine.
Superlative -est: In fact, his are the old<u>est</u> of all.

AN OPTICAL ILLUSION

Three Morphemes -s

Three different morphemes look the same:

◆ Plural for nouns
◆ Third-person singular for verbs
◆ Possessive for nouns

Complicated ambiguous forms such as these can be difficult for nonstandard and nonnative speakers to learn.

INFLECTION OR DERIVATION? ▬▬▬▬▬

Ivan is tall<u>er</u> than me.
He is a basketball play<u>er</u>.
The children are fish<u>ing</u> in the bay.
Fish<u>ing</u> is a relax<u>ing</u> sport.

These cases, -er and –ing, are morpheme homonym pairs. They look the same and sound the same. We use the characteristics of different morphemes as a procedure to decide whether they are inflectional or derivational. The adjective *taller* is <u>inflected</u> to show comparison; the -er is added to *tall* to produce the comparative form, which has the same part of speech. The noun *player* is <u>derived</u> from the verb *play;* it is a different word, meaning "one who plays."

A TEACHING MOMENT

Subject/Verb Agreement

Learners sometimes use a nonstandard past-tense form (*brang* instead of *brought*), or they may have problems with **subject–verb agreement.** Subject–verb agreement means that the subject of the sentence must have the right verb form with it. Plural subjects must have plural verb forms, and singular subjects must have singular verb forms. In speech, people do not always notice subject–verb agreement errors, but in writing they do.

Here are some example sentences taken from conversations and cited in Biber and others (1999):

Page 186: <u>Gary</u>, there'<u>s</u> apples if you want one.
<u>Here'<u>s</u> your shoes.
Page 191: <u>Are</u> you in agreement with her, <u>I</u> say<u>s</u>.

These would be inappropriate in formal academic speaking or writing.

Nonstandard speakers may have the same problems, but in addition they may not use the same inflectional system as standard speakers. For example, some nonstandard dialects of English may not use the plural morpheme or the third-person singular present tense consistently (<u>He</u> *have two book*, or <u>He</u> *don't have three book*). Nonstandard dialects may have different past participles or auxiliaries (*he had went* instead of *he had gone, he done froze the meat* instead of *he has frozen the meat*).

Nonstandard dialect speakers and nonnative English speakers may have a hard time learning inflectional morphology in Standard English (SE). Inflectional morphemes (and function words for that matter) are not salient in speech. They are unstressed and not pronounced fully in many cases. Perhaps this is why people have a hard time learning to use them in speaking and also in writing. While it does not seem to be difficult to grasp what the inflections mean if the learner comes from a language that also has inflections, they seem to be difficult to learn to use procedurally. Some languages have few or no inflectional markings on words, such as Chinese, Vietnamese, or Hmong, and for students of those languages it may be difficult to notice the inflectional ending, to grasp what it is for, and to use it in speaking and writing.

Some verbal inflectional endings appear to be more difficult than others. For example, *-ing* seems to be easier to learn than the third-person singular present tense *-s*, probably because it is more regular, more salient, and more grammatically meaningful.

Another problem, even for advanced Generation 1.5 writers, is leaving off the past participle ending as in sentences like these where the asterisk marks nonstandard usage.

*The tropical fish were release into the water.
*The ranger was annoy.

(Continued)

> Teachers don't often like spending a lot of time drilling students on these rather mechanical details, but these can be stigmatizing errors that Hairston (1981) found to be most serious. People, including college professors, form their opinions about someone's writing ability on the basis of rather superficial details, such as subject–verb agreement errors, different past participles, or missing inflections.

To analyze the word *fishing*, we need to look at each sentence it appears in. In *The children are fishing in the bay, fish<u>ing</u>* is an inflected form, a present participle occurring with the helping verb *are.* In the other sentence, *Fish<u>ing</u> is a relaxing sport, fishing* is the subject of a sentence. Because it is the subject, it must be a noun derived from the verb *fish.* Since there is a change in the part of speech from verb to noun, *-ing* is a derivational morpheme. (Nouns that are derived from verbs by adding *-ing* are called **gerunds.**) The explanation is similar for the adjective **relaxing.** Once again, to answer a question, we use the characteristics of derivation and inflection as diagnostics in the discovery procedure.

EXPLORING CHAPTER PERSPECTIVES

◆ *Discussion Questions*

1. In your Language Notebook, make a list of the word formation procedures discussed in the chapter (e.g., derivation, functional shift, compounding, acronym, back-formation, coinage, and blending). Think of at least one example for each. What part of speech does the word have? Then share your answers with another student. Copy his or her answers into your notebook also if you think they are correct examples. Then, throughout the semester, write down any other words you notice for each procedure.

2. One of the most creative places for word formation is in advertising. Do you remember any innovative uses of words from ads? Make a note of interesting uses of words throughout the semester to add to your Language Notebook and discuss in class.

3. Examine these two sentences and decide what type of morpheme the underlined form is. Once you have decided, articulate how you made your decision (procedural knowledge).

   a. *The news report disturb<u>ed</u> the viewers.*
   b. *The disturb<u>ed</u> viewers called the TV station.*

◆ *Cooperative Exercise: Instant Messaging (IM)*

A. **Homework.** Read the newspaper article titled "IMs Cre8 Worries 4 Some Teachers" and write notes to answer the following questions in your Language Notebook.

1. Do you agree that IM is just a form of shorthand? Why or why not? Use examples in the reading or your own examples from IM.

2. What spelling procedures do you notice in instant messaging? Verbalize how they differ from normal English spelling.

3. What characteristics of IM are the same as or different from Standard Spoken English?

4. In terms of learning or acquiring Standard Written English (SWE) or AE reading and writing skills, what advantages are there to IM for middle and high school learners?

5. In the reading selection, find all the examples of compound words. Remember that compounds are not always written as one word.

IMs CRE8 WORRIES 4 SOME TEACHERS

November 5, 2002

By Chris Cobbs

Reprinted by permission of *The Orlando Sentinel*

Some language watchdogs are fretting over the Internet's effect on the written word.

(1) Orlando, Fla.—Tina Deamicis is teetering on a language high wire. When she's online
(2) with friends or family, the English teacher at St. Cloud High School is an avid user of
(3) the language of instant messaging, with its clipped, slangy style of "u" for "you" and
(4) "lol" for (4) "laughing out loud."
(5) But when she sees that kind of informality turning up in her students' assignments—
(6) along with sentence fragments and missing punctuation—it's no laughing matter.
(7) "Students are prone to use bizarre abbreviations and spellings," says Deamicis, who
(8) blames instant messaging for the shift to slopping writing. "They don't seem to make
(9) distinction between casual and academic language."
(10) Though there's no evidence that anything as radical as "4 skor & 7 yrs ago" is about to
(11) enter the lexicon, teachers are still distressed to see students slipping into the
(12) IM language when writing what is supposed to be formal composition.
(13) Tina Stewart, a teacher at Greenwood Lakes Middle School in Seminole County, Fla.
(14) says her first encounter with IM in a written assignment left her "totally shocked."
(15) "I responded by writing a terse note on the graded paper that I was the teacher and
(16) not an IM buddy," she says. "I then talked to the class about writing for a specific
(17) audience. This use of slang might be OK for notes to their friends and Internet
(18) buddies, but notfor school compositions."
(19) Yet many prominent linguists aren't alarmed.
(20) "We should be encouraged to see a generation of youngsters tapping away at the
(21) keyboard instead of fingering a TV remote," says Leila Christenbury, president of the
(22) National Council of Teachers of English and an English professor at Virginia
(23) Commonwealth University. "Enforcing correct usage is a constant battle, but an
(24) ampersand and the numeral 4 in students' writing are surmountable."

(Continued)

(25) The problem, critics of IM say, is that students get into bad habits and forget to clean
(26) up their errors. When an honors English teacher recently assigned an essay on Beowulf,
(27) she found papers laden with u, r, 2, b/c, and other IM shortcuts, prompting a one-point
(28) penalty for each miscue.
(29) South Lake High School's Melissa Merritt also subtracts points from students' grades.
(30) At the beginning of the year, she just gave warnings. But, when they weren't heeded,
(31) she began deducting points.
(32) "If the problem is too out of control, I return the paper and demand a rewrite," she says.
(33) Some students just don't seem to believe grammar and punctuation apply to them.
(34) "Punctuation? What 's that? It seems to have gone right out the window," Merritt says.
(35) And when she points out students' mistakes, their reply is "It's OK in IM, so why not
(36) in school?"
(37) But a lot of students really do know the difference.
(38) Take Ocoee Middle School seventh-grader Chelsea Price, who's nicknamed the "IM
(39) Queen" because she often chats with a half-dozen members of her buddies list at once.
(40) She has been typing since second grade.
(41) "I like to create excitement in my writing, "Chelsea says. "I put in a lot of exclamation
(42) points, and I use u and r and the @ sign for 'at'."
(43) She may fall into IM style when composing the first draft of an English composition,
(44) but says she knows the difference between IM and formal writing—and her papers are
(45) turned in devoid of the digital shorthand.
(46) Ditto with Ocoee Middle student Nia Phillips, 12. To illustrate how she might write
(47) about her summer vacation in the Bahamas, she composed a paragraph in IM style:
(48) "Lots of tourists wr haggling 4 good prices. I wuz n awe of all da beautiful things. I
(49) bot n anklet dat jingles win I wlk."
(50) The essay she handed in to her teacher, however, was in carefully composed standard
(51) English.
(52) Instant messaging really isn't so different from other forms of shorthand used by
(53) stenographers, reporters or even the telegraph operators of yesteryear. Even
(54) Shakespeare used abbreviations and a different style of capitalization than we do.
(55) "People talk about the instant messaging style with its abbreviations and lowercase
(56) letters, yet people are writing more than ever," says Jesse Sheidlower, North American
(57) editor of the *Oxford English Dictionary*.
(58) "If they're writing more informally, well, so what? The use of shortened forms and
(59) abbreviations was enormously common in Latin in the Middle Ages. The issues are
(60) similar today."

B. **Pair Work.**

1. In your Language Notebook, make three columns labeled "Inflectional Morphemes," "Derivational Morphemes," and "Not Sure." Take a numbered section of the text and put all the morphemes into the correct column.

2. Compare your answers to the previous questions and combine your lists into one to hand in. Try to resolve any you are not sure of.

C. **Class Work.**

　　1. Go over any morphemes still in the "not sure" column. Discuss.

　　2. Hand in the paper from Part B.

◆ *Writing Assignment*

Write a short essay in your Language Notebook in response to one or both of these prompts. Save your essay(s) for later use.

　　1. Imagine you are tutoring a nonnative-speaking learner who makes these mistakes in speaking and writing:

　　　　He always go into the office after class.

　　　　The drugstore usually close at 10 Monday through Friday.

　　　　They wants to speak English very well.

　　　What do you think the problem is? Write an inductive minilecture script to explain third-person singular present tense to your tutee.

　　2. Use ideas from your discussion about the reading passage to respond to this question.

　　　In terms of learning or acquiring SWE or AE reading and writing skills, what advantages and disadvantages are there to IM for middle and high school learners? What future do you predict for IM language?

Introspection

Look at your essay(s) carefully and proofread for spelling, punctuation, and nonstandard or non-SWE usage. Make sure that all the subjects and verbs agree. Underline five words that have derivational morphemes. Divide them into their component morphemes. If you do not have five words with derivational morphemes, can you think of additional information for your compositions that would include such words? Then underline all the inflectional morphemes.

TEACHING TO LEARN

Problems with Verbal Morphology

These are some inflectional problems (or similar) made by some learners in their writing. They might be subject–verb agreement, nonstandard or colloquial forms, or missing inflections. Some might be problems only in academic writing and not in speaking. Divide up into pairs. First say the correct sentence, then explain to your partner which type of problem it is. Make sure that you explain tactfully, as if your partner had made the mistake on a composition. Explain what the correct form should be. The first one is done for you.

1. My dad seen a huge truck coming down our street. *Seen* should be *saw: My dad saw a huge truck coming down our street.*

      The correct past tense for *see* in Standard English is *saw* and not *seen. Seen* is a nonstandard past-tense form that is not appropriate for academic writing.

2. Here's the five reasons for buying that stove.
3. There was too many taxes to pay in that state.
4. Then I says, "Give me all my money right now."
5. The deciduous tree lose all its leaves in winter.
6. My mother going to her office today.
7. The order was cancel because of lack of funds.
8. This flower grow best in full sunlight.
9. They brung their schoolbooks with them.
10. Those kids done their work already.
11. The underlying tone of the wall colors selected were too dark.

Derivation

Description: Word formation is an interesting topic in K–12 because people are curious about words and where they come from. If learners become active observers of words, their metalinguistic awareness increases, and their vocabulary expands. A larger vocabulary improves reading speed and comprehension, and the ability to see to morphemes within words helps learners with grammar.

Goals

Subject area goal: academic vocabulary

English language awareness goals: English word formation processes and derivation

Descriptive grammar goals: morphology and its terms

Procedural goal: form new words with derivational morphemes

Assessment: Assessments stress accurate spelling, usage of a word in context, and knowledge of meaning.

Methodology 1: Each partner takes one column of words. In your Language Notebook, divide the words into their component morphemes. You will probably need a dictionary for some words. Take turns telling your partner what the derivation or origin of the word is.

Column 1	Column 2
multiple	worship
Oldsmobile	handsome
moustache	smog
carpet	lynch
catsup	Massachusetts
tawdry	candy
glamour	perish
antidisestablishmentarianism	supercalifragilisticexpialidocious

Methodology 2: Derivational Morphology and Vocabulary Enhancement

These are some other bound roots. For each, list as many words as you can that contain that root, indicate the word's part of speech, and discuss what the meaning is. How is each example word derived? What is the common meaning for the bound root? Then consult a dictionary to see if you are correct.

-aud-

-cap-

-cert-

-cogn-

-cred-

-fac- or -fact-

-fig-

-mob-

-mort-

-pos-

-rect-

-vac-

Brainstorm some other ways you could encourage learners to build a larger academic vocabulary. Using one or more of the derivational morphemes listed in this chapter, make up a vocabulary-building cooperative activity or game for learners in your preferred grade level. Include part-of-speech information; that is, make sure your activity helps learners see how morphology is a clue to part of speech. Write careful instructions for your activity, show examples of the behavior you expect, give sample materials, and suggest an assessment measure. Share your activity with your group for feedback.

7

Nouns and Noun Phrases

All languages have words functioning as nouns and words functioning as verbs. To explain the universality of nouns and verbs, we might hypothesize that the human mind is hard-wired to understand our environment in terms of either *entities* or *relationships among entities*. If we conceptualize something as an entity in our minds, we refer to it with a noun regardless of whether it has a physical reality or not.

An entity can be a physical thing, such as a *chair* or a *mountain*. It can be an abstract emotional entity, such as *happiness* or *grief*. It can be a concrete countable thing, such as a *finger* or a *bottle*. It can be a concrete but noncountable mass, such as *sand* or *air*. It can even be a situation or an event, such as a *meeting* or the *Revolutionary War*. We can conceptualize a very complex set of facts as an entity and refer to it with the noun *language universal*.

We talk about these or any other concepts with nouns because we think of them as entities. That is why the traditional definition of a noun as a person, place, or thing tells only part of the story, unless we broaden our notion of what a "thing" can be.

For example, we typically think of adjectives as descriptive words and not as "things" at all, yet they occur as nouns as well, as in *She helps out <u>the sick</u> and <u>the injured</u>*. We employ the descriptive properties *sick* and *injured* as nouns to refer to the category of people who have those properties. That explains the fact that these nouns cannot be plural (**the sicks, *the injureds*).

PROTOTYPICAL NOUNS AND THEIR DIAGNOSTICS

Types of Nouns

English has two prototypical types of nouns—**common nouns** and **proper names**—because humans perceive at least two types of entities: classes of things (common nouns) and very specific individuals (proper names). Proper names allow us to identify and talk about particular things, especially people and pets, such as Aunt Geraldine, Dr. Geraldine Page, Buster, Page Veterinary Hospital, American golden retriever, and so on.

Aunt Geraldine,
Dr. Geraldine Page

Buster

In English, proper names are capitalized to make them stand out in a text. Some proper names are composed of common nouns, as in the *Hospital Advisory Committee,* the *Veterinary Complaints Board,* or the *National Animal Lovers Foundation.* The fact that these are capitalized symbolizes that they are being used as proper names of specific entities and not as common nouns, as in *the committee, the board,* or *the foundation.*

If an English noun is not a proper noun, then it is a common noun. Common nouns, which are usually not capitalized, are *hair, veterinarian, woman, dog, fur,* and *tail.* For prototypical common nouns, the category or class of objects is exploited to refer to an individual within the category. In the following picture, one entity fits into the category of *veterinarians,* and one fits into the category of *dogs:*

Hair

Woman

Veterinarian

Dog

Tail

Fur

There are terms for various kinds of common nouns also. **Abstract nouns** refer to entities that have a conceptual reality, that is, a reality in our minds: *concern, grief,* or *intelligence.* **Concrete nouns** refer to entities that have a physical reality: *woman,*

Count and Mass

Native speakers will know the difference between these types of nouns intu-itively, but certain mistakes are common in academic writing. For example, the word *amount* should be used with mass nouns and not with count nouns, as in *a certain amount of candy*, not *a certain amount of books* (which should be *a certain number of books*).

The distinctions between types of nouns (and the determiners that go with them) can be complex for nonnative speakers. The count/mass distinction can be tricky because it is not intuitive for students of English as a second language (ESL). Instead, the meanings are subtly different. What different meaning do you understand with each of these? Who might drink more, Lanny or Lois?

Lanny drank a wine each night before going to bed.
Lois drank wine each night before going to bed.

dog, balloon, finger, or *air.* **Count nouns** refer to concrete things that can be counted: *dog, tail, finger, toe,* or *words.* **Mass nouns** refer to concrete entities that are non-countable, that is, "stuff": *hair, fur, air,* or *wine.* However, these terms are very flexible. We can use an abstract noun very concretely, as in these examples:

<u>Love</u> is a wonderful emotion.

The single great <u>love</u> of her life is wagging her tail.

Count nouns can appear as mass nouns and vice versa:

She gave the dog <u>a hamburger</u>. There was <u>hamburger</u> in the dog food.

As usual, it is the discovery procedure and the diagnostics from noun morphology, syntax, function, or meaning that we use to determine whether a word is a noun and what type of noun it is.

Noun Morphology

Nouns often have specific derivational prefixes and suffixes, such as <u>bi</u>cycle, <u>mega</u>phone, <u>pro</u>gram, <u>pre</u>fix, presenta<u>tion</u>, judg<u>ment</u>, press<u>ure</u>, sani<u>ty</u>, busi<u>ness</u>, intelli<u>gence</u>, brother<u>hood</u>, scholar<u>ship</u>, or social<u>ism</u>. Gerunds are nouns derived from verbs by adding *–ing*, as in *ski/skiing* or *work/working*. Countable nouns take the plural inflection *-s*, as in *fingers, chairs,* or *apples.* Proper names, abstract nouns, and mass nouns occasionally take the plural inflection (the *Browns, waters, wines,* or *intelligences*) as well.

Two Syntactic Templates

Head Nouns in Noun Phrases
Common and proper nouns typically occur as the head of a noun phrase (NP):

[(Det)   (Adjective)   Noun]$_{NP}$

In the template, parentheses mark optional items. For common nouns, determiners and adjectives may or may not be present; for proper names, determiners and adjectives are usually (but not always) missing. This template accounts for each of these noun phrases:

The thick book	(Det Adj N)$_{NP}$
Thick books	(Adj N)$_{NP}$
The books	(Det N)$_{NP}$
Books	(N)$_{NP}$
Luca	(N)$_{NP}$

Descriptive Nouns

Nouns can also modify other nouns in this template:

$$[(Det) \ (N1) \ N2]_{NP}$$

Noun 1 is a descriptive noun, and noun 2 is the head noun. This template represents these options:

some mocha cups	*the brick garages*
mocha cups	*brick garages*
some cups	*the garages*
cups	*garages*

In this template, the first noun describes or classifies the type of the second noun. The phrase can often be paraphrased with "N for N," as in *cups for mocha,* or "N made of N," as in *the garage made of brick.* Descriptive nouns may not take plural or possessive inflections.

Descriptive nouns are very common in English, especially in academic prose. This template is hard to distinguish from compound nouns. One way to distinguish them is by stress pattern. Compounds have a pattern of stress on the first noun, as in '*mink coat* or '*coffee cup.* Descriptive nouns in noun phrases take main stress on the head noun, as in *cloth* '*coat* or *brick* '*wall.*

Distinguishing Descriptive Adjectives and Nouns

The two templates we have seen so far are very similar:

[(Det) (Adj) N]$_{NP}$	*the thick book*
[(Det) (N) N]$_{NP}$	*the cloth coat*

A TEACHING MOMENT

Descriptive Nouns

As with compound words, nonnative speakers tend to substitute paraphrases with *for* or *of* for descriptive nouns in noun phrases in ways that are nonconventional. They may say *the cup for coffee* or *the garage of brick* instead of the more conventional descriptive noun modifier.

> **Box 7.1   Descriptive Noun Versus Adjective Diagnostics**
>
> 1. An adjective usually takes *-er/more* or *-est/most*, but nouns do not:
>
> | | |
> |---|---|
> | *The thicker book* | **the more mocha cup* |
> | *The thickest book* | **the most mocha cup* |
>
> 2. An adjective can take *very*:
>
> | | |
> |---|---|
> | *The very thick book* | **the very mocha cup* |
>
> 3. A noun has the paraphrase with *for* (or *made of*):
>
> | | |
> |---|---|
> | **the book for thick* | *the cup for mocha* |

How can we tell whether a descriptive word is an adjective or a noun in any particular noun phrase? Many people's intuitions have been shaped by the traditional grammatical notion that every word that modifies a noun must be an adjective, so naive syntactic notions are not reliable. Instead, consistent use of the discovery procedure replaces naive syntactic notions. Using diagnostics to gather more information and make a decision is a better strategy than guessing (see Box 7.1).

These diagnostics will differentiate most descriptive nouns and adjectives, but in some cases not all the diagnostics will work. For example, Biber et al. 1999, (p. 68) lists the following to contrast noun-noun combinations with adjective-noun combinations. In these examples, the only diagnostic that works is the third, possibly because both the underlined adjective and the underlined nouns are derived from verbs.

NOUN	NOUN	ADJECTIVE	NOUN
finishing	*school*	*finishing*	*touches*
living	*standards*	*living*	*creatures*
dancing	*classes*	*dancing*	*children*
working	*conditions*	*working*	*mother*

NOUN PHRASES AND THEIR DIAGNOSTICS

According to Biber, Johansson, Leech, Conrad and Finegan (1999, p. 230), noun phrases, especially complex ones, are more common in academic prose than in conversations or simple fiction, where pronouns tend to be more prevalent. Compare these examples in which the noun phrases with common and proper nouns are underlined.

FACE-TO-FACE CONVERSATION

Well I thought you were going to talk to me about <u>Christmas presents</u>.

I have spoken to you about <u>Christmas presents</u>. I've told you about all I can tell you. Why don't you, why don't you sit down and tell me what you want for <u>Christmas</u>? I mean that would be useful.

> *Oh <u>darling</u>, Tut. Nothing I particularly want for <u>Christmas</u>.*
> [unclear]
> *Well you bought me <u>the new vacuum cleaner</u>.*

ACADEMIC PROSE

<u>Nonlinear systems theory</u> is of <u>great importance</u> to anyone interested in <u>feedback systems</u>. It is also true that <u>the theory of feedback systems</u> has made <u>important contributions</u> to <u>nonlinear systems theory</u>. <u>This chapter</u> discusses some <u>chaotic feedback systems</u>, drawn from <u>electronic circuit theory</u> and elsewhere, and show how they may be analyzed. So far, most of <u>the techniques required</u> have been taken directly from <u>the usual differential and difference equation theory</u>, but some results with a <u>more control system-theoretic flavour</u> are now available.

The Unified Syntactic Template

We unify the two noun templates into one noun phrase template to highlight how similar they are:

$$\left[(Det) \left\{ \begin{matrix} (Adj) \\ (N) \end{matrix} \right\} N \right]_{NP}$$

The unified noun phrase template combines descriptive adjectives and nouns into one position marked with curly braces that indicate that either an adjective or a noun, but not both, is an option for any word in that position. However, this is a simplification because more than one descriptive adjective or noun can occur. In noun phrases such as *the excellent old Norwegian peppermint candies* or *a kindly young funny woman comedian,* we have three adjectives followed by a descriptive noun, all of which modify the head noun of the phrase.

Possessive Morphology

Noun phrases that refer to animate beings take the possessive *'s* inflection, as in *Geraldine's nephew, the vet's office,* or *the dog's tail*. The possessive *'s* also appears somewhat commonly with time expressions, as in *tomorrow's meeting* or *today's agenda*.

Noun Phrase Roles

Noun phrases can either <u>refer</u> to specific individuals or <u>describe</u> individuals. **Reference** means that a word in a sentence points to or identifies an entity in a situation. **Description** means that the word merely adds additional information about a preexisting entity in the situation but does not introduce a new entity (see Figure 7.1).

The Apostrophe

Apostrophes began to be used to mark the *-s* possessive in English writing in the late 1600s, but the rules for its usage were not firmly established until the middle of the 1800s (McArthur, 1992). No other language has the preposed possessive noun with an apostrophe *-s*, as in *Mary's school* or *the boy's homework*, so ESL learners need to be encouraged to use them. All in all, there is a lot of confusion about the apostrophe and its use in possessive determiners with noun phrases.

It is quite interesting, given how much confusion and inconsistency there is, that Hairston (1981) found that apostrophe errors with possessive were judged as serious grammatical errors (but not very serious or status marking). Her sample sentence was *Our companys record is exceptional*. In contrast, Connors and Lunsford (1988) found that although apostrophe errors accounted for around 5% of the errors made in the 3,000 papers written by college students in their sample, they were marked 62% of the time by teachers. It was the third-most-marked grammar error. What is going on? First, the error is easy to mark and easy to explain on the students' compositions. Apostrophe errors may be more annoying for teachers than for professional people.

Rules for the Use of the Apostrophe

Singular/irregular plural noun phrases—add 's:
  child's toy,   children's toy

Regular plural—add + s':
  the girls' basketball team, the boys' soccer team

However, there are times when there is little agreement:

  Place names: *St. John's Academy, Pikes Peak*
  Proper names that end with s:
    Mr. Gomes' office, Mr. Gomes's office
    Jesus' desk, Jesus's desk

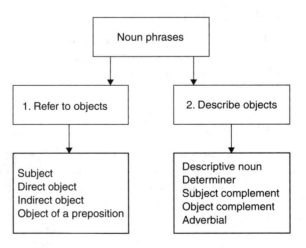

Figure 7.1 *Referential or descriptive noun phrases.*

Referential Roles

Noun phrases spell out, through the order in which they are placed in the sentence, what functional *role* the noun phrase referent takes in the situation. The noun phrase can take any one of these roles: subject, direct object, indirect object, or object of a preposition.

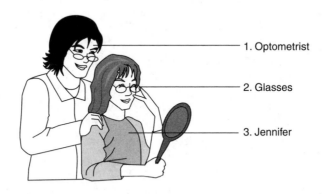

1. Optometrist

2. Glasses

3. Jennifer

Subject

1

The optometrist gave Jennifer her new glasses in her office.

The **subject** identifies the **agent,** or "doer," in the situation being talked about. Prototypically, the subject is placed just before the main verb in the sentence. In this case, the optometrist is the person who did the giving: the giver. The subject also determines what form the verb takes, whether it be singular or plural. Even when there is no real subject, a subject placeholder (*it, there*) must appear in the sentence (*It rains, There are too many people here*).

Direct Object

2

The optometrist gave Jennifer her new glasses in her office.

The **direct object** is the noun phrase that refers to another entity being talked about in the situation, in this case the thing that is given. Direct objects are not always the second entity in the order of words in the sentence. Direct objects are most often inanimate, or at least nonhuman, entities.

Indirect Object

3

The optometrist gave Jennifer her new glasses in her office.

3

The optometrist gave the new glasses to Jennifer in her office.

The **indirect object** is the noun phrase that refers to a third entity, that is, the entity that "receives" the secondary entity in the situation. Jennifer receives the glasses

A TEACHING MOMENT

Missing Subjects

Standard English (SE) and non-SE Speakers may have a problem with missing subjects in Standard Written English (SWE). For SE and non-SE speakers, an omitted subject comes from the differences between Standard Spoken English, which allows for incomplete sentences, and SWE, which requires subjects and complete sentences. Incomplete sentences usually occur as part of a discourse in conversation as add-ons to previous sentences. People are generally very efficient in speech; they do not mention things that are already understood from the context:

What didya eat?
Ate a lot of corn. A whole lot. Three ears.

In writing, the context is lacking, so more information must be clearly referenced.

Some ESL students may also omit subjects because dropping a subject pronoun may be allowed in their first language even in writing, if it can be recovered from the context. In other languages, it is easier to understand who the subject is because some words are marked with inflections. For example, in Spanish, subjects can be dropped because they are unnecessary if the verb carries a specific inflectional ending. The verbal ending of *llueve* (*rains*) is sufficient. Subjects can also be dropped if the adjective is marked as masculine or feminine. That is the purpose of gender marking in Spanish:

Es alto. He is tall.
Es alta. She is tall.

But what makes sense in Spanish is not right in English:

*Is tall.

in this situation, and therefore her name functions as the indirect object (the givee) in the sentence. Indirect objects are usually (but not always) animate entities:

1		2		3
Subject	→	Direct Object	→	Indirect Object
The optometrist	→	*glasses*	→	*Jennifer*
giver		given		givee

Object of a Preposition

Jennifer admired her glasses in <u>the mirror.</u>[2]

Finally, a noun phrase can be the **object of a preposition** in a prepositional phrase. Prepositional phrases often provide information about manner, location, destinations, or time (see Box 7.2).

Box 7.2	**Common Prepositions**			
across	*between*	*in/into*	*over*	
at	*by*	*like*	*to*	
after	*down*	*near*	*under*	
around	*for*	*of*	*up*	
before	*from*	*opposite*	*with*	

Descriptive Roles

Descriptive roles do not point out or introduce any additional entities in the situation that is being talked about in the sentence. These noun phrases only specify another characteristic of a person or thing that has already been mentioned with another noun.

Descriptive Nouns. The descriptive nouns in noun phrases, such as *the <u>cloth</u> coat* or *the <u>brick</u> garage*, are not referential.

Determiners. When noun phrases take the possessive inflection *'s,* as in <u>*Dr. Page's*</u> *beautiful dog,* the underlined expression does not refer to Dr. Page but rather states that the dog belongs to her. In other ways as well, possessive noun phrases act like determiners and not referential noun phrases. They function like *the, a,* or *my*:

> *the very beautiful dog*
> *a very beautiful dog*
> *my very beautiful dog*
> *Dr. Page's very beautiful dog*

Subject or Object Complements. A **subject complement** describes the subject, and an **object complement** describes an object:

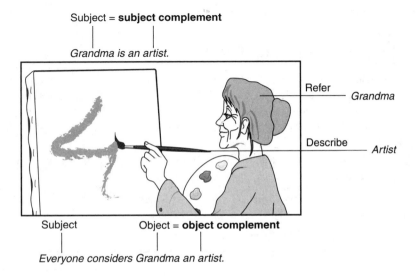

Subject = **subject complement**

Grandma is an artist.

Refer — *Grandma*

Describe — *Artist*

Subject   Object = **object complement**

Everyone considers Grandma an artist.

Adverbials.   In this function, noun phrases provide additional information about the time or place that the situation takes place without introducing any more entities into the situation:

<u>*Tuesday*</u> *Grandma will be painting a picture.*
<u>*Next year*</u> *she'll have an exhibition.*

See Box 7.3 for a summary of the main NP diagnostics.

Box 7.3   Summary of Noun and Noun Phrase Diagnostics

Morphology
　　Noun derivation: prefixes, suffixes
　　　　Inflection: plural in count nouns
　　Noun phrase inflection: possessive's

Syntax
　　Nouns occur in two places within noun phrases:

$$\left[(Det) \begin{Bmatrix} (Adj) \\ (N) \end{Bmatrix} N \right]_{NP}$$

Noun Phrase Function
　　Referential: subject, direct object, indirect object, object of a preposition
　　Descriptive: descriptive nouns, possessive determiners, subject
　　　　　　complement, object complement, adverbial

◆◆◆◆
!　　**TERMINOLOGY CLASH!**
◆◆◆◆　**Adverbial** is a word that refers to the <u>role</u> that a variety of constituents can have in the sentence. In the previous sentences, the noun phrases *Tuesday* and *next year* serve as modifiers in the sentence, so they are called adverbials. However, they are <u>not</u> adverbs; their part of speech is still noun phrase. The term **adverb** refers to a part of speech, such as *quickly, slowly, very, always, then,* or *now.*
　It is important to distinguish different types of grammatical information: the part of speech in line 1 and the role in line 2:

Tuesdays	the artist	always	paints	portraits.
Noun Phrase	Noun Phrase	Adverb	Verb	Noun Phrase
Adverbial	Subject	Adverbial	Predicate	Direct object

EXPLORING CHAPTER PERSPECTIVES ▰▰▰▰▰▰▰▰▰▰▰▰▰▰▰

◆ *Discussion Questions*

Read the newspaper editorial "America in Midst of Apostrophe Catastrophe" by Arianna Huffington and make a note of your own answers to these questions in your Language Notebook. Then discuss the following questions in pairs.

1. How would you describe Ms. Huffington's attitude toward punctuation errors? How is her attitude the same as or different from the attitude expressed in the opinion piece in Chapter 1?

2. What do you imagine was in Isabella's teacher's mind?

3. Does this imply that newspapers use different standards for correct punctuation?

4. Explain the morphological formation process of these terms from the editorial: *apostrodemic, billboards, G.I., jeep, broken-windows, ahold, ad execs,* and *e-mail.* You may need to consult a good dictionary.

AMERICA IN MIDST OF APOSTROPHE CATASTROPHE

Arianna Huffington
December 17, 2002
Reprinted by permission of Tribune Media Services

(1) I'm at the end of my rope. Or maybe I should say "my rope's end"—because what I'm
(2) so worked up about is the growing misuse of that puny piece of punctuation called
(3) the apostrophe. The phenomenon is spreading so rapidly, it's practically, well, an
(4) apostrodemic.
(5) You see the grammatical gaffes everywhere: on billboards, in movie ads, in grocery
(6) stores—even in the hallowed pages of the *New York Times.* Just the other day, I saw a
(7) headline in the "paper of record" that read: "Saudis Seize Kuwaiti in Shooting of G.I.'s
(8) Who are Recovering."
(9) I couldn't help wondering: the shooting of the G.I.'s what? His jeep? His superior
(10) officer? Or perhaps it was in a part of his body too sensitive for a family newspaper to
(11) mention in print?
(12) Now I really hate to make such a big stink about a little squiggle—especially at a time
(13) when life-and-death matters like the march to war in Iraq cry out for our attention.
(14) But sometimes a small thing like this can have much bigger ramifications. Think of it
(15) as the literary equivalent of the broken-windows theory of crime fighting.
(16) Now, I readily admit that putting an end to this scourge of punctuation abuse won't
(17) make the world safer, the environment cleaner, or our political system less corrupt.
(18) But it will lower my blood pressure.
(19) My long simmering irritation over the apostrophe crisis reached a boil the other night
(20) while helping my 11-year-old daughter with her homework. She had written a short
(21) essay about her school camping trip.

(Continued)

(22) She had particularly enjoyed tackling one of those confidence-building ropes courses.

(23) Only she had written it as "rope's courses." I gently brought the error to her attention,

(24) pointing out that she didn't need an apostrophe before the "s" since it was a plural noun.

(25) She didn't take it very well. "You're wrong, Mommy!" she cried.

(26) Even when I insisted that I wasn't, she remained unmoved. Then she played her trump

(27) card: "Well," she sniffed, "this is the way everyone does it here." That hurt, carrying as

(28) it did the implication that my attachment to following quaint rules of punctuation

(29) was due to English not being my mother tongue. In the interest of family peace, I

(30) decided to quash my dissent and let her teacher deal with the matter.

Vindicated Girl

(31) Unfortunately, when Isabella got her paper back, the errant apostrophe had been

(32) allowed to go uncorrected. Her "see, I told you so" grin left me feeling like a chastised

(33) schoolgirl—or the last horse-and-buggy driver in town.

(34) Things only got worse the next morning when, while reading the *New York Times*, I came

(35) across two examples of apostrophes in the wrong place. Flummoxed, I got ahold of

(36) the *New York Times'* manual of style and, to my horror, discovered that the paper's rash

(37) of apostrophe errors had not been the result of sloppy copy-editing but a conscious

(38) executive decision to ignore the rules of proper punctuation.

(39) That's when I decided to do something to stop the madness. It's time for a regime

(40) change in apostrophe land. The good news is that vanquishing this enemy won't take

(41) congressional approval or a U.N. Security Council resolution.

(42) But neither can it be accomplished just by deploying a few unmanned apostrophe

(43) drones. No, this will require a coalition of journalists, copy editors, ad execs,

(44) teachers and people willing to draw a line (albeit a small crescent-shaped one) in the

(45) compositional sand. And, fortunately, we already have the Associated Press and

(46) major newspapers like the *Los Angeles Times*, the *Boston Globe* and the *Washington Post* on

(47) our side.

(48) It's really not that complicated. To make a word plural, you simply add an "s" (ropes).

(49) To make the word possessive, you add an apostrophe and an "s" (rope's). To make a

(50) plural noun ending in "s" possessive, add only the apostrophe (ropes'). And the same

(51) rules apply to acronyms and abbreviations like CEO, GI and CD.

(52) OK, students, class dismissed. And leave those apples—or more likely, brickbats—in

(53) my e-mail box.

◆ *Cooperative Exercise: Compounds and Other NPs*

A. **Homework.** Draw the categories in your Language Notebook and divide the expressions from Huffington's essay into the four categories in the following table.

Note: Do not guess, as guessing relies on your existing intuition, which may not be well honed. Instead, use the diagnostics to distinguish descriptive adjectives from nouns so that you can acquire new intuitions.

It is sometimes difficult to distinguish noun-noun compounds and descriptive noun-nouns. Once you have established that the expression is a noun-noun sequence, try to distinguish compounds from descriptive noun-noun sequences. To do so, say the expression out loud. The stress pattern for compounds tends to place primary stress on the first word and secondary stress on the second. The opposite is true for the descriptive noun-noun sequences. If, after trying this diagnostic, you are still not clear on the more precise answer (either category 3 or category 4), leave the expression in the more general category 2.

Be prepared to explain your answers in class.

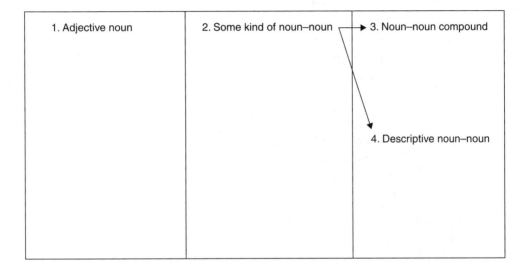

1. Adjective noun	2. Some kind of noun–noun → 3. Noun–noun compound	
		4. Descriptive noun–noun

growing misuse

puny piece

grammatical gaffes

movie ads

grocery stores

hallowed pages

superior officer

family newspaper

big stink

little squiggle

small thing

bigger ramifications

literary equivalent

crime fighting

punctuation abuse

blood pressure

simmering irritation

apostrophe crisis

plural noun

trump card

quaint rules

mother tongue

family peace

vindicated girl

errant apostrophe

chastised schoolgirl

wrong place

apostrophe errors

proper punctuation

regime change

apostrophe land

good news

congressional approval

copy editors

ad execs

compositional sand

brickbats

e-mail box

B. **Group Work.** In class, compare your answers and decide which are correct using diagnostics together. Then analyze the structure of these expressions. What word formation processes are involved?

broken-windows theory

life-and-death matters

school camping trip

confidence-building ropes courses

"see, I told you so" grin

horse-and-buggy driver

sloppy copy-editing

conscious executive decision

U.N. Security Council resolution

unmanned apostrophe drones

C. **Class Work.** Correct answers. Model the use of the diagnostics for the difficult ones. Are complex noun phrases typical of news?

D. **Reflect on the cooperative process**.

◆ *Writing Assignment*

1. Write about the parent-teacher conflict discussed by Arianna Huffington. Have you been involved in any parent-teacher conflicts either when you were a child or with your own child? How were they resolved? Explore the conflict from the perspective of the teacher. Would you do things the same way or a different way?

2. Do newspaper usage rules from grammar books influence the way you write? Should everyone follow the same grammar rules?

Introspection

Proofread your essays and make any necessary corrections. After finishing them, underline all nouns and noun phrases and identify the the referential or descriptive role it is playing in the sentences you wrote.

TEACHING TO LEARN

Capitalization

Capitalization is relevant to nouns and noun phrases and is the source of problems in SWE and Academic English. Some rules are fairly rigid:

Capitalize:	
The first word of a sentence	This is a sentence.
A proper name	Juan Ortega, Anne Smit, Uncle Lou
A definite description	The Awards Committee
Subject matters	English, Linguistics, Special Education
Days and Months	Monday, March
Nationality, cultures, religions, and languages	Rome, Arabic, English
Nouns	Roman (but the roman alphabet)
Adjectives	Arabic (but arabic numerals)

Variable Rules

Titles: Capitalize all content words versus capitalize only the first word: "IWM: Integrated Waste Management" versus "IWM: Integrated waste management"

After a colon: Clearly there are exceptions to all grammar rules: H/how should they be presented to learners?

Some of the following sentences (but not all) have errors in capitalization norms. If there is an error, take turns with your partner explaining the error and the correction, imagining that your partner made the errors in a composition.

1. Edward decided that he wanted to become an English Teacher because he loved shakespeare.

2. The most commonly spoken languages in the world are chinese and english.

3. I bought a book about mexican food for aunt Giselle.

4. When was the roman calendar invented?

5. We learned that thursday is named after thor and wednesday is named after woden; thor and woden are both ancient Gods.

6. The general development fund lost some money last year.

7. I think he's a physical education major.

8. Compounding is a common english word formation process.

LEARNING TO TEACH

Sentence Combining and Expanding

Description: The more distant the language that children use at home from the language that is used in school, the more they will need to learn. If children's home language is generally lacking in complex noun phrases, they may need to learn to read and write complex noun phrases for syntactic maturity. **Sentence-combining** activities are often recommended to promote syntactic awareness and maturity. In sentence-combining activities, children are given two or more sentences to combine into one. Here are some examples with descriptive adjectives and nouns:

The cat was black.

The cat lived in a barnyard.

The cat liked to catch mice.

The black barnyard cat liked to catch mice.

Luna put the crown on her head.

The crown was golden.

The crown was for a princess.

Luna put the golden princess crown on her head.

Sentence-combining activities can also benefit nonnative-speaking students and Generation 1.5 students. Their need is probably more acute than that of native speakers because they may have acquired only basic conversational English, which lacks nouns and complex noun phrases. If so, the transition to understanding and using the academic language that is used in school, which is necessary for success in higher education, must be supported.

In these activities, teachers highlight a particular modifying structure (noun–noun combinations, adjectives, adjectival clauses, prepositional phrases, and so on) and explain them in simple words, using appropriate grammatical labels.

A sentence-combining activity gives all the information in two or more sentences, and the learner needs to integrate all the information into one sentence using modification:

I bought shoes on my trip. They are red tennis shoes.

I bought red tennis shoes on my trip.

A sentence-expanding activity gives the original sentence, and learners are invited to add more original details to the sentence:

I bought shoes on my trip.

I bought red tennis shoes on my trip to New York.

Goals

Subject area goal: descriptive writing

English language awareness goals: use of modifiers; syntactic awareness

Descriptive grammar goal: names of modifiers

Procedural goal: writing more mature sentences

Assessment: Check for correct structures and for transfer from the exercises to the learner's free writing.

Methodology: After choosing the grade level that you are most interested in teaching, think of a creative and interesting activity or a game to work with noun-noun compounds, descriptive noun-noun combinations, or adjective-noun combinations. Make your grammatical explanation match your grade level.

If your chosen grade level is fourth grade or lower or is composed of learners with low English proficiency, you might consider whether to make your activity oral or written. For these learners, the activity can also be based on pictures and not a text to be read. For any other learners, the activity should be both oral and written. How would you assess learning after your activity? Share your activity with your partner.

8

Determiners and Pronouns

Determiners and pronouns are both classes of function words that are closely related to noun phrases. The most basic way to state their difference is that determiners occur *inside* noun phrases *with* nouns but that pronouns *are* noun phrases and occur *instead* of nouns. There are, in fact, two noun phrase templates:

$$\left[(Det) \begin{Bmatrix} (Adjective) \\ (Noun) \end{Bmatrix} Noun \right]_{NP}$$

$$[Pronoun]_{NP}$$

DETERMINERS WITH NOUNS IN NOUN PHRASES

Determiners have an important purpose in the noun phrase: they tell us how we are to perceive the entity pointed out by the noun. For example, if the entity has not been discussed before or if it is a new entity that is being introduced, the introduction usually takes place with *a/an*:

1. *An elephant suddenly walked into the campsite.*
   Note that *campsite* uses the definite determiner *the,* presumably because there is only one campsite and the speaker has already alluded to it earlier or the listener can readily identify its referent through the context. In contrast, the following sentence seems vague, abrupt, and unrelated to anything in our immediate surroundings. It could even be the start of a joke, that is, a line to set the scene.
2. *An elephant suddenly walked into a campsite.*

Box 8.1   A List of Determiners

Definite:	*the*
Indefinite:	*a/an*
Possessive:	*my, your, his, her, its, our, their*
Demonstrative:	*this, that, these, those*
Quantifying:	*some, any, no, every, each, many, much*
Numbers:	*one, two, second, eighth*
W*h*-words:	*which, whose, whatever*
Possessive noun phrases:	*Homer's, the student's, the students'*

A TEACHING MOMENT

Language Variation in Determiners

Determiners can be very hard for nonnative speakers. The problem that each student faces depends on his her native language. Some languages, such as Spanish, have similar determiners, but they are used somewhat differently. For example, English prefers an indefinite determiner in a subject complement construction having to do with professions: *I am a teacher*. The corresponding sentence in Spanish, *soy profesora*, does not have a determiner. In Spanish, abstract nouns take a definite determiner, *la felicidad*, but in English they do not, *happiness*. Spanish also avoids using possessive determiners in places where English has them. This is especially true with parts of the body:

English: *My hand hurts.*
Spanish: *Me duele la mano.*   (*To me hurts the hand.*)
                                The hand hurts me.

Some languages do not have determiners at all, including Japanese, Chinese, and Hmong. Students from those languages have a great deal of difficulty using determiners and selecting the right one to convey the meaning they are after.

In the noun phrase template, there was one determiner position, but in fact more than one determiner can occur in English noun phrases. There are three types of determiners: **predeterminers, central determiners,** and **postdeterminers.** Examples of noun phrases with more than one determiner are <u>*all the*</u> *pretty flowers* and <u>*the first seven*</u> *intelligent students*. In this template, "Determiner" is a place holder for the three positions of predeterminer, central determiner, and postdeterminer:

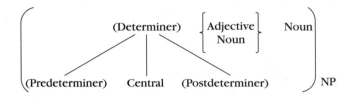

Predeterminers

Words such as *all* or *both*, fractions (*half*, or *one quarter*), and multipliers (*double*, *three times*, or *once*) are predeterminers.

Predeterminers

1. $\left\{\begin{array}{l} \underline{All} \\ \underline{Both} \\ \underline{Half} \end{array}\right\}$ *the guides jumped to their feet.*

2. *The elephant was* $\left\{\begin{array}{l} \underline{three\ times} \\ \underline{double} \\ \underline{twice} \end{array}\right\}$ *their height.*

Central Determiners

The **definite article** *the* and the **indefinite article** *a/an* are central determiners. In addition, central determiners include **demonstratives** (*this, that, these, those*), **possessives** (*my, your, his, her, its, our, their, Mary's, John's*), **wh-determiners** (*which, whose, whatever*), and **quantifiers** (*no, some, any, neither, either, every, each, enough, little, less, few, fewer*).

Central Determiners

1. *I wanted* $\left\{\begin{array}{l} \underline{a} \\ \underline{the} \\ \underline{this} \\ \underline{whatever} \\ \underline{either} \\ \underline{your} \end{array}\right\}$ *camera.*

2. *I took* $\left\{\begin{array}{l} \underline{some} \\ \underline{no} \\ \underline{enough} \end{array}\right\}$ *photos of the elephant.*

Postdeterminers

If there is a postdeterminer, it will be an ordinal number or similar word (*first, last, third, next*) or a quantifier (*two, three, other*). There can be more than one in the sentence:

The elephant took $\left\{\begin{array}{l} \textit{the } \underline{last\ three} \\ \textit{his } \underline{other\ two} \\ \textit{those } \underline{few\ other} \end{array}\right\}$ *ripe bananas.*

A TEACHING MOMENT

Less and Fewer

Less is the comparative of *little*, and *fewer* is the comparative of *few*. In Standard Written English (SWE) and Academic English (AE), *less* is used with mass nouns and *fewer* is used with plural count nouns. However, in Standard Spoken English (SSE), many people use *less* with plural count nouns:

> *After that, there were *less people on the safari.*
> (Compare *little people)
> *After that, there were fewer people on the safari.*
> (Compare *few people*)
> *Less* is correct with mass nouns or abstract nouns:

> *After that, there was less trouble on the safari.*
> *After that, there were fewer problems on the safari.*

A TEACHING MOMENT

Unstressed Determiners

Determiners are unstressed in speech; that is, they are spoken with little emphasis, loudness, and force. The lack of stress on determiners makes them hard to hear, so English learners do not get much exposure to determiners in listening to native speakers. Therefore, the most effective methodology would be for teachers to raise the learners' awareness of determiners as they are used in reading material, asking them to focus attention on them as they are reading. It is easy for learners to skip over them and consider them unimportant. Unfortunately, if they do, they are throwing away the main source of exposure to accurate determiner usage.

It is important to take the time to go over the differences in meaning among the determiners, and many English-as-a-Second-Language (ESL) grammar books have charts that attempt to codify the way the English speaker uses determiners. However, ultimately the best way to learn to use determiners is to examine how they are used in the context of English writing, so teachers should encourage English learners to be active observers of their target language so that they form hypotheses about determiner usage and test them in their own speaking and writing for feedback. Once they are aware of determiners and how they work, they will be ready to practice them in workbook exercises and computer-assisted language learning exercises.

PRONOUNS ARE NOUN PHRASES ▬▬▬▬

A common intuition about pronouns is that they take the place of nouns, but that intuition is not quite right. It is more accurate to say that pronouns function the same way that entire noun phrases do. They refer to people and things in the context or in the conversation, but because they are function words and not content words, they are highly efficient. With a minimum of effort and no fuss at all, they refer to anything at all. We can use the word *it,* for example, to refer to any inanimate or nonhuman entity (*the yeti*), any event (*your birthday party*), or any complex situation (*the war against terrorism*) anywhere at any time (See Figure 8.1). Pronouns do not have consistent morphology, and their template is simple: [Pronoun]$_{NP}$. They have the same referential roles as noun phrases, but some of the roles are unlikely.

Personal Pronouns

These pronouns often function as subjects, direct objects, indirect objects, and objects of a preposition. It is possible but rare to use pronouns as subject complements (*I am I/me, You are you*) or as object complements (*?They considered me her*):

Subject	*I like tofu burritos and sauerkraut.*
	They are a filling combination.
Direct object	*Grandma made it for dinner last week.*
	We thanked her.
Indirect object	*She made us that combo last night.*
	She gave me a serving with onions.
Object of a preposition	*She also served a tuna salad with it.*
	I ate in front of her.

Figure 8.1 *A pronoun refers to a variety of NPs efficiently.*

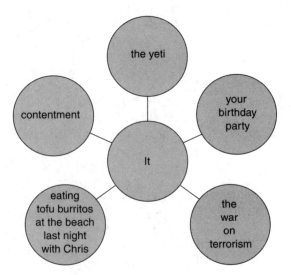

Box 8.2 Personal Pronouns		
Person	**Subject**	**Object**
First singular	I	*me*
First plural	*we*	*us*
Second plural	*you*	*you*
Third singular masculine	*he*	*him*
Third singular feminine	*she*	*her*
Third singular impersonal	*it*	*it*
Plural	*they*	*them*

A QUESTION OF STYLE

In conversation, most people use object pronouns after the verb *be*. This is also common in fiction and news. Biber et al., 1999, (p. 335) gives these examples:

Hello gorgeous, it's me! (conversation)
Carlo immediately thought it was me who had died. (fiction)
Some people say it was him that wrote it. (fiction)

There are not any examples from academic prose because the construction is extremely unusual in that style. The rule that requires subject pronouns after *be* (*It is* I) is imported from Latin, but it has affected only the speech of people most concerned with correctness. In writing, purists would prefer these:

Carlo immediately thought it was I who had died.
Some people say it was he who wrote it.

When a writer is in doubt about which one to use, paraphrasing the sentence is a common resolution.

Possessive Pronouns

Expressions such as *He's a friend of mine* with a possessive pronoun have a different and more indefinite meaning than *He's my friend*, which uses a possessive determiner. Possessive noun phrases with *'s* can also function as possessive pronouns in expressions such as *He's a friend of Bill's.*

? A QUESTION OF STYLE

SWE and AE require subject forms for all subjects of sentences, and with "normal" subjects, most people oblige. However, with conjoined subjects (two subjects with *and* or *or* in the middle), some people, even highly educated people, use object forms. This occurs almost exclusively in conversation or reported conversations, as in these examples from Biber et al., 1999, (p. 337):

Me and her mother split up about two years ago. (news)
And you and me nearly—nearly didn't get on the train. (conversation)
Him and Ed stink, both of them. (conversation)

However, object pronouns in subject position are not appropriate for SWE or AE. Instead, the previous sentences should be *Her mother and I split up*, *You and I nearly didn't get on the train*, and *He and Ed smelled* or *Ed and he smelled*. Generally, SWE and AE prefer the first person (I) to be the last one mentioned in any conjoined pronoun subject.

Teachers have harped on this for years, but learners have not gotten the message quite right. Instead, they have internalized the notion that it is <u>always</u> better to use subject pronouns, so they often use them in prepositional phrases when it is correct to use object pronouns. A very common example is *between you and* I instead of *between you and me*. This is called **hypercorrection.** When people hypercorrect their speech or writing, it means that they feel insecure about their usage, have learned a usage rule incorrectly, and/or misapply the usage rule to instances it should not cover. These examples are from Biber et al., 1999, p. 338:

Well there's two left in there and that's not enough for you and I. (conversation)
Balthazar says that the natural traitors like you and I are really Caballi. (fiction)

When *as* and *than* are considered prepositions, it is standard to use the object pronouns. Otherwise, they are subordinators and take a subject and a verb:

He has as many toys as me.
He has as many toys as I do.

He has more toys than me.
He has more toys than I have.

In AE prose, writers generally avoid referring to themselves or using the pronoun I in order to make their statement seem more objective or scientific. This is not a hard-and-fast rule, but it is generally best to edit out expressions such as I *think*, I *feel*, or I *know*.

TERMINOLOGY CLASH!

Compare the possessive pronouns above with the possessive determiners: *my, our, your, his, her, its,* and *their.* Determiners are used *with* nouns; pronouns are used *instead of* nouns:

Make <u>*my coffee*</u> black, please.
Make <u>*mine*</u> black, please.

<u>*Her paper*</u> was used up.
<u>*Hers*</u> was used up.

Box 8.3   Possessive and Reflexive Pronouns

Person	Possessive	Reflexive
First singular	*mine*	*myself*
First plural	*ours*	*ourselves*
Second	*yours*	*yourself/ves*
Third singular masculine	*his*	*himself*
Third singular feminine	*hers*	*herself*
Third singular impersonal	*its**	*itself*
Plural	*theirs*	*themselves*

* *Its* is a possible form, but it is rare. The *piece of kibble is the dog's. It's its.*

A TEACHING MOMENT

Reflexive Pronouns

The form of standard reflexive pronouns is irregular because sometimes the reflexive pronouns are a compound of the possessive determiner + *self* (*herself, myself*) and sometimes they are a compound of the object pronoun + *self* (*himself, themselves*). Given this irregularity, it is not surprising that in some dialects of English nonstandard reflexives are found: (*hisself, theirselves*). However, these are stigmatized usages in SSE and SWE.

Reflexive Pronouns

Reflexive pronouns usually refer back to a noun phrase elsewhere in the sentence, often the subject. The noun phrase and the reflexive pronoun are said to **co-refer,** because both point to the same entity. Reflexive pronouns are most often direct objects or objects of a preposition, as in these examples from Biber et al., 1999, (p. 342):

> *I'm cooking for <u>myself</u> tonight.* (conversation)
>
> *Universal envy setting <u>itself</u> up as a power is only a camouflaged form of cupidity which re-establishes <u>itself</u> and satisfies <u>itself</u> in a different way.* (academic)

Reflexive pronouns are sometimes used in subject position in conversation and in reported conversations in fiction and news (Biber et al., 1999, p. 339). In these examples, there is no **co-reference:**

> *Paul and myself went up there didn't we?* (conversation)
>
> *My three associates and myself are willing to put big money into the club to get the best players for the team.* (news)

Biber suggests that this use is a strategy to avoid the problematic choice between a subject pronoun and an object pronoun. That is, the speaker avoids saying either *Paul and I* or *Paul and me.* The reflexive pronoun in subject position is rare in academic prose, but reflexive pronoun usage without co-reference is common in academic prose, as in these examples (Biber et al., 1999, p. 346):

> *This explains why the representation of the totem is more sacred than the totemic object itself.* (academic)
>
> *The subskills themselves are not the purpose of the activity, but they must be developed to serve the needs of the higher-level complex activity.* (academic)

On the whole, personal pronouns (except for *it* and *they/them*), all the possessive pronouns, and reflexive pronouns (except for *itself* and *themselves*) are exceptionally rare in academic prose.

Demonstrative Pronouns

Singular	**Near**	*This*
	Distant	*That*
Plural	**Near**	*These*
	Distant	*Those*

Demonstrative pronouns serve to introduce or identify entities:

This is my favorite dinner.

That's a good cook.

They also refer to a particular situation, fact, or event described in a previous or following sentence. This usage is very common in Academic English (Biber et al., 1999, p. 348):

> *We are identifying children who have needs but we're not providing the resources to solve the problem. We are waiting until they crash land and <u>that</u> is no good.* (news)

TERMINOLOGY CLASH!

All demonstratives are either determiners or pronouns:

That elephant stomped on the food supply.
That was a big problem for the safari.

The word *that* is very confusing because it also occurs as a degree word in conversation, often referring to a gesture:

The elephant was that tall.

That is a relative pronoun also:

The elephant that stomped on the food ran off.

It can also be used to link a main sentence with a subordinate sentence:

I know that she'll be back tonight.

> *This is vintage Havel: creating a work that is both specific and universal, tragic, and comic.* (news)

Those occurs very commonly with an expression that identifies a group:

> *The insurance men were willing to admit that the safe driver is subsidizing those who have accidents.* (news)

Indefinite Pronouns

In the following list, the compounds with *one* are more common than the compounds with -*body*, except in conversation. Indefinite pronouns are not common in academic prose because most writers prefer a specific noun with quantifying determiners (*every human, some details, any answer, no object*), which occur more frequently.

Every: *everybody, everyone, everything*
Some: *somebody, someone, something*
Any: *anybody, anyone, anything*
No: *nobody, no one, none, nothing*

Relative Pronouns

Relative pronouns introduce adjective clauses (to be discussed later). Word processing grammar checkers prefer *that* as a relative pronoun and mark other relative pronouns with an underline. However, SSE or SWE has a relative pronoun specifically for humans:

He is the guide who scared away the elephant.
He is the guide who the elephant detested.

A TEACHING MOMENT

**Indefinites and
Subject–Verb Agreement**

Nonnative speakers sometimes miss the fact that the quantifying determiner *every* and the compound indefinites with *every* are not plural. They are singular, take singular forms of verbs, and other singular determiners and pronouns like *his* or *her*. One way to make this move clear is to equate *every* with *each*:

Everyone need<u>s</u> a backpack.
Everyone need<u>s</u> his/her backpack.
Each one need<u>s</u> a backpack.

Very formal English has two forms. In this sentence, *who* is the subject of the verb *frightened*:

Subject: *He is the guide <u>who</u> frightened away the elephant.*

In this sentence, *whom* marks the object of the verb *detested*:

Object: *He is the guide <u>whom</u> the elephant detested.*

For animals or inanimate objects, *which* is a possibility:

The elephant <u>which</u> stomped on the food ran away.

Reciprocal Pronouns

Each other and *one another* express the idea that an action is mutual. *Each other* is more common than *one another*, which some people reserve for those contexts where there are more than two entities:

They looked at each other. (two people)
They looked at one another. (two or more people)

One

The pronoun *one* (not the number) substitutes for a noun phrase with a count noun. It has a plural form, *ones*, which substitutes for plural nouns (not noun phrases), possessive forms (*one's* or *ones'*), and a reflexive pronoun (*oneself*). These forms refer back to indefinite entities that have been mentioned before or that can be inferred from the context. These examples are from Biber et al., 1999, (p. 353):

An artist cannot fail, it is success to be <u>one</u>. (academic)
It's like everything else in the world, he said. You get some bad <u>ones</u> and you get some good <u>ones</u>. (fiction)

One is also an impersonal pronoun for those situations when we use *you* in less formal conversation and writing. In some cases, as in the third sentence in the fol-

A QUESTION OF STYLE

When writers use an indefinite determiner or pronoun, they sometimes are unsure about how to finish off the sentence. With singular forms such as *everyone* or *every student*, the traditional resolution was to use the masculine singular pronouns, as in these examples from Biber et al., 1999, (p. 316):

Each novelist aims to make a single novel of the material he has been given. (academic)
Each individual is thus the recipient of the accumulated culture of the generations which have preceded him. (academic)

However, more recently, style manuals for news and academic speech and writing prefer a gender-neutral resolution:

A geologist studying fossiliferous rocks in the field needs only an average knowledge of paleontology in order to make a fairly accurate estimate of the epoch in which the rocks he or she is studying belong. (academic)
Anyone with English as his or her native language does not need other languages. (news)
Thus the user acts on his/her own responsibility when executing his/her functions within his/her task domain. (academic)

An alternative in both SSE and even SWE (but rarely in AE) is the use of the third-person plural forms. This alternative has resisted the best efforts of English teachers and language critics to stamp it out for years. Biber et al., 1999, (p. 316) gives these examples:

Everybody remembers where they were when JFK was shot. (news)
Nobody likes to admit that they entertain very little or that they rarely enjoy it when they do. (news)

One way to avoid all these problems is to make everything plural, as in this example from Biber et al., 1999, (p. 317):

Now they expect responsible customers to pay for their folly. (news)

lowing examples from Biber et al., 1999, (p. 354), the author uses *one* to refer very obliquely to himself or herself:

One doesn't raise taxes with enthusiasm, but the alternative is public sector borrowing going through the roof. (news)
Success and acclaim were seen as a means of validating one's existence. (news)
One does not wish to repeat oneself unduly and the reader is referred to other parts of this book. (academic)

A summary of determiner and pronoun diagnostics is shown in box 8.4.

A TEACHING MOMENT — **The Multiple Negative**

Some dialects permit multiple negative expressions with combinations of negative verbs, the negative quantifying determiner (*no*), and the indefinite pronouns (*nothing, no one, nobody*), but this usage is highly stigmatized in SSE, SWE, and AE. However, it is not an illogical usage and has a long history in English. The standard forms are the quantifying determiner and the indefinite pronouns with *any*, to be used with negative verbs.

He doesn't know nothing about it.
He doesn't know anything about it.
You didn't care about nobody else.
You didn't care about anybody else.

There is one emphatic usage that is accepted:

You can't not respond to this attack.

Box 8.4   Summary of Determiner and Pronoun Diagnostics

Determiner
 Syntax: No consistent morphology

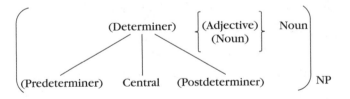

 Function: Gives grammatical information about how to view the noun.

Pronoun
 No consistent morphology
 Syntax: [Pronoun]$_{NP}$
 Function: Takes the place of a noun or refers to a noun.

EXPLORING CHAPTER PERSPECTIVES

◆ *Discussion Questions*

1. English does not have a distinction between singular *you* and plural *you*, but it would seem to be an important distinction that speakers would need to make at times. How have different dialects of English repaired this lack in English? Do you think those forms are appropriate or inappropriate in formal academic writing? What is your prediction for the future of these forms?

2. Explore the issue of a new third-person singular pronoun besides *he/she/it* further. What would such a pronoun be useful for? Who could initiate the use of such a pronoun? What factors might make it catch on? What strategy do people use to refer to another person if they want to conceal the gender of the person?

3. If there are speakers of other languages in the class, contrast English subject pronouns and subject pronouns in other languages. How do the pronoun systems differ?

4. English has "natural" gender that is not marked morphologically for the most part. Pronouns and nouns that refer to males have masculine gender, and pronouns and nouns that refer to females have feminine gender. Pronouns and nouns that refer to inanimate things are neuter. The gender system in many European languages is called "grammatical." How is it different from English? Is there any gender in Chinese or Hmong pronouns and nouns?

◆ *Cooperative Exercise: A Survey on Pronoun Usage*

A. **Individual Work.** Make 10 photocopies of this survey and ask 10 people you know to record their impressions of their own speech. Choose a variety of people of different ages, education levels and so on. (Articulate the difference between each pronoun in terms of form and usage for yourself, but don't tell your consultants until they are finished, if they ask.)

Age _____   Sex _____
Last year of school completed _____

(Percentages should add up to 100% for each question.)
1. What percentage of the time do you use either of these?
      It's me. _____%
      It's I. _____%
2. What percentage of the time do you use either of these?
      He's the one whom I know. _____%
      He's the one who I know. _____%
3. What percentage of the time do you use either of these?
      Between you and me _____%
      Between you and I _____%
4. What percentage of the time do you use either of these?
      Every student needs their backpack for the trip. _____%
      Every student needs his/her backpack for the trip. _____%

When you are finished, examine your results to see if there are any consistent patterns in the responses in your class with respect to age, educational level, or sex of students.

Fill out this form with the average percentage per age-group and sex.

Males

age	under 20	20–40	40–60	60 and over
me				
I				
whom				
who				
you and me				
you and I				
their				
his/her				

Females

age	under 20	20–40	40–60	60 and over
me				
I				
whom				
who				
you and me				
you and I				
their				
his/her				

A. **Pair Work.** Average each individual's results and enter them onto this form:

Males

age	under 20	20–40	40–60	60 and over
me				
I				
whom				
who				
you and me				
you and I				
their				
his/her				

Females				
age	under 20	20–40	40–60	60 and over
me				
I				
whom				
who				
you and me				
you and I				
their				
his/her				

Do the patterns hold? Are there any new patterns? (You can also analyze the results for education levels.)

B. **Class Work.** Each pair of students summarizes what they found in a few sentences. Fill out the form one more time with all the results.

◆ *Writing Assignment*

Write a short essay in your Language Notebook in response to one or both of these prompts. Save your essay(s) for later use.

1. Write an inductive minilecture script that explains the difference between using *the* or *a/an*. Imagine that your learners are non-native speakers of English from a language where there are no determiners. You may need to refer to a pedagogical grammar for assistance.

2. Write a deductive minilecture to explain the use of subject pronouns in conjoined phrases in SWE and AE versus the common use of object pronouns, as in *Chin and me spelled the word correctly*.

Introspection

Proofread your essays and make any necessary corrections. Underline all pronouns and determiners in your essays and identify what they are.

TEACHING TO LEARN

Pronouns and Determiners

What would you say to your learners in order to improve their academic writing? In groups, take turns explaining what the problem in each sentence is and suggesting a more formal AE alternative. Make sure to identify if the problem is with a determiner or a pronoun.

1. Everyone must remove their personal items from their lockers as soon as the semester is over.

2. This math problem is too difficult for Sheila and I.

3. In public speaking, you don't want to leave your audience without a clear idea of your conclusion.

4. The three men saw each other as soon as the smoke cleared.

5. Mario and me performed the chemistry experiment last week.

6. Trisha and myself were the only ones who understood the question.

7. Each athlete should consult with his adviser once a week.

8. Each student has an archaeological dig in the making in their backpacks.

9. Wendy did not approve of Sue and I and what we think.

10. A doctor should never make his patients wait more than 15 minutes.

| LEARNING TO TEACH |

Graphic Organizers and Games

Description: Graphic organizers can be converted into grammar games. For example, this "determiner flower" is a semantic network made into a matching game in which learners cut out the petals (labels) and attach them to the circle (category) to form a sunflower shape:

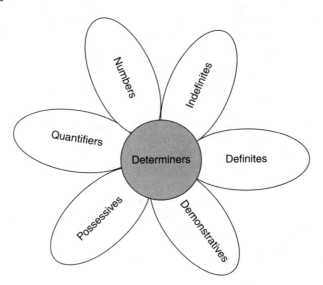

Games make grammatical learning a visual and hands-on experience that appeals to some learners. As learners manipulate the labels and forms (*my, your, his, her, its, our, their*), they will learn them, especially if they say the words as they are assembling the flower.

With grammar instruction, you must always ask yourself, "What are my alternatives?" The traditional methods, writing the forms in response to a question or filling in the blank—may not lead to retention, but a dynamic visual matching game may engage the learner enough for learning to take place.

Goals

Subject area goal: Types of determiners or pronouns

English language awareness goal: Metalinguistic awareness

Descriptive grammar goal: Metalanguage

Procedural goals: Sort labels or forms into categories

Assessment: Successful completion of the game and transfer of knowledge to other contexts.

Methodology: Make up a graphic game based on pronoun or determiner labels, forms, or categories for your preferred grade level. Share your games within your cooperative group. At the end of the activity, evaluate whether the games led to learning.

9

Adjectives and Adverbs

In the past, there was no sharp distinction between adjectives and adverbs in English, and the demarcation between them remains fuzzy to this day. That may be why adjective/adverb usage is a source of insecurity for some people.

ADJECTIVES

Adjectives attribute such qualities as color, size, shape, personal characteristics, and value to nouns (Biber et al., 1999, p. 508–509):

Color: *black, white, bright, dark*
Size: *tall, short, wide, narrow*
Shape: *round, square, rectangular*
Personality: *intelligent, wise, kind, happy*
Value: *good, bad, useless, useful*
Others: *appropriate, complex, empty, practical*

Adjectives are frequent but mostly optional open-class words. Because they occur in complex noun phrases, they are more frequent in academic prose and news than in conversation. In the following example of Academic English (AE) prose (Biber et al., 1999, p. 504), the adjectives are underlined. One is a **predicate adjective,** that is, an adjective placed after a linking verb as a subject complement within a verb phrase. The others are **attributive adjectives,** which are located before a noun inside a noun phrase:

> *Thus HIV infection is <u>likely</u> to remain with us for the <u>foreseeable</u> future. The <u>full</u> impact of HIV infection will be felt over decades. The virus does not need to spread rapidly in a population to have a very <u>marked</u> and gradually <u>expanding cumulative</u> effect. The two major factors influencing the risk of <u>individual</u> infection are the prevalence of HIV infection and <u>individual</u> behavior.*

Evaluative adjective–noun collocations that occur frequently in AE include the following (Biber et al., 1999, p. 514–515):

good	*judges, readers, separation, communication, relations, fortune, yields, indication*
important	*changes, advances, step, part, consequences, respect, role, point, factor*
special	*cases, process, regulations, class, types, method*
right	*principles, level, relation, direction, answer, criteria*

Contrasting pairs of adjectives frequently used in AE include these:

large/small	*long/short*	*young/old*
low/high	*final/initial*	*previous/following*
general/ particular	*same/different*	*simple/complex*
primary/secondary	*necessary/possible*	*positive/negative*

Adjectives in a Series

When attributive adjectives occur in a series, there tends to be a prescribed order: general, physical state, proper (or general) adjectives, noun, and head noun.

Predicative adjectives have a weaker tendency, and some orders are more awkward than others. Different orders convey different meanings.(Note that the comma before *and* in a series of more than two adjectives is optional.):

The peppermint candies are excellent, old and Norwegian.

The peppermint candies are old, excellent, and Norwegian.

The peppermint candies are Norwegian, excellent and old.

A TEACHING MOMENT

Adjective Orders

Native speakers learn these preferred orders from exposure to their language as they are growing up. Even so, sentence-combining and other activities encourage syntactic maturity.

At a very rudimentary level, English learners may have problems placing adjectives before nouns, and for more advanced learners the orders of adjectives and descriptive nouns can be a problem. They should notice the adjectives in their reading and translate the modifiers into their first language. Translations should not be word for word but rather by meaningful chunks, keeping the meanings the same.

Sentence-combining activities are also useful. This exercise can review *a/an* if you have alternative adjectives and nouns that begin with either vowel or consonant sounds:

The camera is Japanese.
The camera is expensive.
The camera is new.
I bought a camera.

I bought an expensive new Japanese camera.

Characteristics of Prototypical Adjectives

Prototypical adjectives have morphological, syntactic, and functional characteristics that identify them.

Derivation

These suffixes are frequent: *-al* (*final, social*), *-able* (*provable*), *-ent* (*different*), *-ive* (*active*), *-ous* (*serious*), *-ate* (*appropriate*), *-ful* (*beautiful*), and *-less* (*endless*) (Biber et al., 1999, pp. 531–532).

Inflection

Some adjectives form their comparatives with *-er* (*taller*) and their superlatives with *-est* (*tallest*). Some adjectives occur with *more* and *most* (*more beautiful*, *most beautiful*). The rules are not hard and fast, but there are some trends described in Biber et al., 1999, pp. 522–523.

TAKING *-ER/-EST* (AND *LESS/LEAST*):

- Adjectives of one syllable, except for *right*, *wrong*, and *real*
- Two-syllable adjectives that end in *-y*, as in *angry*, *busy*, *crazy*, *dirty*, and *pretty*

TAKING *MORE/MOST* (AND *LESS/LEAST*):

- Two-syllable adjectives with no apparent morphology, such as *common*
- Adjectives longer than two syllables
- Adjectives that end in *-ful*, *-less*, *-al*, *-ive*, or *-ous* (*useful*, *mindless*, *musical*, *effective*, or *zealous*)
- Participial adjectives (*excited*, *exciting*)

VARIABLE USE OF *-ER/-EST* AND *MORE/MOST*:

- Some monosyllabic adjectives, such as *fair*, *full*, *fierce*, *proud*, and *rude*
- Adjectives that end in *-ly*, such as *costly*, *deadly*, *friendly*, *lively*, *lonely*, *lovely*, *lowly*, and *ugly*

A TEACHING MOMENT

Comparative and Superlative Adjectives

Children and learners of English as a second language may not know which adjectives form their comparatives and superlatives in which way. In addition, with adjectives that end in *-y* or *-ly*, there is a spelling change that can be confusing, as in *pretty* to *prettier* and *early* to *earlier*.

English learners might learn these adjectives in their inflected forms: *best, better, earlier, easier, greater, greatest, higher, highest, larger, largest, lower, older, smaller,* and *wider*. Other than *best, greatest, highest,* and *largest,* very few superlative adjectives are common in academic prose probably because mature writers avoid making strong claims in academic writing.

- Adjectives that have unstressed endings, such as *-ow* (*mellow, narrow*)

Syntax of Adjectives in NPs and VPs

The adjective phrase (AdjP) template looks like this:

$$[(Adv) (Adj^*) Adj (Adv)]_{AdjP}$$

The first adverb, the first adjective, and the last adverb are optional, and the asterisk means that there can be more than one optional adjective. The head adjective is obligatory. An adjective phrase is located within a noun phrase (NP) or a verb phrase (VP) with a linking verb, as in *is too tall, are very accommodating, seem smart enough* or *will be clever indeed:* as in *a very beautiful sunset* or *the slightly sodden newspaper*:

Attributive Adjective Template
$$[(Det) (AdjP) (N) N]_{NP}$$

Predicate Adjective Template

$$\left[V \left\{ \begin{array}{l} (AdjP) \\ (NP) \end{array} \right\} \right]_{VP}$$

Some adjectives exhibit strong preferences to be either attributive or predicative but not both. Adjectives that tend to be attributive are *mere*, as are adjectives ending in *-al*, such as *general, industrial, local, national,* and *social*. Adjectives that tend to be predicative are *glad, ill, impossible, ready, sure, anxious, as well as unable, aloof, able, aware,* and *asleep,* as are most other adjectives that begin with *a-*, such as *abed, ablaze, afraid, aghast,* and *aglow* (Biber et al., 1999, p. 511–516).

Figure 9.1 *Attributive and predicative adjectives in academic prose.*

Attributive Adjectives			
simple	individual	total	oral
basic	lower	various	physical
common	particular	local	public
following	similar	natural	sexual
higher	specific	normal	

Predicate Adjectives			
common	present	important	sure
dependent	similar	necessary	wrong
equal	useful	clear	possible
equivalent	able	small	ready
essential	true	available	aware
greater	different	better	likely
large	impossible	hard	unlikely
low	unable	right	

Adjective Function

Classifying Adjectives

In addition to their descriptive function, adjectives often serve a classifying function, especially in academic prose writing. They classify their head nouns in terms of their relationship to others of the same group, origin, subject area, and so on:

> **Relation:** *average, chief, internal, left, main, maximum, standard, previous* (all these are "defined" with relation to another or a group)
>
> **Origin:** *American, Catholic, British, Indian, Navajo*
>
> **Subject area:** *chemical, commercial, environmental, legal*

Complements

Predicate adjectives are subject complements. Object complements, in which the linking verb is implied but not really there, are also adjectives or nouns:

> *The candies are <u>tasty</u>.*
>
> *We all considered the candies (to be) <u>very tasty</u>.*

Other Syntactic Positions for Adjectives

Not all adjectives meet the template for predicate or attributive adjectives:

1. Adjective phrases can be preposed in a sentence as a kind of displaced modifier or transition word:
   <u>Too tired to move</u>, [she] stayed there. (fiction) (Biber et al., 1999, p. 521)
   <u>Still more important</u>, children who grew up in elite homes enjoyed advantages that helped them maintain their elite status. (academic)
2. Adjectives occur after indefinite pronouns:
   It's a shame if you haven't got anyone <u>musical</u> here. (conversation)
   Try as they might, no one <u>close</u> to Frankie Howerd could ever improve his image. (news)
3. Some adjectives (*involved, available, concerned*) can occur after their head nouns:
   He said the only details <u>available</u>, apart from the death certificate, had come from Mr. Garrod's family.
4. Very complex adjective phrases often shift to a position after the noun. Placing the "heavy" adjective phrase after the noun makes it easier for the listener or reader to find the noun and connect it with the other constituents of the sentence. The heavy adjective phrase becomes more salient in the sentence, as shown in these examples (Biber et al., 1999, p. 519):
   It's a lounge <u>not much bigger than the one we've got now</u>.
   McDeere is a great student, <u>dedicated, hardworking, and ambitious</u>.
5. Exclamations in conversations and in fiction, as in *Great! Wonderful!* or *Beautiful!* are adjectives. These are very uncommon in academic prose.

Box 9.1 provides a summary of the diagnostics of the prototypical adjective.

Syntactic Maturity with Adjectives

Developing writers unfamiliar with alternative locations for adjective phrases benefit from sentence-combining activities to acquire syntactic maturity.

Box 9.1   Summary of Diagnostics of the Prototypical Adjective

Morphology
   Derivation: *-tion, -ness, -hood*, etc.
   Comparative/superlative inflections

Syntax
   Take degree or intensifying adverbs like *very*
   Occur in a noun phrase or verb phrase and other positions

Function
   Attributive or predicative description, subject or object complement

---

Nonprototypical Adjectives

Some adjectives do not meet all the defining characteristics of prototypical adjectives. **Classifying adjectives** are frequently incompatible with comparative/superlative or degree words, as in **the very chemical reaction* or **the chiefer reason*. **Nongradable adjectives** are absolute words, such as *unique, perfect, dead, alive, lone,* or *pregnant*. They are absolute because an entity either does or does not have the quality; there is no relativity involved. If something is *unique*, then there is no other like it. If something is *perfect*, then it is logically impossible to be more perfect. In Standard Spoken English (SSE), people use absolute adjectives with intensifiers or degree words, sometimes to say something about appearance. For example, if someone is *very pregnant*, she appears to be very advanced in her pregnancy.

   Participial adjectives come from present or past participles, verbs ending in *-ing* or *-ed*, and they are not always easy to distinguish from the verbs they come from. In this complex noun phrase from the Gettysburg Address, for example, the underlined words could either be adjectives or past participles:

> *this nation (which was) <u>conceived</u> in liberty and (which was) <u>dedicated</u> to the proposition that all men are created equal*

Applying the diagnostics for adjectives, we find that **very conceived* does not sound right but that *very dedicated* does and that **more conceived* does not sound right but that *more dedicated* does. However, *conceived* is an absolute adjective, and these characteristics naturally follow from that. We conclude that these words are adjectives and not verbs. (Note that the adjective phrases follow their head noun because they are heavy.)

Perfect/Unique

Absolute adjectives do not lend themselves to comparison or degrees in academic writing, although they sometimes occur that way in SSE. Language purists avoid using expressions such as *very unique* or *more perfect*.

Participial Adjectives

English learners might have problems understanding the difference between the two types of participial adjectives. Being *bored* is not the same as being *boring*:

The student is never bored.
The student is never boring.
The class is never boring.

In addition, some learners omit the *-ed* suffix from the participial adjective. Their instructors should point out the suffix in reading to raise students' awareness and provide for instruction and practice in writing once the concept has been learned.

The meanings of participial adjectives depend on the participle they come from. The *-ing* adjectives (*boring, interesting, amazing, exciting, following*) have a progressive or active meaning. The *-ed* adjectives (*advanced, alleged, bored, complicated, excited, exhausted*) have a completed or passive meaning:

The work has <u>exhausted</u> me. (main verb past participle)
I was <u>exhausted</u> by the work. (main verb past participle)
I was <u>exhausted</u> every day. (adjective derived from past participle)
The work was <u>exhausting</u> me. (main verb present participle)
The work is very <u>exhausting</u>. (adjective derived from present participle)

Comparative Expressions

The most common comparative in conversation, news, fiction, and academic writing has this template:

$$\left[(adv) \left\{ \begin{array}{l} \text{Adj -er} \\ \text{more/less \quad Adj} \end{array} \right\} \text{than} \right]$$

Internodes are <u>longer</u> and sheaths <u>relatively and progressively shorter than</u> the internodal length.

> **Box 9.2   More Comparative Constructions**
> **(Biber et al., 1999, pp. 527–529)**
>
> As + adjective + *as*
> *The last tinkle of the last shard died away and silence closed in <u>as deep as</u> ever before.* (fiction)
> So + adjective + *that*
> *His personality was <u>so subdued that</u> it seemed to fit in with anything he did.* (fiction)
> So + adjective + *as to*
> *And if anybody was <u>so foolhardy as to</u> pass by the shrine after dusk he was sure to see the old woman hopping about.* (fiction)
> *Too* + adjective + infinitive
> *I mounted the black scaffold, which was almost <u>too hot to touch</u>.* (fiction)
> Adjective + *enough* + infinitive
> *I was <u>old enough to do</u> it for myself.* (fiction)

A TEACHING MOMENT

A Wide Range of Comparative Expressions

Academic prose is simpler than fiction in comparative constructions. To read and write academic prose successfully, the main comparative construction is *adjective -er than* or *more/less adjective than*. For reading or writing fiction or for writing descriptive works, readers must understand and use a wider range of comparatives. English learners may need sentence-combining practice.

> *But a small sample for comparison is <u>better than</u> nothing at all.*
>
> *The cost of installing the device would have been <u>higher than</u> the discounted cost of the accident.*

Box 9.2 shows some sample comparative constructions.

ADVERBS

Adverbs are very versatile modifying words. The conventional thinking is that adverbs modify verbs, but, in fact, they modify other adverbs, adjectives, noun phrases, indefinite pronouns, predeterminers, determiners (numbers), prepositional phrases, and particles, as these examples (Biber et al., 1999, pp. 546–548) show:

Adverb: *They'll figure it out <u>really</u> fast.* (conversation)

Adverb: *The do-it-yourself builder <u>almost</u> always uses a water-repellent plywood, oil-tempered hardboard or fibre-cement sheet.* (academic)

A QUESTION OF STYLE

It is good style in academic writing to place the adverb near the word that it modifies and to delete informal adverbs that do not add much to the meaning. Common adverbs that should be deleted are *just, very, really, actually, so, right, way, pretty*:

> The <u>only</u> modification was ~~only~~ to the wing span and shape. (Note that the adverb becomes a determiner.)
> The subjects ~~just~~ had to fill out the questionnaire before completing the test.
> They reported the test as ~~pretty~~ hard.

Noun Phrase: <u>*"It came as quite a surprise," said one.*</u> (news)

Indefinite Pronoun: <u>*Almost nobody, it seemed, could eat what they were given*</u>. (fiction)

Predeterminer: *I've done <u>about</u> half a side.* (conversation)

Number: *It's still not clear whether the <u>approximately</u> 250 people still listed as missing include those whom ex-detainees say were still alive in May.* (news)

Prepositional Phrase: *But there's a hell of a lot—<u>well</u> into their seventies.* (conversation)

Particle: *It's really filled the room <u>right</u> up.* (conversation)

Four Types of Adverbs

Time and Place Expressions and/or Adverbs of Frequency
now

then

everyday

here

there

always

sometimes

usually

often

never

Morphology: These adverbs have no consistent morphology.

Syntax: The placement of time and place expressions is variable.

A TEACHING MOMENT

More Double Negatives

Double Negatives: Some of the adverbs of frequency (*seldom, never*) are negative in meaning and should not be used with negative verbs in Standard Written English (SWE) or AE:

He *never studied as hard as that day.*
*He didn't never study as hard as that day.

Hardly is not an adverb of frequency, but it acts like one syntactically. It should not be used with a negative verb:

He *can hardly understand the issue.*
*He can't hardly understand the issue.

English learners need assistance with the location of adverbs in the sentence, especially the inverted sentences:

Seldom have I seen such complex concepts.
Never has she asked such confusing questions.

Adverbs of frequency tend to be placed before the main verb in a sentence unless it is the verb *be*:

They <u>often</u> eat handmade candy.
The candy is <u>sometimes</u> sticky.

Some adverbs of frequency appear at the beginning of the sentence and trigger a change in the verb:

Hiro had never studied as hard as that day.
Never had Hiro studied as hard as that day.

Degree Words/Intensifiers
very
too
a little
slightly *(and other words that end with –ly)*
so
quite
pretty
way

A QUESTION OF STYLE

Some intensifiers are appropriate for SSE; and some are proper to SWE and AE: *real, pretty, kind of, sort of,* and *way* are used in conversation and not in academic prose.

Morphology: There is no consistent morphology.

Syntax: These adverbs occur before adjectives, other adverbs, noun phrases, and prepositional phrases.

Function: These adverbs indicate the degree or intensity of the modified expression:

The candy is <u>too</u> sticky.

The candy is <u>kind of</u> sticky.

Adverbs of Manner

Common: *fast, well, slow*

Descriptive: *obviously, rapidly*

Classifying: *chemically, politically*

Morphology: The suffix *–ly* derives descriptive and classifying adverbs from the corresponding adjective.

Syntax: The template for adverbs of manner shows that they occur within an adverb phrase with other adverbs as modifiers:

$$[(\text{Adv}) \quad \text{Adverb of manner} \quad (\text{Adv})]_{\text{AdvP}}$$

| *very* | *happily* | *indeed* |
| *not* | *easily* | *enough* |

Sentential adverbs

Simple: *not, too, also,*

Complex: *frankly, of course,*
       nevertheless, however,
       in general, on the contrary

Morphology: There is no consistent morphology, but *–ly* appears in some complex sentential adverbs.

Syntax: Simple sentential adverbs have variable locations, usually within a sentence. Complex sentential adverbs occur at pre-, mid-, or postsentence positions.

Function: Sentential adverbs are frequent in academic discourse because they reflect the speaker's or author's stance toward the statement or add a transition linking two or more ideas.

Adjective or Adverb?

Sometimes learners are not sure whether to use an adjective or an adverb. Which sentence is correct?

I *felt bad about the accident.*
I *felt badly about the accident.*

The first sentence is correct. The confusion lies in the distinction between a linking verb and a main verb. Linking verbs are *be, seem, feel, taste,* and other verbs of sensation. With linking verbs, we use an adjective (or a noun) as a subject complement.

With main verbs, we use an adverb to modify the action of the verb. Because so many people have overgeneralized the idea that "adverbs modify verbs," they hypercorrect I *feel bad* to I *feel badly.* These sentences are correct but unusual:

The towel felt bad. (It was rough when I touched it.)
My fingertips felt badly after they were burned. (They were unable to feel. They had no sensation.)

Good is an adjective, and *well* is an adverb:

I *was in good health.* I *felt good.* (healthy)
It *was soft and smooth.* It *felt good.*
My car got a tune-up. It *worked well.*
The immigrants always did good and donated to charities.
The immigrants always did well at that company.

When we are talking about health, *well* can be an adjective that means *not sick*:

I *was in good health.* I *felt well.* (not sick)

  A QUESTION OF STYLE

Split infinitives: Adverbs of manner (and adverbs of time also) modify infinitives:

a. *to boldly go*
b. *to go boldly*
c. *to sometimes contemplate*
d. *to contemplate sometimes*

Language purists often reject the placement of adverbs between the infinitive marker *to* and the verb, as in a. or c. They prefer b. or d. where the adverb is outside the infinitive. Writers might want to avoid the split infinitive in their most formal academic writing. One option is to delete the adverb if it does not add much to the meaning of the expression:

to ~~*sometimes*~~ *contemplate*

A QUESTION OF STYLE

Some language purists have pet peeves about sentential adverbs; for example, they reject *hopefully* or *irregardless*. Although these may be common in SSE, it is best to avoid them in academic writing.

Differentiating the Adverbs

Context helps determine what type of adverb a particular word is because the same form occurs in various ways:

Intensifier	*He is so tall.*
Sentential adverb	*So the thing to do is put up the ladder.*
Adverb of manner	*Tony went off to work happily.*
Sentential adverb	*Happily, Tony likes his job.*

Adverbs in Different Registers

Nowhere is the difference between conversation and academic prose more evident than in the use of adverbs. In conversation, *pretty, real, good,* and *right* are commonly used:

You could remember that number pretty well.

She did pretty good, didn't she?

It would have been real bad news.

In conversation, over 60% of the adverbs are simple adverbs such as *again, always, already, far, here, never, now, soon, still, then, yet, very, rather, quite,* and *pretty.* Only about 20% of the adverbs are *-ly* forms.

In academic prose, it is the opposite. About 55% of the common adverbs are *-ly* forms such as *generally, possibly, probably, certainly, obviously, rapidly, entirely, carefully, relatively, particularly, exactly, approximately,* and *slightly.* Only 30% of the adverbs are simple adverbs (Biber et al., 1999, pp. 540–541).

Both conversation and academic prose use multiword lexical units that are adverbs, but they are very different. In conversation, the most common units are *at least* and *as well.* In academic prose, many of the fixed expressions are Latin abbreviations, such as *etc.* or *e.g.* and terms such as *in general* or *in particular* (Biber et al., 1999, pp. 886–889).

Four sentential adverbs, *so, then, anyway,* and *though* appear in conversation especially frequently. The transition word *so* is usually placed at the beginning of a sentence. The others appear at the end of a sentence:

He twisted it and a fragment of the tooth came off and hit me straight in the eye. So I've got a little pinprick in my eye. So I'm just hoping I'm not gonna get an infection in it. (conversation)

AN OPTICAL ILLUSION:

To, Two, Too

1. *to* = preposition/infinitive marker:
   I want to$_{Inf}$ take the dog to$_{Prep}$ the park for a romp. Will you go with me?
2. *two* = determiner/pronoun
   It's more fun walking the dog with two$_{Det}$ people.
   Would you like me to invite my sister too?
   No, two$_{Pro}$'s company, three's a crowd.
3. *too* = intensifier or sentential adverb:
   I'd like my sister to go along too$_{SA}$.
   She's not too$_{Int}$ busy for a walk.

It's the spears don't work—they slide off the spears that's the problem.
Well use your spoon <u>then</u>. (conversation)

They've got loads of dressy things for girls, not for boys <u>though</u>. (conversation)

Speaker A: *I can't remember unpacking it—it's not in the er—in the ski bag.*
Speaker B: *worry about*
Speaker A: *can always get another one <u>anyway</u>.* (conversation)

Although the most common sentential adverbs in academic prose are *however, thus, therefore*, and *for example*, there is great variety in transition words in academic prose because authors have individual preferences:

The Venezuelan government has encouraged the Piaroa to form larger communities in downriver positions closer to the administrative centre. <u>Thus</u>, although I use the present tense, the physical organization of communities and the economic organization that I discuss are more relevant to the pre-1970 period (academic). (Biber et al., 1999, p.889)

In academic prose, sentential adverbs generally occupy the position in front of their sentence because they identify for the reader exactly what relationship there is between the two sentences.

EXPLORING CHAPTER PERSPECTIVES

◆ *Discussion Questions*

1. This chapter discusses a number of grammatical structures that are avoided by language purists. Select several of them and decide what you think about them. Discuss your opinons with your partner.

2. Read the following paragraph from Ricento (1998, pp. 86–87) in the Cooperative Exercise and answer the questions:

    a. What does this quote say? Put it in your own words.

    b. How do you know this is AE ?

    c. What specific structures might be difficult for an English learner to understand?

    d. Can you find the example of the split infinitive? How would you modify the infinitive in question?

◆ *Cooperative Exercise: Language Policies*

A. **Homework.** In the following quotation, some of the adjectives and descriptive nouns are underlined. Decide whether the underlined word is a descriptive or classifying adjective, or a descriptive noun, or a combination of these. Use morphology, syntax, paraphrase, and function as cues; do not guess. Use both positive and negative evidence. (If you can figure out that a word is not an adjective, it must be a noun. If it is not a noun, it must be an adjective.) Identify the word each one modifies as well. Make a note of any problems you have.

(1) Unlike Canada, which passed the <u>Official Languages</u> Act of 1969, and Australia, with
(2) its <u>National</u> Policy on Languages (1987) and the <u>Australian Language and Literacy</u>
(3) Policy (1991), the United States has never attempted to articulate, let alone
(4) implement, a <u>national language</u> policy. When <u>language</u> matters are addressed at the
(5) <u>federal</u> level, usually in legislation or in <u>higher court</u> rulings, goals usually center
(6) around the solution of <u>long-standing social</u> problems, most frequently to redress
(7) violations of <u>constitutional</u> and <u>statutory civil</u> rights. Therefore, to accurately
(8) characterize <u>language</u> policies, one must situate such <u>government</u> actions within
(9) <u>broader social policy</u> issues and <u>sociohistorical</u> processes. For example, to
(10) understand the goals of the <u>Bilingual</u> Education Act of 1968, one needs to
(11) understand why that legislation was passed when it was passed, whose interests
(12) were being served, what the <u>general policy</u> framework was with regard to <u>minority</u>
(13) languages and speakers of those languages, what sort of support was or wasn't
(14) provided to implement the legislation, what the <u>prevailing social</u> attitudes were at the
(15) time regarding bilingual education, and so on.

B. **Pair Work.** Take turns explaining why you identified each word as either an adjective or a noun, providing for your partner a number of forms of evidence. Do you agree on each answer?

C. **Class Work.** Discuss any answers that are controversial.

◆ *Writing Assignment*

Write a short essay in your Language Notebook in response to one or both of these prompts. Save your essay(s) for later use.

1. Put the information from Ricento's paragraph into your own words in a written paragraph. Then compare your answer to a partner's. What similarities and differences do you find in your "translations"? What specific linguistic factors are different from the original?

2. Look up one or more of the language policies mentioned in the paragraph on the Internet. Summarize what you find out about them.

Introspection

Proofread your essays and make any necessary corrections. Underline and identify all the adjectives and adverbs. (Make sure to separate out any noun modifiers. They do not count.) Identify what type of adjective or adverb you have underlined. If you do not have many adjectives or adverbs, can you add some?

TEACHING TO LEARN

Adverbs

In pairs, imagine that you are giving your students some individual feedback on their compositions about a science experiment they did. Their compositions should not be written in conversational style.

Some of these sentences are good, so praise your "student" (your partner) and point out any correct use of adverbs. Some sentences have errors or nontypical usage with adverbs and their placement. If so, please point out the error and tell your partner what to do to fix it. The adverb may need to be replaced with an adjective. The adverbs may be too informal or slangy and may need to be replaced with something more academic. The adverb may be placed incorrectly in the sentence and need to be moved, or the adverb should be deleted because it does not add much to the sentence. A sentence could have more than one error or no error at all. You may need to make other suggestions as well to make sentences sound more academic.

1. On Tuesday, the experiment we did in class turned out good for our group.
2. It was pretty interesting to immediately see what happened when we mixed up the two chemicals in the test tube.
3. Experiments always aren't possible to do right.
4. Our team did the experiment quickly and effectively.
5. Hopefully, all of our experiments will be just as easy to perform.
6. We shook the test tube right up and stood way back to see what would happen.
7. The result was so spectacular!
8. The experiment ended in a bang which involved mixing two chemicals.
9. The smoke smelled badly and afterwards, we smelled badly too.
10. Irregardless of the outcome, the teacher said we did very good.

```
LEARNING TO TEACH
```

Chunking and Unscrambling

Description: There are two activities that improve syntactic awareness and knowledge of AE without any use of metalanguage, so teachers use them for all learners at all levels, provided that the text materials are appropriate for them. Both help learners notice the structure of complex sentences. They are very controlled; little creativity is allowed.

The first, **chunking,** is the easiest. It involves dividing the text into meaningful syntactic units of around five to seven words (or fewer if the text is complex). The units are usually the five phrases—NP, Aux/VP, AdjP, AdvP, and PP—although it is usually best to avoid these metalanguage terms at first. Reading in chunks facilitates comprehension. (Note that the Reciento quote on page 170 is not correctly "chunked." Did this make the text more difficult for you to understand?)

The second, **sentence unscrambling,** is more complex. It requires learners to take scrambled phrases and reassemble them into coherent sentences in AE. The following examples are designed for high school students.

Goals

Subject area goals: Reading comprehension and controlled writing

English language awareness goals: Advanced syntactic awareness and complex sentences

Descriptive grammar goals: Development of syntactic awareness in preparation for eventual metalanguage instruction

Procedural goals: Divide complex sentences into coherent phrases, reassemble phrases into sentences

Assessment: With these methods, there is no one right or wrong way to assess learners, but there are better ways to do than others. Teachers assess chunking through oral reading. In sentence-unscrambling activities, if the resulting sentence makes sense it is correct. It does not need to replicate the original, but it should convey the same meaning.

Methodology

1. *Chunking.* Divide this text into "chunks" that are approximately five to seven words in ways that are faithful to their phrasal properties based on what you have learned from this chapter. (You will also find some subordinate sentences that you have not studied yet.) The first sentence in each is done for you. When you are finished, read the passage in chunks or "breath groups".

This academic prose selection is from, Leap p. 152 (1993). This section deals with influences of other languages on Native American languages.

ANCESTRAL LANGUAGE DIVERSITY AND TRIBAL MULTILINGUALISM

Entirely new linguistic codes // also emerged // in some of these settings, // through a synthesis // of European and Indian language grammars // and rules of discourse. . . . // That there were non-Indian speakers of these language "hybrids" is apparent from these brief descriptions, though how extensively non-Indians used these languages outside of particular economic and political settings of interest to individual speakers, or how long such usage was retained, is difficult to assess in most cases. . . . Two other nonindigenous language traditions contributed to language diversity among the tribes during the colonial period and western expansion that followed it, and both had particularly powerful effects on the knowledge of English taking shape in Indian country during this period. First were the varieties of nonstandard English that are the antecedents to today's Black English vernacular, introduced into the Indian Southeast in the early years of the seventeenth century as a result of the slave trade and the commercial ties between the southern colonists and the Caribbean. Second, though somewhat later (mid-nineteenth century), were the many forms of Pidgin English introduced into the Indian West by the Chinese laborers who helped build the railroads and worked in the mines.

---

2. *Unscrambling.* With four sentences from the previous quotation, scramble the phrases and let your partner reassemble them without looking at the original. Remove capitalization and punctuation so that it can be added later. An example is done for you:

  of European and Indian language grammars

  in some of these settings

  entirely new linguistic codes

  through a synthesis

  and rules of discourse

  also emerged

  _____

  _____

  _____

  _____

10

Verbals and Verb Phrases

A verbal (a more inclusive term than *verb*) identifies the relationship among the entities referred to with nouns. Also, I am using the term *relationship* in a very inclusive way to include states of being, physical activities, mental activities, emotional activities, experiencing activities, and others. Most verbals are content words, but two types—auxiliaries (helping verbs) and modal auxiliaries—are function words.

Verbals can be finite or nonfinite. **Finite verbals** have past or present tense (e.g., *am, is, are*; *go, goes, went*; *can, could*). **Nonfinite verbals** are **bare infinitives** *(go)*, **infinitives** *(to go)*, or **participles** *(going, gone)*.

Verbals are numerous in fiction and conversation, less numerous in news, and even less numerous in academic prose (Biber et al., 1999, pp. 359–360). In the following examples, the finite verbals are underlined, and the nonfinite verbals are in capital letters:

CONVERSATION

Those hyacinths in the corner <u>are</u> TAKING a long time TO COME OUT, <u>aren't</u> they? I'<u>d</u> HAVE THOUGHT the tulip in the coal scuttle, the tulips in the cauldron, I <u>thought</u> they'<u>d</u> HAD it, they <u>were</u> lying DOWN completely.

I <u>know</u>, but they'<u>ve</u> STRAIGHTENED OUT.

ACADEMIC PROSE

Internal heat, volcanism, and the kinds of igneous and metamorphic rocks that <u>are</u> PRODUCED by thermal processes <u>are</u> the subjects of the first group of chapters. The structure of the interior as DEDUCED from seismology, gravity, and magnetism <u>is</u> then EXPLORED, in preparation for a detailed systematic explanation of plate tectonics.

Regular English verbal inflectional morphology is important but meager when compared to some other languages. Most verbs have four different inflected forms:

FINITE VERBAL MORPHOLOGY:

Third-person present tense *-s*	*plays, collects, talks*
Past tense *-ed*	*played, collected, talked*

NONFINITE VERBAL MORPHOLOGY:

Progressive participle *-ing*	*playing, collecting, talking*
Past participle *-ed*	*played, collected, talked*

A QUESTION OF STYLE

The verbs in the academic example are passive. Writing teachers often advise their students to avoid overusing the passive verbal *be* and the past participle in writing and to prefer active descriptive verbs. Yet, as you can see from the example of academic prose, scholarly writers do not always follow this advice.

A TEACHING MOMENT

Verb Inflections

English learners may have a lot of trouble with English-inflected verb forms despite how usual they are in conversation. Some languages, such as Chinese and Hmong, do not have verbal inflections at all, so learners of these languages have little awareness of inflections. Other languages have inflections, but learners still have difficulty choosing the correct inflection in English. English learners' typical errors are like these: He *go to the store* or *Yesterday he study his algebra*.

FINITE VERBALS

Main verbs, auxiliaries, and modal auxiliaries have present- and past-tense forms. The terms **past** and **present** refer to verb <u>forms</u>, that is, what the verb looks like, and not the <u>time</u> it refers to because verb forms in English are only indirectly related to time concepts. That is, we can talk about past, future, and present times, but there are only two tenses: present and past. These two simple tenses account for approximately 90% of all verb usages (Biber et al., 1999, p. 461).

Characteristics of Main Verbs

Morphology
Verbs have typical derivational endings such as *-ize (cauterize)* or *-ate (mediate)*, but for main verbs, inflections are more informative.

Present Verbs
Present verbs have regular inflectional morphology; they have two forms:

$$
\left\{\begin{array}{l} \text{I} \\ \text{You} \\ \text{We} \\ \text{They} \\ \text{The students} \end{array}\right\} \text{eat} \qquad \left\{\begin{array}{l} \text{He} \\ \text{She} \\ \text{It} \\ \text{The student} \end{array}\right\} \text{eat\underline{s}}
$$

However, three common irregular verbs in the present are the verbs *to be, to do,* and *to have:*

$$I \quad am \qquad \left\{ \begin{array}{l} He \\ She \\ It \end{array} \right\} is \qquad\qquad \left\{ \begin{array}{l} You \\ We \\ They \end{array} \right\} are$$

$$\left\{ \begin{array}{l} I \\ You \\ We \\ They \end{array} \right\} do \qquad\qquad \left\{ \begin{array}{l} He \\ She \\ It \end{array} \right\} does$$

$$\left\{ \begin{array}{l} I \\ You \\ We \\ They \end{array} \right\} have \qquad\qquad \left\{ \begin{array}{l} He \\ She \\ It \end{array} \right\} has$$

Common in conversations, the present tense refers to past time (as in jokes or news reporting), present time (as in sports), or future time:

After the fire, one man <u>says</u> to the other . . .

She <u>jumps</u>, she <u>shoots</u>, she <u>scores</u>.

Then next Sunday, they <u>go</u> to Belgium.

A TEACHING MOMENT Subject–Verb Agreement

Many learners make mistakes matching present tense verbs with their subjects. They sometimes match the verb with the closest noun phrase instead of the true subject of the sentence, which may be farther away. There is an intervening phrase that separates the verb from its real subject:

The condition of California's roads makes drivers feel that their taxes are wasted.

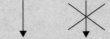

The cost of the supplies is too high for anyone to pay right now.

With the expression *there is/are*, the verb matches the noun phrase after the expression, but in Standard Spoken English (SSE), many people use the contracted form *there's* with plural noun phrases. This usage should be avoided in academic speech and writing:

There's are too many detail<u>s</u> in this report.

Unfortunately, there's are too many garish colors in the painting.

In academic prose, the present tense expresses facts that are not limited to a specific time frame (Biber et al., 1999, p. 458):

> *A fault tree analysis <u>reveals</u> the logical connections existing between an undesired event in a technical system and component and operating failures which <u>lead</u> to it. In the case of safety analyses for process plants the undesired event usually <u>is</u> a fire, a release of toxic substances or an explosion. In other cases it <u>is</u> simply an outage of the system. The method of analysis <u>is</u> deductive and <u>is</u> normally used for calculating the probability of occurrence of the undesired event. A qualitative investigation of the system <u>is</u> a prerequisite for it. This <u>requires</u> knowledge about the dynamic behavior of the system.*

Past Verbs

Past verbs have either regular or irregular morphology. Regular verbs are easy; they have only one form, but these are some spelling conventions that must be observed.

$$\left.\begin{array}{l} \text{answer} \\ \text{bake} \\ \text{call} \\ \text{study} \end{array}\right\} \text{ed}$$

Three common irregular verbs in the past are *to be, to do,* and *to have:* Other common irregular verbs are listed in Figure 10.1.

$$\left.\begin{array}{l} \text{I} \\ \text{He} \\ \text{She} \\ \text{It} \end{array}\right\} \text{was} \quad \left.\begin{array}{l} \text{You} \\ \text{We} \\ \text{They} \end{array}\right\} \text{were}$$

Had   (not *haved)
Did   (not *doed)

Finite Verb Phrase Syntax

Transitive verb phrases, intransitive verb phrases, and linking verb phrases are the three prototypes.

A TEACHING MOMENT

Past-Tense Verbs

Do you got is common in SSE, but *Do you have* and *Have you got* are acceptable in Standard Written English (SWE) and Academic English (AE).

Used to is a past-tense verb. Learners sometimes leave off the past-tense ending because they hear the sound of the *t* right after it:

He <u>used</u> to smoke three packs a day.
He didn't <u>use</u> to jog around the block.

Figure 10.1 *Verbs irregular in the past.*

Patterned (three forms)

Simple Form	Past Form	Past Participle
speak	spoke	spoken
choose	chose	chosen
forget	forgot	forgotten
get	got	gotten (*got* in British)
take	took	taken
shake	shook	shaken
write	wrote	written
ride	rode	ridden
drive	drove	driven
give	gave	given
bid	bad(e)	bid(den)
hide	hid	hidden
bite	bit	bitten
wear	wore	worn
bear	bore	borne, born
know	knew	known
draw	drew	drawn
fly	flew	flown
show	showed	shown
mow	mowed	mown
drink	drank	drunk
sing	sang	sung
swim	swam	swum

Unpatterned

dive	dived/dove	dived
fall	fell	fallen
do	did	done
go	went	gone
see	saw	seen
eat	ate	eaten
lie	lay	lain

Two Forms

Simple	Past/Past Participle
bring	brought
buy	bought
teach	taught
think	thought
sell	sold
tell	told
hang	hung/hanged
stick	stuck
bend	bent
sent	sent

Figure 10.1 *(continued)*

Two Forms *(continued)*

Simple	**Past/Past Participle**
find	found
wind	wound
feed	fed
lead	led
read	read (spelling same)
feel	felt
mean	meant
pay	paid
say	said
lay	laid

Unpatterned

make	made
have	had
sit	sat
build	built

One Form

Simple/Past/Past Participle

put, set, hurt, fit, cast, cost, cut, shut, quit, knit

Transitive Verb Phrases

Transitive verb phrases relate two entities to each other directly in a situation. The first entity is the subject (the agent or experiencer of the action), and the second entity is the direct object (the receiver of the action or that which is experienced). The negative sentence and the question are formed with *do/does* as an auxiliary. Indirect objects and objects of a preposition may also appear in the sentence:

SUBJECT	**ACTIVE VERB**	**DIRECT OBJECT**	
Miguel	*tosses*	*the napkin*	*into the air.*
doer		receiver	

SUBJECT	**ACTIVE VERB**	**DIRECT OBJECT**	
Miguel	*felt*	*the wind*	*on his face.*
experiencer		that which is experienced	

QUESTION
Does Miguel feel the wind?

NEGATIVE
Miguel doesn't feel the wind.

ACTIVE TRANSITIVE VERB PHRASE TEMPLATE

	[V	NP	X*]ᵥₚ
Miguel	*eats*	*the burrito*	*reluctantly.*
Isaac	*kisses*	*Mary*	*on the cheek.*
Betty Boop	*lets out*	*a big squeal*	*suddenly.*
The clouds	*swallow up*	*the ballon*	*on the horizon.*
The girl scouts	*donate*	*two hours.*	

Intransitive Verb Phrases

Intransitive verb phrases have no direct object, only a subject. If there are other nouns in the sentence besides the subject, they are usually in a prepositional phrase.

ACTIVE INTRANSITIVE VERB PHRASE TEMPLATE

	[V	X*]ᵥₚ
Miguel	*snores*	*loudly.*
Isaac and Mary	*kiss*	*under the apple tree.*
Betty Boop	*squeals*	*into the microphone.*
The balloon	*vanishes.*	
The two hours	*go by*	*very quickly.*

Linking Verb Phrases

Linking verb phrases with *be, seem, become,* or *turn into* are intransitive because they link the subject to a subject complement—either a noun phrase or an adjective phrase. Subject complements do not introduce a new entity into the situation and do not refer to anyone. They merely describe the subject, and that is what makes linking verbs intransitive.

LINKING VERB PHRASE TEMPLATE

	[V	{ADJP} NP	X*]ᵥₚ
Miguel	*is*	*a sound sleeper*	*in the morning.*
Isaac and Mary	*become*	*very good friends*	*later.*
Betty Boop	*seemed*	*excitable*	*to her manager.*
The balloon	*gets*	*very high.*	
The two hours	*turned out*	*very interesting*	*for the Scouts.*

Auxiliaries, Aspect, and Voice

The **auxiliaries** *have* and *be* are finite verbals that mark verb phrases with aspect or voice. **Perfect aspect** indicates that the situation talked about occurred in the past but is still relevant to the present. **Progressive aspect** indicates that the situation described is still in progress, not completed. **Passive voice** contrasts with the simple active templates mentioned earlier. In the passive voice, the subject is not the agent or

---

*The variable X stands for anything that can occur in a verb phrase that is not a noun phrase.

◆◆◆◆
! TERMINOLOGY CLASH!

Have and *be* are both content words and function words. They are prototypical main verbs by themselves (a) and auxiliaries that are used with nonfinite main verbs, either the present or the past participle (b):

a. The little puppies <u>are</u> cute.
b. The little puppies <u>are</u> ROLLING around on the floor.

a. The children <u>have</u> some peppermint candy.
b. The children <u>have</u> CHEWED some peppermint candy.

---

the experiencer; rather, the entity that would normally be the direct object is the subject of the passive verb.

Aspects	**Perfect**	*Vince <u>has written</u> three papers for this class so far.*
	Progressive	*Vince <u>is writing</u> a paper right now.*

Voices	**Active**	*Vince Carulo wrote those papers.*
	Passive	*Those papers <u>were written</u> by Vince Carulo.*

Perfect Aspect

When *have* is the auxiliary and the nonfinite main verb is the past participle, the verb has perfect aspect. Perfect aspect is an invitation to view the relationship expressed by the verb as completed with respect to another vantage point of time, usually the present (*They <u>have already</u> <u>eaten</u>*), sometimes the past (*They <u>had</u> already <u>eaten</u> before going to the movie*), or the future (*They will <u>have</u> already <u>eaten</u> before they arrive here*). Five to 10% of all verb forms in conversation, news, fiction, and academic prose have perfect aspect (see Box 10.1).

PERFECT ASPECT TEMPLATE

	[HAVE V + -ED/-EN	X*]_{VP}
Yang	*has chewed*	*that piece of gum for 8 hours.*
The boys	*have chewed*	*bubble gum all their lives.*
The boys	*had chewed*	*bubble gum every day until last year.*

Progressive Aspect

When *be* is the auxiliary and the main verb is the present participle, the verb has progressive aspect. This means that we are to view the relationship expressed by

---

*The variable X stands for any other material that could be part of a verb phrase.

Box 10.1   Verbs Commonly in Perfect Tense in Academic Prose and News

agree	*criticize*	*prompt*	*implicate*
appoint	*draft*	*vow*	*master*
campaign	*experience*	*witness*	*report*
circulate	*pledge*	*document*	

Source: (Biber et al., 1999, p. 463)

A TEACHING MOMENT

Variation in Auxiliaries and Past Participles

Some nonstandard dialects have different aspects, different past participles (e.g., *went* instead of *gone*), and different uses of auxiliaries. One nonstandard auxiliary is *ain't*, which is a negative form for *am not, is not,* and *has not.* Learners of all kinds leave off the inflection on the past participle, as in this example: *They have prove their hypothesis.*

In addition, English learners often have difficulty understanding when to use the present perfect and what distinguishes it from the regular past tense. The regular past tense implies that the situation is completed, over and done with; the present perfect implies that the situation still has some relevance to the present:

He always took a shower before class.
He's always taken a shower before class.

They never ate all the canapés.
They've never eaten all the canapés.

---

the verb as in progress or as continuing over a period of time. (Sometimes this verb form is called **continuous.**) This aspect is a little less frequent than the perfect aspect in news, fiction, and academic writing, but in conversation the progressive is twice as common as the perfect (Biber et al., 1999, p. 462). Perhaps that explains why native-speaking children learn this verb form early and English learners have fewer problems with it. Of course, it is also a very regular form. Certain verbs, especially verbs of mental state, rarely appear in the progressive because their meaning is not compatible with it: *understand, believe, know, comprehend, mean, doubt, want,* and *prefer.*

*I am wanting a soft drink.

*He is understanding the lesson right now.

PROGRESSIVE ASPECT TEMPLATE

[BE   V + ING   X]_{VP}

where X stands for any other material that could be part of a verb phrase:

The puppy	*is*	*rolling*	*around on the floor right now.*
The puppies	*are*	*rolling*	*around on the floor.*

Perfect Progressive Aspect

The perfect and progressive templates can be combined in a more complex verb form, but these are somewhat uncommon:

	Present	**Perfect**	**Progressive**
The boys	*have*	*been*	*studying.*

	Past	**Perfect**	**Progressive**
The boys	*had*	*been*	*studying.*

Passive Voice

In passive sentences, the focus shifts from the entity that is the subject to the entity that is normally the direct object. Passive uses the auxiliary *be* and the past participle. Authors use passive verbs when they are trying to convey a certain detachment and objectivity in their writing. They choose the passive to deemphasize the agent, especially if they are not sure who it is. If the agent is present, it appears in a prepositional phrase with *by*. Passives account for 25% of all verbs in academic prose but only 2% in conversation (see Box. 10.2):

> (Academic prose) Three communities on a brackish marsh of the Rhode River, a subestuary of the Chesapeake Bay, <u>were exposed</u> to elevated carbon dioxide concentrations for two growing seasons beginning in April 1987. The study site and experimental design <u>are described</u> in Curtis et al. (1989a). One community <u>was dominated</u> by the perennial carbon 4 grass spartina patens.

Active: *Miriam planted the tree.*

Passive: *The tree was planted by Miriam.*

Box 10.2 Passive Verbs Common in Academic Prose and News

done	designed	accused	effected	labeled
born	developed	announced	entitled to	linked to
told	discussed	arrested	flattened	/with
said	examined	beaten	inclined	located
expected	explained	believed	obliged	at/in-
held	formed	charged	positioned	plotted-
achieved	identified	delighted	situated	recruited
associated	illustrated	hit	stained	stored
defined	introduced	injured	subjected to	transferred
expressed	limited	jailed	approved	viewed
measured	noted	killed	composed of	coupled with
obtained	observed	named	confined to	associated
performed	presented	released	designed	with
related	recognized	revealed	distributed	attributed
applied	regarded	shot	documented	to
calculated	replaced	sold	estimated	classified
chosen	represented	aligned with	extracted	as
compared	studied	base on	grouped with	diagnosed as
derived	suggested	deemed	intended	

(*Source:* Biber et al., 1999, p. 477)

PASSIVE VOICE TEMPLATE

	BE	V + -EN/-ED	X*]VP
This word	*is*	*spelled*	*wrong.*
The children	*are*	*taken*	*to school in the bus.*
The race car	*was*	*repaired*	*by Mario.*
Those plays	*were*	*written*	*in Tagalog.*

Perfect Passive

The perfect passive combination occurs frequently in academic prose and news.

PERFECT PASSIVE TEMPLATE

	[HAVE BEEN		V + -EN/-ED	X*]VP
This word	*has*	*been*	*spelled*	*wrong.*
The children	*have*	*been*	*taken*	*to school in the bus.*
The race car	*has*	*been*	*repaired*	*by Mario.*
Those plays	*had*	*been*	*written*	*in Tagalog.*

*The variable X stands for any other material that could be part of a verb phrase:

A TEACHING MOMENT

Passive Voice

To be supposed to is a passive verb form with a past participle that ends with *-ed*. People sometimes omit the inflectional ending in writing because of confusion with the *t* that begins the word *to* right after it. English learners need to learn a variety of verb tenses for conversation, but for academic writing, the present tense and the passive are important to learn and practice. The form *be* often stands on its own as a main verb or as an auxiliary in a passive verb phrase.

OPTICAL ILLUSIONS

Its/it's; there/their/they're

These words are **homophones;** that is, they sound alike but are written differently. If learners do not understand their syntax, they are unable to discriminate between them in their writing. They often select one form to write always or arbitrarily use one or the other without understanding which is which:

Its/it's
Possessive determiner (or pronoun):
   Is that your dog? <u>*Its*</u> *face is so cute!*
Contracted subject with verb or auxiliary BE:
   Yes, it is. Well, really <u>*it's*</u> *my mother's dog.* (The apostrophe does not mean possessive.)

Their/there/they're
Possessive determiner:
   See those people? <u>*Their*</u> *dog is a pit bull.*
Adverb or dummy subject:
   That's the pit bull over <u>*there*</u>. <u>*There*</u> *are two beagles next to it.*
Contracted subject/verb:
   <u>*They're*</u> *not afraid of it.*

Contracted Forms

In speech, we usually give less stress to auxiliaries, so they blur into the words surrounding them. When we write informally, this blurring of speech is represented as contracted forms. Examples of contracted forms are *he's, she's, it's, isn't, don't,* and *hasn't*. Very formal writers avoid contracted forms in academic style, but others use them.

Modal Auxiliaries

Modal Auxiliaries (e.g., *can, could, will, would, shall, should, must*) are function words and finite verbals. They are called auxiliaries because they support the main

A QUESTION OF STYLE

One issue for some learners is the difference between *can* and *may*. Some people reserve *can* for ability and *may* for permission, but common usage today is for *can* to mean both ability and permission. Other expressions like modals are *ought to, had better, used to,* and *be supposed to.* These are sometimes called **semimodals** and are more common in conversation than in academic prose. People often say *He better go,* but the standard for writing is *He'd better go. Shall* is used for future or to ask permission, but it is rare.

verb, and they are called modals because they contribute to the **mood** that the verb has. Mood refers to concepts such as ability, possibility, future, conditionality, permission, obligation, necessity, hypothesis, and so on. A modal combines with a simple nontensed main verb, called a **bare infinitive** because it is not marked with *to.* In these examples, the modal auxiliary is underlined, and the bare infinitive is in capital letters:

> *Miguel <u>will</u> SNORE loudly tonight.*   (future)
>
> *He <u>would</u> LIKE to stop snoring.*   (present)
>
> *If he <u>could</u> STOP snoring, his wife <u>would</u> be happy.*   (present hypothetical, present conditional)
>
> *Isaac and Mary <u>may</u> KISS under the apple tree.*   (present or future possibility)
>
> *Betty Boop <u>can</u> SQUEAL for a long time.*   (present ability)
>
> *Betty Boop <u>could</u> SQUEAL for a long time.*   (past ability or possibility)
>
> *The balloon <u>might</u> VANISH very quickly.*   (present or future possibility)
>
> *The girl scouts <u>could</u> GO home.*   (present possibility or permission)
>
> *They <u>should</u> STOP for dinner on the way.*   (future obligation)
>
> *They <u>must</u> CHECK for ticks when they get there.*   (future necessity)

To express the past with modals (underlined), we combine them with present perfect verbals (capital letters), in which *have* appears as a bare infinitive and the main verb as a past participle. Many of these are rare:

> *Miguel <u>would</u> HAVE LIKED to stop snoring, but he never did.*
>
> *If he <u>could</u> HAVE STOPPED snoring, his wife <u>would</u> HAVE BEEN happy.*
>
> *Isaac and Mary <u>may</u> HAVE KISSED under the apple tree.*
>
> *Betty Boop <u>could</u> HAVE SQUEALED for a long time.*
>
> *The balloon <u>might</u> HAVE VANISHED very quickly.*
>
> *The girl scouts <u>could</u> HAVE GONE home.*
>
> *They <u>should</u> HAVE STOPPED for dinner on the way.*
>
> *They <u>must</u> HAVE CHECKED for ticks when they got there.*

> **A TEACHING MOMENT**
>
> When people say *could have gone* or *should have eaten*, the auxiliary *have* is pronounced with very little stress on it, so it sounds like the word *of*, which some people mistakenly write. Others sometimes try to write a contraction, which is also not standard in SWE or AE:
>
> *They should ~~of~~ stopped for dinner.*
> *They should've stopped for dinner.*
> SWE: *They should have stopped for dinner.*

> **A TEACHING MOMENT**
>
> English learners may have some difficulty learning and using auxiliaries and modals. Their typical errors might be like these.
>
> *She walking down the street* (missing auxiliary)
> *She don't can swim* (incorrect negative)
> *Do she can swim?* (incorrect question form)
> *They can might go.* (two auxiliaries)
>
> Modal auxiliary meanings are subtle and the differences among them are very fuzzy. Because they are unstressed in spoken English, they can be hard to hear, so students may lack oral knowledge of them to apply in their writing. When they write, they may avoid using modals altogether because they seem so complicated.

Modals occur in approximately 15% of all verb phrases. (Biber et al., 1999, p. 486) *Can, may, must,* and *should* are common in academic prose, possibly because they lend a speculative mood of logical possibility to scientific claims. The modals *should* and *must* combine with the passive voice discussed earlier, as in this example of academic prose from Biber et al. (1999, p. 497):

To produce the best results, the plant <u>should be supplied</u> with water which carries no contamination.

NONFINITE VERBALS

Nonfinite verbals occur within verb phrases, but they do not have any tense of their own. They consist of the bare infinitive *(take)*, the infinitive *(to take)*, the present participle *(taking)*, and the past participle *(taken)*. Their contribution to the verb phrase, when paired with an auxiliary or a modal auxiliary, has to do with aspect or voice. They occur with main verbs as well. Examples of nonfinite verbals are the following:

With auxiliaries	*can <u>sit</u>, is <u>speaking</u>, have <u>written</u>*
With main verbs	*let <u>go</u>, plan <u>to do</u>, remember <u>seeing</u>, got <u>burned</u>*

Auxiliaries and Nonfinite Verbals

We have already seen some combinations of finite and nonfinite verbals, all of which involve auxiliaries, modals, or both. For a review, see the following and Box 10.3:

NONFINITE VERBALS	FINITE + NONFINITE VERBALS
Bare infinitives ⟶	**Modal + bare infinitive**
(without *to*)	*can go, will study, may eat*
Present participles ⟶	**be + present participle**
(with *-ing*)	*is/are studying* (progressive)
Past participles ⟶	**have/be + past participle**
(with *-ed* or irregular)	*has/had studied* (perfect)
	is/are studied (passive)

Of course there are other complex finite/nonfinite combinations we have already studied as well. Some of these combinations have specific tense, mood, aspect, and voice labels:

MODAL + *BE* + PRESENT PARTICIPLE

Future Progressive:	*will be going*
Conditional Progressive:	*would be eating*

MODAL + HAVE + PAST PARTICIPLE

Future perfect:	*will have taken*
Conditional perfect:	*would have made*

MODAL + *BE* + PAST PARTICIPLE

Future Passive:	*will be taken*
Conditional Passive:	*would be made*

It is possible to carry these combinations even further, and the labels always follow the contents of these complex combinations:

MODAL + HAVE + *BE*/PAST PARTICIPLE + PARTICIPLE

Future Perfect Progressive:	*will have been living*
Conditional Perfect Passive:	*would have been tested*

Box 10.3 Summary of Verbal Diagnostics

Morphology
    Derivation: *-ize, -ate*
    Inflection:
        finite present/past: *-s, -ed*
        nonfinite: *-ing, -en/-ed*
        + irregular verbs of various types

Syntax
    Transitive, intransitive, linking V | V (NP)|$_{VP}$
    With auxiliary (*have/be*)
        Aspect: perfect, progressive
        Voice: passive
    Mood: modal auxiliary + bare infinitive
    Main verb + nonfinite verbals

Function
Verbals express relationships among entities

Main Verbs and Nonfinite Verbals

Main verbs are also coupled with nonfinite verbals. Not all verbs can occur in these verb phrase constructions, but the construction with infinitives is very productive. When a main verb and a past participle occur together, the verb phrase usually has a passive meaning. To discuss all the possibilities is beyond the scope of this textbook, so only a few examples of each are given:

NONFINITE VERBALS		FINITE + NONFINITE VERBALS
Main Verb + Bare Infinitive	⟶	*let go (of), make do with*
Main Verb + Infinitive	⟶	*plan to paint, want to read*
Main Verb + Present Participle	⟶	*get moving, sat thinking*
Main Verb + Past Participle	⟶	*got burned, seemed disturbed*

EXPLORING CHAPTER PERSPECTIVES

◆ *Discussion Questions*

1. There used to be many more irregular verb forms in the past than there are now. Can you think of any verbs that used to be irregular but that are now regular? One example is *hang*, which has two past tenses *(hung and hanged)*. Why might this state of affairs have come about?

2. What are some past-tense forms that children often mistake? Can you explain the mistakes they make?

3. Have you noticed that in speech, people sometimes substitute *all* for *say* or *said*: *And I'm all, "Go on then. Eat it."* What can you say about this use of *I'm all?* Does it act like a verb?

4. Read the following paragraph from Wolfram (1991, pp. 265–267) and discuss the answers to these questions below. In this section of the book, Wolfram details what language arts teachers need to know about the community language(s) spoken by their learners. He mentions knowledge of a "nonpatronizing respect" for the community language, the structural details of the community language systems, and community resources in the language arts (e.g., storytellers and writers). In addition, he argues that teachers must have knowledge of community language conventions, values, and beliefs.

   a. What are language conventions?
   b. What are turn-taking styles?

COMMUNITY LANGUAGE

(1) Knowledge of community language must also involve *an understanding of*
(2) *community conventions for language use.* These conventions may dictate how
(3) students from different communities will participate in classroom situations,
(4) ranging from students' turn-taking styles to students' direct and indirect use of
(5) language in discussing particular topics. On one level, such knowledge provides a
(6) perspective for understanding student language behavior. On another level, this
(7) information may provide an important contrastive basis for the eventual
(8) socialization of students into the norms of language behavior expected in a
(9) classroom context. Knowledge of language use conventions must also include
(10) information about community values and beliefs with respect to language use.
(11) What kinds of language styles are positively and negatively valued in the community,
(12) and how is school language valued in the community by comparison? Is it
(13) associated with "acting white," as found in some working-class black communities?
(14) Is it associated with acting "uppity," as it may be in some working-class white
(15) communities? Understanding values about the relative social significance of
(16) community language and school language is not a frivolous adjunct for the
(17) language arts or English teacher; information of this type may impact the
(18) language arts curriculum in a fundamental way and determine how students respond
(19) in very practical ways to the English language objectives set forth in the classroom.

   c. What are direct versus indirect uses of language?

   d. Why is knowledge of these conventions important?

   e. What are some examples of community values and beliefs about language use besides those suggested here?

   f. Do you agree that this knowledge is not frivolous?

◆ *Cooperative Exercise: Community Language*

A. **Individual Work.** Read the excerpt from Wolfram again.

   1. Underline all the finite and nonfinite verbals in the paragraph and identify their tense, aspect, voice, and mood (modal). Be careful not to underline gerunds (nouns ending in –*ing*) or present or past participial adjectives, if there are any.

   2. Note the structure of the questions. How does the word order in the verbals in question found in differ from that found in statements?

B. **Pair Work.** Compare your answers with your partner and make a master list of verbals with their labels to hand in. Make a note of any problems you have.

C. **Class Work.** Spot-check some of the answers. Discuss any lingering questions and issues.

◆ *Writing Assignment*

Write a short essay in your Language Notebook in response to one or both of these prompts. Save your essay(s) for later use.

   1. Summarize what Wolfram says about community language conventions, values, and beliefs. Do you agree that knowledge of these issues is not a "frivolous adjunct"?

   2. Describe any experience with positive or negative community attitudes toward school language from your own life, from the media, or from films.

Introspection

Proofread your essays and make any necessary corrections. When you are finished, underline all the finite and nonfinite verbs, avoiding those expressions that merely look like verbals.

TEACHING TO LEARN

Passive Voice

Your Generation 1.5 students and those who speak English as a second language made these mistakes with passive sentences. Role-play with a partner. Take turns imagining that you are explaining to a learner what his or her error is in a one-on-one writing conference. Errors have to do with missing or incorrect helping verbs or modals, past participles, subjects/objects, prepositions, or other errors. Tell your partner if the errors obscure the meaning the writer is trying to convey (global error) or if they are details that readers notice (local).

After explaining the nonstandard usage, tell your partner what the correct sentence is. Ask him or her to make up a similar correct sentence:

1. Spanish spoken in my country.
2. My city found in 1800 for missionaries.
3. This book is wrote by Jack London.
4. They cans be prove the results by the scientists.
5. The details will added later.
6. One not smoke here.
7. He was disturb by the news.
8. This word is spell wrong.
9. The paragraph was described the landscape.
10. The hamburgers been eaten already.
11. The president of the company was consider an expert.
12. The speeder for stop the police.

LEARNING TO TEACH

Sentence Transforming

Description: Many learners benefit from focused practice on forms and labels without the distractions of a "real" context. These practice exercises can be done as games or competitive/ cooperative team activities to add interest.

Goals

Subject area goal: English language

English language awareness goal: English verb system

Descriptive grammar goal: Mastery of verb forms and tense aspect and voice labels

Procedural goal: Conscious manipulation of tense, aspect, and voice

Assessment: Group self-assessment and whole-class assessment of winning teams.

Methodology: Do the following exercise as a competitive game to bring an element of fun and interest to it. The first group that finishes wins. This exercise can be done more than once to provide opportunities for more teams to win. (However, if one team wins all the time, mix up the team members.)

In groups of four, each student takes out a piece of lined paper and writes a short **simple active transitive** (but imaginative and alliterative) sentence in the **present** tense on the top. Example: *Petra ponders a new poem.*

All students check to make sure their sentences are correct. Each student passes his or her paper to the student on the right. That student writes the same sentence in **present progressive** and passes it on to the student on the right: *Petra is pondering a new poem.* Students go on passing the sentences around the group. Each time the paper returns to its original owner, everyone stops and makes sure that all the sentences are correct. Use all these tenses in this order:

Present

Present progressive

Past progressive

Conditional progressive (with *could*)

Past

Present perfect

Past perfect

Future perfect

Present passive

Past passive

Conditional passive

Clarify any errors or difficulties experienced by the group members and make sure that all the sentences are correct. The winning group members must read all their sentences out for other students to check.

11

Prepositions and Particles

English speakers use the forms *up* and *down* as **prepositions** and as **particles**. Although both are function words, there are important differences between the two parts of speech:

> *The cook walked slowly <u>up the street</u> looking at houses for sale.*
>
> *Her income <u>went up</u> in recent months.*
>
> *The cook strolled <u>down the next block</u> still looking at houses.*
>
> *Housing prices <u>came down</u> this year.*

Prepositions are transitive; that is, they link their object noun phrases (called the object of the preposition) to other phrases in the sentence. Particles are intransitive; they do not take an object. Particles are derived originally from prepositions, but they split off from them and now, combined with verbs, form compound words, such as *go up, come down,* and *eat up.* The particle modifies the verb, changing its meaning in subtle ways.

The difficulty is that prepositions look like particles and vice versa, and only syntactic or semantic characteristics differentiate them:

	PREPOSITION	PARTICLE
Is there an object?	Yes	No
Does it influence the meaning of a verb?	No	Yes

PREPOSITIONS

Some prepositions look like subordinators, such as *as, before, after, since, than,* and *like.* A **subordinator** connects an embedded sentence to a main sentence, and that is the way to distinguish subordinators from prepositions. A preposition is followed by a noun phrase and forms a prepositional phrase [P NP]; a subordinator is followed by a sentence, that is, a subject and a verb.

Prepositional phrase	<u>*As*</u> *[a cook]$_{NP}$, she was very accomplished.*
Subordinator	<u>*As*</u> *[she worked]$_S$, she made careless errors.*
Prepositional phrase	*No one baked better <u>than</u> [her]$_{NP}$.*
Subordinator	*No one baked better <u>than</u> [she did]$_S$.*

Prepositional phrase	*No one's pastry tasted <u>like</u> [hers]$_{NP}$.*
Subordinator	*No one's pastry tasted <u>like</u> [her pastry did]$_S$.*

People also confuse prepositions with adverbs. Adverbs are intransitive, but prepositions are transitive. Note that the same form can be used as an adjective also.

Adverb	*She worked <u>inside</u>.*
Prepositional phrase	*She worked <u>inside</u> the hot kitchen.*
Adjective	*Give me the <u>inside</u> story on the problem.*

Characteristics of Prepositions

Morphology

Prepositions take no inflections and have no consistent derivational patterns. However, they themselves have either simple or complex morphological structures, with many multiword lexical units as shown in Box 11.1.

Box 11.1   Common Prepositions

The most common single-word prepositions from Biber et al. (1999, pp. 74–75):

about	at	from	of	than
after	by	in	off	to
around	down	into	on	towards
as	for	like	round	with
			since	without

The most common two-word prepositions are compounds made up of a first word followed by *as, for, from, of, on, to,* or *with*:

such as	away from	out of	due to
but for	ahead of	depending on	next to
except for	because of	according to	thanks to
apart from	instead of	close to	along with
			together with

Three- and four- word prepositions usually have the form Prep + (Det) + N + Prep:

as far as	in place of	in addition to
as well as	in spite of	in contrast to
in exchange for	in view of	in relation to
in return for	on account of	with regard to
by means of	on top of	with reference to
by way of	as a result of	with respect to
for lack of	for the sake of	in comparison with
in front of	in the case of	in contact with
in lieu of	in the event of	in line with
in need of	with the exception of	

Prepositional Meaning

Prototypical single-word prepositions have to do with connecting entities and relationships or situating them in space and time. Multiword prepositions, common in Academic English (AE), have abstract meanings and express complex relationships.

Prepositional Phrase Syntax

A prepositional phrase is made up of a preposition and a noun phrase, as in this simple template:

$$[P \quad + \quad NP]_{PP}$$

The P stands for a single word or multiword lexical unit. The NP can be of any type, including a **gerund:** a noun formed from a verb by adding *-ing:*

She made her living by cooking.

She liked baking instead of cooking.

She liked baking in addition to cooking.

Locations

Prepositional phrases freely occur in a variety of locations in a sentence. For example, they can modify a sentence if they are placed at the beginning of it:

In the mornings the cook always reads the newspaper.

They modify a noun in a noun phrase, an adjective in an adjective phrase, or a verb in a verb phrase:

the pastry cook with red hair

the pie with peach filling

proud of herself

ecstatic at the news

ate the bagel with a fork

beat the eggs for a minute

If the prepositional phrase is part of the verb phrase, it can often be shifted to the front of the sentence for added interest or to change the focus. This is called **preposing**.

Down the street the cook strolled.

Preposition Stranding

The object of the prepositional phrase sometimes moves to a different part of the sentence, leaving a stranded preposition in its original place after the verb. This is common in questions, but other sentences also have preposition stranding:

Which bakery did she come from?

What meeting was she late for?

What did she rush to the door with?

Tardiness is the only crime she is accused of.

A QUESTION OF STYLE

Some people believe that good writers avoid ending a sentence with a preposition, maybe because it is impossible to strand prepositions in Latin. Standard Spoken English (SSE) and Standard Written English (SWE) generally allow preposition stranding, but in AE the writer might consider whether "to strand or not to strand." Often, the unstranded sentence is awkward. (Awkward sentences are things up with which most writing teachers cannot put.) Few other languages, if any, allow preposition stranding, so English learners may not be familiar with this syntactic possibility:

From which bakery did she come?
For what meeting was she late?
With what did she rush to the door?
Tardiness is the only crime of which she is accused.

Prepositional Verbs

Some verb + preposition collocations occur so frequently that the words have "fused" into one **prepositional verb** unit. The accompanying noun phrase is a direct object of the verb, not the object of the preposition:

The pastry cook <u>depends on</u> her oven.

The wire whisk <u>belongs to</u> her.

Alternatively, some prepositional verbs occur in this template in either active or passive voice:

$$[V + NP + Prep + NP]_{VP}$$

The server <u>blamed the mess on</u> the cook.

She had <u>used the whisk as</u> a fly swatter.

With a prepositional verb, the preposition and the direct object are not free to shift away from the verb. If we try to prepose the preposition and the direct object, the resulting sentence is ungrammatical or awkward and marked with an asterisk. This characteristic gives us a diagnostic to distinguish a prepositional verb from a free occurrence of a prepositional phrase. Preposition stranding is common, however:

Preposed:	*˚Of the letter the secretary approved.*
Stranding:	*What letter did she approve of?*
Preposed:	*˚With this keepsake I couldn't part.*
Stranding:	*What keepsake did you part with?*
Preposed:	*˚For the bus I waited.*
Stranding:	*What bus did you wait for?*

Prepositional Phrase Function

Some prepositional phrases, such as those that occur with prepositional verbs, are *obligatory*. Some verbs require prepositional phrases to form a grammatical sentence. For example, in the sentence *The cook's assistant put the wrong flour* _____, the blank might take an adverb of place *(here, there)* or a prepositional phrase of location *(in the bowl, in the bin)*. Other obligatory prepositional phrases are similar to subject complements:

> The cook was <u>in the doghouse</u>.
> The complaint was <u>against her</u>.

Optional prepositional phrases merely provide additional information about the entities or situation being described in the sentence. In the following sentences, the prepositional phrases are underlined. As you are reading, decide if each prepositional phrase is optional or obligatory. The answers are not always clear:

> <u>On Tuesday, in the early morning</u>, the assistant cook, <u>in her perky new cook's cap</u>, arrived <u>at the bakery</u>. She was late <u>for work</u>! She rushed <u>to the door</u> <u>with the key in her hand</u> and put the key <u>in the lock</u> <u>on the old door</u>. <u>With a great effort</u> she twisted the key <u>in the lock</u>. The door opened <u>with a squeak</u>.

Prepositional Phrases in Different Registers

Sentences in the newspaper and academic prose are packed with prepositional phrases, far more than conversation and more than fiction as well (see Box 11.2). The reason is that prepositional phrases permit a very dense concentration of information, as in the following example of academic prose; (Biber et al., 1999, p. 607):

> Mortality <u>among stocks</u> <u>of eggs</u> stored outdoors <u>in the group</u> averaged 70%; eggs collected the following spring <u>from a large number</u> <u>of natural habitats</u> <u>in the central part</u> <u>of the province</u> suffered a 46% reduction <u>in viability</u> which could only be attributed to this exposure <u>to cold</u>. Further evidence <u>of the association</u> <u>of winter egg mortality</u> <u>with sub-zero temperatures and snow cover</u> was reported <u>by Riegert (1967a)</u>.

◆◆◆◆
! **TERMINOLOGICAL CLASH!**
◆◆◆◆

Prepositional phrases that are optional in a sentence are **adverbials,** but they are not adverbs. The word **adverb** refers to a part of speech, but the word **adverbial** refers to a single modifying function that a number of parts of speech might have in a sentence. All the underlined phrases are adverbial in their sentences, but they are not all adverbs:

[On Thursday]_{PP} the new cook was hired.
[Saturday]_{NP} she was fired.
[Very unhappily]_{AdvP} she scanned the Sunday ads.

Box 11.2 Some Common Prepositional Verbs in Academic Prose

be used in	refer to	allow for
depend on	be expressed in	be required for
be based on	think of	occur in
be associated with	add to	depend on
look at	be known as	belong to
look for	be seen in	account for
deal with	be regarded as	consist of
be applied to	be seen as	differ from
be made of	be considered as	be based on
be aimed at	be defined as	be involved in
be derived from	lead to	be associated with
be divided into	come from	be related to
obtain NP from	result in	be included in
use NP as	contribute to	be composed of

Prepositional verbs are common in conversation, fiction, news, and academic prose (Biber et al., 1999, p. 414):

> For example, the 'library manager' <u>reminded members</u> of the procedures for ordering library stock. (academic)
>
> I think the media <u>is</u> falsely <u>accused</u> of a lot of things. (news)

PARTICLES ▬▬▬

Particles combine with common verbs to form compound verbs called **phrasal verbs:**

> My teenaged son goes <u>out</u> every Friday night.
>
> He comes <u>in</u> late.
>
> He wakes <u>up</u> when I turn <u>on</u> the light.

Particles are sometimes called "intransitive prepositions," which makes sense because they do not take objects. However, there are some good reasons to give particles a completely different name and their own identity. First, particles do not form phrases with noun phrase objects. Second, they do not occur in as many different places in the sentence. For example, they do not occur as modifiers in noun phrases and adjective phrases, and they do not appear at the beginning of a sentence as a modifier. Third, they generally appear with verbs and with some "verby" adjectives, such as *tired out* or *prettied up* (see Figure 11.1).

Particles also look and act much like adverbs, so some grammarians lump them with adverbs modifying the verb that they occur with. However, particles are function words, and adverbs are content words. In addition, to express the right verbal

Figure 11.1 *Verbs and particles mix and match. (Can you come up with some phrasal verbs? Careful! Not all these work!)*

Verbs	Particles
bring	about
call	across
come	back
do	down
get	in (to)
give	off
go	out
hand	over
hold	to
keep	up
look	(up) on
make	with
pass	
pick	
put	
run	
take	
turn	

meaning, particles are obligatory, not optional, and they make one unit with the verb, unlike adverbs, which are variable. In addition, like other compound words, there is a common stress pattern on phrasal verbs. The verb is stressed much more than the particle. If there is a noun phrase after the phrasal verb *(turn on the light)*, the NP is the direct object of the phrasal verb. That is, *the light* is the direct object of *turn on*.

Characteristics of Particles

Morphology
With no consistent morphology themselves, particles simply combine with verbs to form phrasal verb compounds.

Syntax of Particles in Verb Phrases
Phrasal verbs contrast syntactically with both prepositional phrases and prepositional verbs. There are two diagnostics to distinguish them:

Preposing: We can move true prepositional phrases to another location in the sentence without changing the meaning or grammaticality of the sentence. Prepositional verbs and particles do not allow this.

Pronoun Shift: For both prepositional phrases and prepositional verbs, if the object of the preposition is a pronoun, it stays in its usual place after the preposition. If the object after a particle is a pronoun, it shifts to a location between the verb and the particle.

> **Box 11.3 Diagnostics for Prepositional Phrases, Prepositional Verbs, and Particles: A Summary**
>
> | | Preposed? | Pronoun Shift? |
> |---|---|---|
> | Verb+PP | Yes | No |
> | Verb+Prep NP | No | No |
> | Verb+Part NP | No | Yes |

Prepositional phrase [V + PP]: *The car turned quickly <u>on the next street</u>.*

Preposing: <u>*On the next street*</u>, *the car turned quickly.*

Pronoun in situ: *The car turned quickly <u>on it</u>.*

Prepositional verb [V-Prep + NP]: The ugly dog turned <u>*on its master*</u>. (attacked or betrayed)

Preposing: *<u>On its master</u> the ugly dog turned.

Pronoun in situ: The ugly dog turned <u>*on him*</u>.

A phrasal verb has two possible templates:

[V-Part + NP]	The mechanic *<u>turned on</u>* the light.
[V + NP/Pronoun + Part]	The mechanic *<u>turned</u>* the light *<u>on</u>*.

The diagnostics reveal a difference in syntax. Preposing is not allowed, and the pronoun must shift to a position between the verb and the particle (see also Box 11.3):

Phrasal Verbs

Preposing: *<u>On the light</u> the mechanic turned.*

Pronoun Shift: *The mechanic *<u>turned on</u>* it.*

                The mechanic <u>turned it on</u>.

Particle Meaning

Like the simple prepositions they come from, the literal meanings for particles have to do with spatial location and time: *across, back, down, in (to), off, out, over, to, up, (up) on,* and *with.* Despite that, the meaning that the particle contributes to its phrasal verb is elusive. There are some tantalizing generalizations; for example, *up* generally means either *ascend* or *do something completely:*

The brokers <u>bought up</u> all the cheap stocks.

They <u>filled up</u> their portfolios.

The stock prices <u>went up</u>.

The stocks <u>climbed up</u> to their highest value ever.

The brokers <u>cleaned up</u> when they sold the stocks.

AROUND/CAUSE	BEHIND/RETURN	DOWNWARD
bring about	bring back	bring down
come about	call back	come down
go about	come back	get down
turn about	get back	go down
	give back	hand down
	go back	hold down
	hand back	keep down
	hold back	look down
	keep back	put down
	look back	run down
	pass back	take down
	put back	turn down
	run back	
	take back	
	turn back	

Many phrasal verbs have figurative meanings as well as literal ones:

run down/denigrate	make out/understand, perceive
come across/find	make up/reconcile a quarrel
run into/meet by accident	pick on/tease
look after/take care of	

Particles in Different Registers

Phrasal verbs are informal and slangy, and people use them in requests and commands in conversation and informal SWE. Although phrasal verbs are not overly frequent in

---

A TEACHING MOMENT

Take a minute to combine the verbs with the particles in the previous lists and provide a context. You might come up with examples such as these:

bring in the cake	*take in the sights of the city*
bring on your best hitter	*take on the other team*
bring down the house	*take down the notes*
bring up that topic	*take up skiing*

English learners who are genuinely new to English are often baffled by phrasal verbs and need practice with them, especially meaningful practice with common collocations (phrasal verb + direct objects) that they can associate with meanings. Generation 1.5 learners who have grown up speaking English as their dominant language are proficient with phrasal verbs. However, they may not know the alternatives that are preferred in academic prose.

AE, Biber et al. (1999, pp. 408–409) lists a few phrasal verbs typical of formal written prose: *carry out, take up, take on, set up,* and *point out.* Generally, each phrasal verb corresponds to a word with a similar meaning in formal academic writing:

carry out—accomplish, complete
make up—invent
take up—begin, occupy
take on—become, assume
set up—establish, plan
point out—indicate, signal

LOOKING BACKWARD AND FORWARD

This section has examined the four categories of content words (nouns, verbs, adjectives, and adverbs) and a number of important functional categories (determiners, pronouns, auxiliaries, modals, prepositions, and particles). We define these categories morphologically, syntactically, and functionally, and the definitions yield a discovery procedure that students of grammar use to determine the part of speech of a particular word. The definitions and the discovery procedure are an improvement on traditional semantic definitions that do not give students much help in determining a word's part of speech.

While it is empowering to master the categories, their definitions, and the discovery procedure, there is still more to learn about grammar. Word categories combine with each other in a system. The next advance in metalinguistic awareness is to understand that system.

EXPLORING CHAPTER PERSPECTIVES

◆ *Discussion Questions*

1. Occasionally someone tries to write an entire story using only the verb *get* in combination with different prepositions and particles. Go around your classroom telling such a story. Begin with the sentence *I got up very early this morning . . .* When you are finished, identify the particles and the prepositions.

2. Recently I heard someone say, *I healthied up this recipe by lowering the fat and sugar content.* What kind of word formation procedure(s) does this innovative form come from? Does *I healthied this recipe* have the same meaning?

3. Make a list of five or more phrasal verbs with each of these particles: *in (to), off, out,* and *over.*

   a. Make sure the verbs from question 3 are phrasal verbs by making up a sentence with a pronoun object. Does it come between the verb and the particle?
      The monks took in <u>the refugees</u>.
      The monks took <u>the refugees</u> in.
      The monks took <u>them</u> in.

b. Discuss the literal meaning you get from your sample verbs. Which verbs have figurative meanings? What are they?

4. Discuss the paragraph in the text that has optional and obligatory prepositional phrases. Do all students agree?

◆ *Cooperative Exercise: Successful Acquisition*

Read this excerpt from page 6 of Hinkel and Fotos's (2002) "From Theory to Practice: A Teacher's View." Hinkel and Fotos begin by pointing out that there has been quite a bit of research on communicative interaction as a causative factor in the acquisition of grammar. They suggest that the learner's "internal factors, particularly the noticing and continued awareness of structures," may be even more significant in successful acquisition.

A. **Class Work.** Discuss the meaning of the excerpt. Articulate the main ideas.

Individual Work
Underline all prepositional phrases. Circle all particles. Make sure to avoid infinitives—a verbal marked with *to*—because those are not prepositional phrases.

FROM THEORY TO PRACTICE: A TEACHER'S VIEW

(1) The psycholinguistic foundations for this view involve the distinction between two
(2) types of grammatical knowledge: explicit and/or declarative knowledge, which is
(3) conscious knowledge about grammatical rules and forms developed through
(4) instruction; and implicit or procedural knowledge, which is the ability to speak a
(5) language unconsciously developed through acts of meaning-focused
(6) communication. Whereas in the past these two knowledge systems were often
(7) treated as separate, it has recently been suggested that they are connected and
(8) that one possible interface is learner awareness or consciousness of particular
(9) grammatical features developed through formal instruction (Schmidt, 1990). Once
(10) a learner's consciousness of a target feature has been raised through formal
(11) instruction or through continued communicative exposure, the learner often
(12) tends to notice the feature in subsequent input (Ellis, 1996; Schmidt, 1990, 1993).
(13) Such noticing or continued awareness of the feature is suggested to be important
(14) because it appears to initiate the restructuring of the learner's implicit or
(15) unconscious system of linguistic knowledge (Ellis, 1996; Schmidt, 1990, 1993;
(16) Sharwood Smith, 1993). When a language point is noticed frequently, learners
(17) develop awareness of it and unconsciously compare it with their existing system of
(18) linguistic knowledge, unconsciously constructing new hypotheses to accommodate
(19) the differences between the noticed information and their L2 competence.
(20) Then they test these new hypotheses—again unconsciously—by attending to
(21) language input and also by getting feedback on their output using the new form
(22) (Swain, 1985). In this way, implicit knowledge has been created.

A. **Pair Work.** Compare your answers and discuss: Does the number of prepositional phrases versus particles help identify this as academic prose? What other linguistic factors show this to be AE?

B. **Class work.** Check to make sure everyone has identified the prepositional phrases, particles, and infinitives correctly.

◆ *Writing Assignment*

Write a short essay in your Language Notebook in response to one or both of these prompts. Save your essay(s) for later use.

1. Do a written translation of the previous reading from AE into your own words. Then write about the differences between your paragraph and those of the reading. What linguistic factors would make this reading easy or difficult for people unfamiliar with AE?

2. Can you give an example of explicit declarative knowledge turning into implicit procedural knowledge? Possible examples might be learning to drive or learning to read. How might the conversion of declarative to procedural knowledge work in the case you mention? Are they similar or different from what is proposed here for grammar learning?

TEACHING TO LEARN

Particles or Prepositions

In pairs, go over each of these sentences and decide if it has a prepositional phrase, a prepositional verb with an object, or a phrasal verb with an object. Do not guess; use the diagnostics to make sure. Are there any you are unsure of? Discuss those as a whole class.

1. The student is <u>waiting for</u> the bus.

2. I am <u>eating up</u> all the cookies no matter what you say.

3. The construction engineer <u>looked over</u> the foundation and approved it.

4. The construction engineer <u>looked over</u> the foundation and saw the horizon.

5. My brother told me to <u>get out of</u> the car quickly.

6. Please try to <u>get out</u> the stain on this shirt.

7. She <u>spoke on</u> the phone for 20 minutes.

8. The lecturer <u>spoke on</u> the subject of English morphemes.

Language Analysis

Description: Taking grammar out of the classroom and into the everyday life of learners bridges the gap between declarative and procedural knowledge and theory and practice. One way to do this is to use materials that resonate with learners, such as simple, familiar songs, poems, advertising copy, and jingles. For example, the song "In the Middle of the Night" by Billy Joel is excellent for prepositional phrases. However, teachers need to identify text appropriate for their learners that has the desired grammatical characteristics. Avoid nonstandard or non-SWE usage unless a comparison between dialects or variants is part of the lesson plan, too. These materials can be used at any point in a lesson plan or minilecture, even as assessment, as long as learners are familiar with and can apply the discovery procedure.

Goals

Subject area goals: Language analysis and appreciation of a popular text

English language awareness goal: Analysis of a particular English structure in a real context

Descriptive grammar goals: Structures in context and their labels

Procedural goals: Identifying parts of speech or other grammatical information using the discovery procedure

Assessment: Once the cooperative groups have prepared their analyses of language and put them on overhead transparencies, they report to the class. Teachers and other students engage in informal, interactive instruction: listening, expansion and elaboration, questioning, and dialogue.

Methodology: Select a text (song, poem, jingle, or paragraph from popular prose) and write classroom cooperative learning materials that ask your future middle or high school learners to distinguish content from function and then to identify the nouns, verbs, adjectives, and adverbs. More advanced learners can identify phrases, sentence types, and subordinate clauses. If possible, use a picture or graphic organizer to make your materials more interesting or more clear.

SECTION 3

The Macroscopic Perspective

The macroscopic perspective presents a larger view of English grammatical structure: the complete sentence. Sentences are combinations of noun phrases, verb phrases, adjective phrases, adverb phrases, and prepositional phrases. For the macroscopic perspective, we use generative grammar, a dynamic and visual approach that organizes the details from earlier chapters into a consistent grammatical context.

In the generative approach, a grammatical category symbol is a variable that stands for any constituent of that type. For example, S is a variable that stands for any sentence, NP stands for any noun phrase, VP stands for any verb phrase, Aux stands for any auxiliary, and so on.

A sentence (S), such as *Bob can dance,* is made up of a noun phrase (NP), an auxiliary (Aux), and a verb phrase (VP). That information can be spelled out as a generalization:

$$S \rightarrow NP\ Aux\ VP$$

Putting this into words, we read it as a permission statement, "S can be rewritten as NP Aux VP." We write the variables in a graphic organizer called a **phrase structure tree,** a visual representation of the generalization that looks like an upside-down tree with branches. The lines connecting the variables take the place of the $\rightarrow$, or the words "can be rewritten as":

The generalization, the sentence, and the tree represent the same information about the structure of English sentences:

$S \rightarrow NP\ Aux\ VP$ S can be rewritten
                as NP Aux VP

Generative insights help students and teachers in training learn descriptive grammar in several ways. Its dynamic nature appeals to kinesthetic learners (people who learn by doing), and its graphic nature appeals to visual learners. Knowing how the constituents of the sentences relate to each other as a consistent system makes teachers versatile, flexible, and overall more able to respond to the needs of all their learners. Generative rules and formalisms equip students of grammar with a discovery procedure to understand the syntactic structure of sentences. Finally, this is where the details from the microscopic perspective fall into place and metalinguistic awareness expands.

Chapter 12 is about simple sentences, sentence diagrams, and instructions for drawing diagrams. Chapter 13 deals with sentences that are not declarative, that is, negative sentences, questions, imperatives, and exclamations. Chapter 14 is about complex sentences (main sentences that have at least one subordinate sentence) and the most common types of subordinate sentences: noun clauses, adjective clauses, predicate adjective complements, and adverb clauses. Chapter 15 is about compound constituents and some complex verbal structures.

12

Declarative Sentences

We often think that people should always use complete sentences to express "complete thoughts," but that is a naive way of thinking. In fact, the constituents used to express complete thoughts in Standard Spoken English (SSE) are different from those used in Standard Written English (SWE). For example, in conversation, a basic element is the phrase. Biber et al. (1999, p. 225) contains the following conversation composed largely of noun and prepositional phrases. It is clear from reading this conversation that its coherence is less obvious than the coherence required for standard writing. The coherence, such as it is, rests on a notion of "synergistic" coherence, that each utterance is incomplete on its own but is completed when it is understood in the context of the other thoughts in the context:

A: Where do you go for that, Bath Travel for that then Neil?

B: Where?

A: For that brochure.

B: Bath Travel, where's that?

A: No, where do you get the—thing from then?

B: What?

A: Butlins?

B: Well—I got it from that travel agent's.

A: Oh.

B: er the one

A: In the precinct?

B: by, yeah, by Boots.

A: Oh yeah.

Therefore, it is sometimes hard to understand real conversations that are written down. They are somewhat like the paragraph we saw in an earlier chapter in which the function words, which supply the grammatical context, were missing. In real conversations that are written down, the sentential context is also missing and must be

>
> **Sentence Fragments**
>
> SSE permits the use of phrases as a basic element without any problem, but when writers transfer this license to their writing, they run the risk of producing "fragments." A fragment is an artifact of writing, a so-called incomplete thought, even though we can, in fact, understand what the fragment means and its relationship to the other phrases and sentences. Many readers notice fragments and object to them. Only very accomplished writers are allowed to get away with writing sentence fragments because they are doing so intentionally and not as an "error." For novice writers, it is best to use complete sentences with a subject and a predicate and edit out any fragments.

supplied by the reader, who infers the connection to other phrases. That is why plays and fiction do not and probably cannot reproduce SSE accurately (for which we should probably be thankful).

However, phrases sometimes occur by themselves in standard writing. In fact, sentence fragments occur in informal prose in newspapers or academic style. These examples, from Biber et al. (1999, pp. 224–225), give the impression that the author is speaking or perhaps giving a lecture:

> *Safari jackets are still favourites with more mature male travellers. <u>Often worn with pale, open-necked sports shirts and dodgy cravats</u>. <u>Very Alan Whicker</u>. <u>Velcro</u>. (news)*

> *Now there is no bar to having more than one particle in each state. <u>Quite the contrary</u>. (academic)*

> *But what is that? Is it a number? <u>Well . . . yes</u>. It can't be a real number since its square is negative. <u>Of course</u>. (academic)*

In the rest of this chapter, complete declarative sentences occupy our interest. Any sentences that are not negatives, questions, commands, or exclamations are **declarative.**

A DISCOVERY PROCEDURE FOR CONSTITUENTS

Native speakers divide sentences into their phrasal constituents on the basis of their natural implicit knowledge of grammar. However, a more systematic way to determine the constituents of a sentence is by using **substitution frames.** A substitution frame is a sentence with an empty slot into which we insert candidate constituents to test them. A substitution frame is a discovery procedure or test to determine what the constituents of the sentence are because it asks and answers the question, "What constituent goes into the slot and makes a good sentence?"

Phrasal Constituents

The simplest complete English sentence has two phrasal constituents: a noun phrase constituent and an intransitive verb phrase constituent.

NP	VP
Bill	*went.*
The boy	*stayed.*
The guest	*visited too long.*

For example, the noun phrase slot in _____ *ran* can be filled only by phrases such as *the boy, Bill, the big boy,* or *Mary and Bill.* That is good evidence that all these phrases fall into one kind of grammatical category in the sentence. If all the phrases are equivalent to each other in the substitution frame, they are equivalent to each other in terms of their grammatical category. Putting nonequivalent expressions (*bumbled, as soon as, eery*) will not lead to good English sentences. Therefore, we know that those expressions are not noun phrases:

*Bumbled ran

*As soon as ran

*Eery ran

In the substitution frame *The boy* _____, we can insert *ran, ran quickly, drank the milk,* or *is sleeping.* In fact, these expressions are all verb phrases:

NP		VP	
The boy	*ran.*	*The boy*	*ran.*
Bill	*ran.*	*The boy*	*ran quickly.*
The big boy	*ran.*	*The boy*	*drank the milk.*
Mary and Bill	*ran.*	*The boy*	*is sleeping.*

At least some verb phrases contain noun phrases as well. These are transitive verb phrases because the noun phrase is the object of the verb:

	V	NP
The boy	*drank*	*the milk.*
		a glass of juice.
		Pepsi.

Continuing this segmentation process with a variety of substitution frames, we confirm that five types of phrasal constituents, occuring over and over again in different combinations, make up prototypical sentences in English. The phrases are the ones already seen in earlier chapters: the noun phrase, the verb phrase, the adjective phrase, the adverb phrase, and the prepositional phrase.

Lexical Constituents

We also use substitution frames to segment phrasal constituents into their **lexical constituents,** which are single word-level categories, such as noun, verb, adjective, adverb, or preposition. This substitution frame tells us what can be a common concrete count noun, such as *I put my elbow on a/an* _____. Inserting the words *apple, wall,* or *computer* makes possible English sentences, but the words *General Powell, air,* or *happiness* yield ungrammatical or strange sentences because the words are not common concrete or count nouns. Grammarians use substitution frames as a discovery procedure to deconstruct sentences into their lexical and phrasal constituents, but once they have determined the structure, they can reassemble sentences with the knowledge that they have gained.

INVENTORY OF SYNTACTIC AND LEXICAL VARIABLES

S	sentence	N	noun
NP	noun phrase	V	verb
VP	verb phrase	Det	determiner
AdjP	adjective phrase	P	preposition
AdvP	adverb phrase	Adj	adjective
PP	prepositional phrase	Adv	adverb

PHRASE STRUCTURE TREES

Grammarians display sentence structure in the form of an upside-down tree showing the divisions between the major phrases and the lexical items in the sentence. A tree is a specialized semantic network, organized from top to bottom:

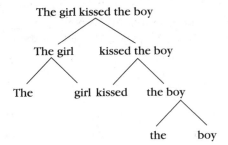

Phrase Structure Information

This tree displays two types of information relevant to syntax besides the words themselves: the **linear order** of the words and the **structural hierarchy** of the constituents:

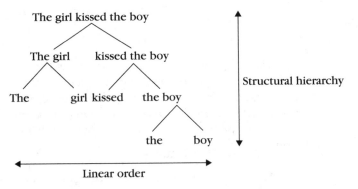

The linear order of the constituents determines much (but not all) of the meaning of the sentence. *The boy kissed the girl* has the same words and the same syntactic structure as *The girl kissed the boy,* but they have entirely different meanings because the constituents are arranged in a different order. Linear orders are **language specific,** meaning that while most languages allow for similar constituents in sentences (noun, verb, and adjective phrases), the same constituents occur in different orders. For example, in English, the adjective phrase is before the noun in the noun phrase, but in Spanish, the adjective phrase is usually after the noun in the noun phrase.

The structural hierarchy tells us that *the boy* is within the verb phrase and therefore is the **direct object.** *The girl* is outside the verb phrase as a direct offshoot of the top sentence, so it is the **subject** of the sentence. Structure hierarchy tends to be very similar from language to language, although their linear orders are not. However, this tree diagram represents only one sentence. It is not general enough to represent the immense number of other sentences just like this one but with other words.

We can make a more general and informative tree by replacing the words with **variables** that stand for the phrasal and lexical categories, except for the bottom line of the tree, where the actual words are inserted:

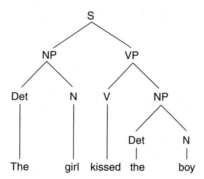

This tree simply substitutes a syntactic variable that stands for the part of speech of each word and phrase in the earlier tree. It also gives the same information about linear order and structural hierarchy as the earlier one, so it is more informative overall. It duplicates the syntactic templates we have already seen, but it shows how they relate to each other within the sentence. The bottom line of the tree diagram, which contains the lexical items (words), is the **lexical line.** Simply by changing the lexical line, the same phrase structure tree will work for a large number of sentences besides this one.

STOP AND PRACTICE

Check to make sure that each of these sentences also has the same tree diagram as the previous tree:

1. The elephant ate the peanut.
2. A student passed the exam.
3. Some women threw a ball.
4. The boys left their books.
5. Pedro's brother ate a pickle.
6. Her dog licked up the water.

This is an extremely important metalinguistic insight for the student of grammar: Instead of an infinite number of different and confusing English sentences with no relationship to each other, there are only a relatively few syntactic structures that occur over and over again with different words. If students look beyond the superficially distracting words and perceive the common underlying grammatical patterns, they see and understand a syntactic system instead of a random assortment of sentences.

Ambiguity

If a single sentence has two very different meanings, it is **ambiguous.** There are two types of ambiguity: lexical and structural.

Lexical Ambiguity

If a sentence contains a word with more than one meaning, then the whole sentence might be understood two ways, even though they have the same phrase structure tree diagram. Because the words *bank* and *mouse* have different meanings, each sentence can be understood in more than one way:

The children sat by the <u>bank.</u>

I saw the <u>mouse</u> under the desk.

Structural Ambiguity

When a sentence has two different tree diagrams, even though the lexical line is the same in each structure, the sentence is structurally ambiguous. In other words, although the linear order the constituents have (the horizontal axis of the tree) is the same, the structural hierarchy (the vertical axis of the tree) is different. What happens is that the phrasal and lexical variables (noun phrase, verb phrase, sentence, noun, verb) combine with each other in different ways to make the difference in the two meanings:

They are hunting dogs.

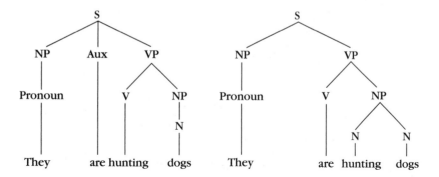

In the first sentence, *hunting* is the main verb, so it means that some plural group (say, farmers) is hunting and that the object of their hunting is *dogs* (say, feral dogs that attack sheep). In the second sentence, the main verb is *are,* and *hunting* is an attributive noun modifying *dogs,* so the sentence merely identifies a plural group of a certain type of dog used for hunting.

Instructions for Drawing Trees

There are other methods for diagramming a sentence, but many of them have at least one important flaw for the student of grammar: The student needs to know what the structure of the sentence is and what the parts of speech are before drawing the diagram. In contrast, in this method, by following some simple rules the student applies a discovery procedure and determines the structure of the sentence and the phrasal and lexical categories while diagramming the sentence.

The first rule is to start with *S* (for *sentence*) and on the next line, under the S, to put *NP VP* and connect them to the S with lines. (For now, we will skip the question of any auxiliaries, such as *can* or *will.*) A sentence is composed of a noun phrase and a verb phrase because each sentence has two main phrasal constituents—a noun phrase (subject) and a verb phrase (predicate):

A noun phrase might be a single lexical constituent (a noun), and a verb phrase might be a single lexical constituent (a verb) if it is intransitive:

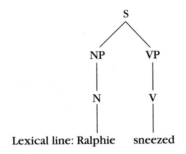

But a noun phrase might have two lexical constituents—a determiner and a noun:

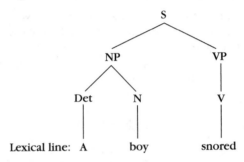

Likewise, the verb phrase can have a noun phrase in it if it is transitive. Does this tree look familiar?

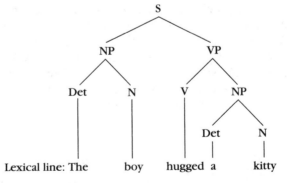

These instructions for drawing trees can be summarized in the following concise way:

PHRASE STRUCTURE RULES A

1. S   →   NP   VP
2. NP   →   (Det)   (Adj)   N
3. VP   →   V   (NP)

    where ( ) marks any element that is optional.

The rules are permission statements:

1. If you have an S on the left of the arrow, you may rewrite it (→) as NP VP.
2. If you have an NP on the left, you may rewrite it as any one of these options:

$$\left\{ \begin{array}{ccc} \text{Det} & \text{Adj} & \text{N} \\ \text{Det} & & \text{N} \\ & \text{Adj} & \text{N} \\ & & \text{N} \end{array} \right\}$$

3. If you have a VP on the left, you may rewrite it as either a transitive or an intransitive verb:

$$\left\{ \begin{array}{cc} \text{V} & \text{NP} \\ \text{V} & \end{array} \right\}$$

Following the rules while keeping the outcome sentence in mind at the same time, you usually find only one way to diagram the sentence, unless it is ambiguous. Ambiguous sentences make it clear that you also need to consider meaning.

However, these rules will not permit a tree for the sentence *The man with red hair kissed the woman with black hair.* We need to add a prepositional phrase rule 4. and make a revision to the noun phrase rule in the previous rule 2:

2. NP = (Det)   (Adj)   N   (PP)
4. PP = P   NP

The new rule 2 allows the insertion of a prepositional phrase within the noun phrase because the prepositional phrase modifies the noun. That is, *with red hair* modifies *man,* so the prepositional phrase is inside the same noun phrase that contains *man.* Rule 4 says that a prepositional phrase is always made up of a preposition and a noun phrase:

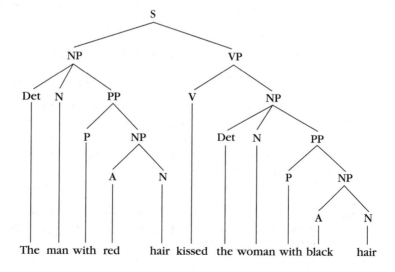

—————————— **STOP AND PRACTICE** ——————————

Compare the previous tree to the rules to see if all four rules are followed at each step of the way. Following the rules, draw tree diagrams for these sentences:

7. Jesse laughed.
8. Koko hugged the kitten.
9. Larry turned on the television in the bedroom.
10. The engineer saw the woman with long hair.
11. A careful reading of the book reveals some important errors of judgment.

Although rules 1 to 4 allow trees for some very complicated sentences, they do not allow us to draw the sentence *I ate the donut <u>in the cafeteria</u> <u>very quickly</u>*. The problem is that the prepositional phrase *in the cafeteria* does not modify the word *donut*, so it cannot be part of the noun phrase. Instead, it modifies the verb *ate*, telling us where the eating took place. Thus, we revise our set of rules (rule 3) to allow a prepositional phrase in the verb phrase. Also, *very quickly* is an adverb phrase made up of an adverb of manner, *quickly*, modified by the intensifier *very*. None of the rules allows an adverb phrase to be inserted into a verb phrase, but revised rule 3 and rule 6 allow that. Furthermore, an intensifying adverb such as *very* modifies an adjective such as *careful*, so we need to make a space for more than one word in the adjective phrase, as in the following rule 5. Nouns also frequently modify other nouns; rule 2 now permits that:

REVISED PHRASE STRUCTURE RULES B
1. S → NP   VP
2. NP → (Det)   (AdjP)   (N)   N   (PP)
3. VP → V   (NP)   (PP)   (AdvP) *
4. PP → P   NP
5. AdjP → (Adv)   Adj   (Adv)   (e.g., *very careful indeed*)
6. AdvP → (Adv)   Adv   (Adv)   (e.g., *very carefully indeed*)

—————————— **STOP AND PRACTICE** ——————————

Follow revised phrase structure rules B and diagram these sentences:

12. The extremely confused grammar students laughed nervously.
13. Some students without books snored during class loudly.
14. Students in the class enjoyed the tough exercise on English grammar inordinately.
15. A very candid answer to the question confused the old professor from the English Department yesterday.

*Note that adverb phrases can occur in many other locations in sentences, but at this point it becomes too complex to include them in all possible places in the phrase structure rules. With formalisms, it is best to stop before they become too complex.

16. The tall student with the torn shirt passed the very difficult test in the afternoon extremely easily indeed.
17. A woman saw the boys with binoculars. (two trees)

The phrase structure rules generate sentences with transitive verb phrases:

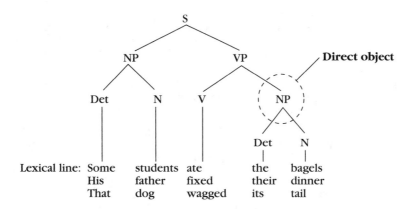

The very same tree structure, however, is also associated with **subject complements,** structures in which the main verb is a linking verb and the following noun phrase (or adjective phrase) gives additional information about the subject without introducing a new entity into the meaning. A revision to the verb phrase rule (rule 3) is necessary:

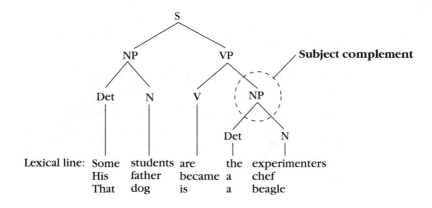

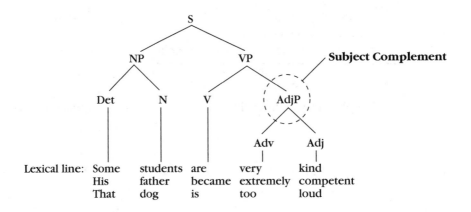

REVISED PHRASE STRUCTURE RULES C

1. S → NP   VP
2. NP → (Det)   (AdjP)   (N)   N   (PP)
3. VP →   { V (NP) (PP)   (AdvP)* }
           { V AdjP (PP)   (AdvP)* }
4. PP → P   NP
5. AdjP → (Adv)   Adj   (Adv)
6. AdvP → (Adv)   Adv   (Adv)

─────────────────── **STOP AND PRACTICE** ───────────────────

Use revised phrase structure rules C to diagram these sentences:

18. A student in this class became a parent recently.
19. Her name is Jody.
20. Her little son is Cody.
21. The tiny baby seems healthy.
22. Jody looks very serious to me.
23. Cody looks very sleepy in his cute pajamas.

THE AUXILIARY AND THE VERB

Auxiliaries are the helping verbs *have* and *be* and the modal auxiliaries *can, could, will, would, shall, must, should, may, might,* and *ought to.* In English, we can refer to a lot of different past, present, and future times, but our verbal inflections directly mark only present and past. Therefore, in our phrase structure tree, the tense (tns) is either present (pres) or past:

*Note that adverb phrases can occur in many other locations in sentences.

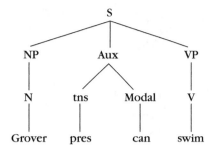

Auxiliaries

The phrase structure rules need further revision because now S (sentence) has three variables coming off of it: the noun phrase, the auxiliary, and the verb phrase (rule 1). We also introduce a new rule that extends all the possibilities for the auxiliary verb (rule 3) and a new rule that allows the two tense forms in English: present and past (rule 8).

1. S   →   NP   Aux   VP
3. Aux   →   tns   (M)   (have—perf)   (be—prog)   (be—pass)
8. tns   → $\left\{ \begin{array}{l} \text{pres} \\ \text{past} \end{array} \right\}$

Rule 3 permits the following:

- ◆ Tense (tns)
- ◆ Modals such as *can, will,* and *might* (M)
- ◆ Perfect aspect, such as *have eaten* (have—perf)
- ◆ Progressive aspect, such as *are eating* (be—prog)
- ◆ Passive voice, such as *is eaten* (be—pass)
- ◆ Combinations of tense, modals, aspect, and voice

This rule generates a series of separate morphemes such as *pres, be, past, have,* and *can* in the lexical line, and then **morphological rules** unscramble the morphemes into the proper order:

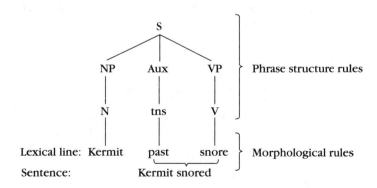

SAMPLE MORPHOLOGICAL RULES

perf + *eat* = *eaten*
prog + *eat* = *eating*
pass + *study* = *studied*
pres + *can* = *can*
past + *can* = *could* (past form, not past meaning)

pres + *be** = $\begin{Bmatrix} am \\ is \\ are \end{Bmatrix}$

past + *be** = $\begin{Bmatrix} was \\ were \end{Bmatrix}$

pres + *have** = $\begin{Bmatrix} have \\ has \end{Bmatrix}$

past + *have* = *had*

*Note that the correct form matches the subject.

REVISED PHRASE STRUCTURE RULES D

1. S → NP Aux VP

2. NP → $\begin{Bmatrix} \text{(Det) (AP) (N) N (PP)} \\ \text{Pronoun} \end{Bmatrix}$

3. Aux → tns (M) (have—perf) (be—prog) (be—pass)

4. VP → $\begin{matrix} V \\ V \end{matrix}$ $\begin{Bmatrix} \text{(Nonfinite) (NP) (PP) (AdvP)*} \\ \text{AdjP (PP) (AdvP)*} \end{Bmatrix}$

5. PP → P NP
6. AdjP → (Adv) Adj (Adv)
7. AdvP → (Adv) Adv (Adv)

8. Tns → $\begin{Bmatrix} \text{Past} \\ \text{Pres} \end{Bmatrix}$

Note additional updates to rules 2 (pronouns) and 4 (nonfinite verbals).

Naturally, a sentence with *all* the possible auxiliary elements is highly unlikely:

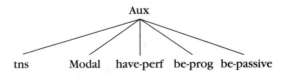

Few sentences have more than two or three of the possible auxiliary elements. Recall that we mark *optional* elements in the phrase structure rules with parentheses, so the only obligatory element in the auxiliary is tense:

*Adverb phrases also occur elsewhere.

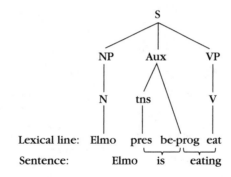

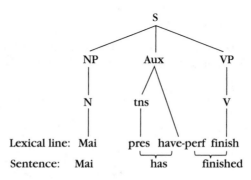

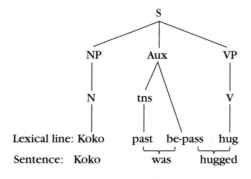

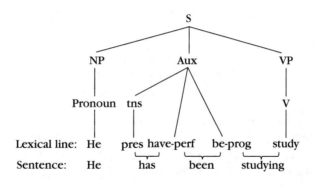

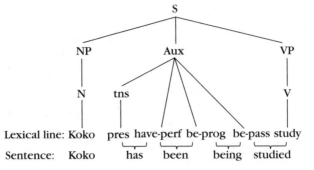

Finite Main Verbs

Finite main verbs are marked inflectionally with either present or past tense, so they also need an auxiliary, even if it contains only tense:

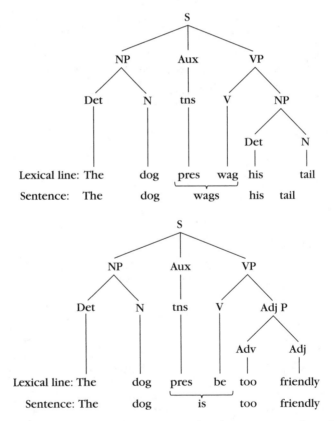

The following tree represents a sentence with a finite main verb and various nonfinite verbals. The same structure would work for all combinations of finite and nonfinite verbals. The triangle is a shorthand method to treat the nonfinite verbals as whole morphologically unanalyzed chunks:

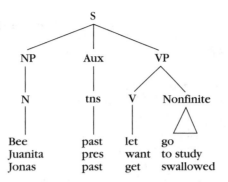

```
                    S
          ┌─────────┼─────────┐
         NP        Aux        VP
          │         │      ┌───┴───┐
          N        tns     V    Nonfinite
          │         │      │      /\
          │         │      │     /  \
         Bee       past   let    go
        Juanita    pres   want   to study
        Jonas      past   get    swallowed
```

───────────────── **STOP AND PRACTICE** ─────────────────

Draw tree diagrams for these sentences:

24. My brother likes olives with anchovies.
25. Kenny can swallow four olives at the same time.
26. Green olives are his very favorite food.
27. Black olives were his preference in 2001.
28. The dear boy has devoured a jar of olives every day since 2002.
29. He has been diagnosed with an eating disorder.
30. Kenny may have acquired a food addiction.
31. The poor creature will be undergoing rigorous therapy very soon.
32. He will need to change his habits.
33. My poor brother has to focus his attention on his food issues.

───────────────── **STOP AND PRACTICE** ─────────────────

Draw tree diagrams for these sentences:

34. Jennifer sat thinking in the library cubicle.
35. She planned to speak to her roommate about the dishes.
36. The new roommate avoided washing the dishes.
37. The dishes started to pile up in the sink.
38. Jennifer got stuck with the dishes every weekend.
39. She couldn't let go of her cleanliness addiction.

EXPLORING CHAPTER PERSPECTIVES

◆ *Discussion Questions*

Read the following excerpt from "*Language Minorities*" by Corson (1999, pp. 171–176) and discuss the answers to these questions:

1. What are some examples of the three types of language minorities in your area?
2. Do you agree with Corson's assessment of the policy in the United States?
3. What would it mean for Spanish or Ebonics speakers if the United States observed policy 6?

LANGUAGE MINORITIES

Reprinted by permission of Lawrence Erlbaum Associates.

(1) Language policies are now receiving worldwide attention because of the great population shifts that occurred over the last two or three generations. These shifts highlight language issues that once went unnoticed, even in those countries where there were always significant language minorities. Reporting from his studies of OECD countries, Churchill (1986) saw major changes everywhere in national attitudes to language minorities. He saw the most potent factor in this move to be the recent development of an international climate of opinion favoring the more open and tolerant treatment of minorities. Changes in international law have resulted, and other distinctive structural arrangements are being set in place (Hastings, 1997; Skutnabb-Kangas, 1997).

(2) Broadly speaking, there are three main types of language minorities in modern societies:

◆ *Ancestral peoples*, including those aboriginal groups long established in their native countries, like the Amerindians, the First Nations, and the Inuit in North America.
◆ *Established minorities*, including the long-standing Spanish-speaking communities in the United States, the Acadian French in North America generally, or the franco-ontarian community in Ontario.
◆ *New minorities*, including immigrants, refugees, or asylum seekers, foreign workers living semipermanently in their new home, and expatriates serving in countries tied in a loose community.

Classifying Minority Language Policies in Education

(3) There are many ways of comparing across countries and evaluating the treatment that different language minorities receive. Churchill (1986) located OECD countries at various points on an ascending ladder of six levels. His ranking was based on each country's policy response in recognizing minority language communities and in implementing suitable educational policies. The most basic level of development is when a country simply ignores the special educational needs of language minority groups, which is still a common response in parts of the Americas. But all OECD countries now have some policies reflecting at least items 1 or 2 in the list that follows, and the major English-speaking countries are rather similar in their sets of policies. In practice, this means that language policies in English-speaking countries for new arrivals fall under one or more of the following three categories:

1. The existing policy sees the new language minority groups as lacking English, and the typical policy response is to provide extra teaching in English (ESL), with a rapid transition expected to a use of English.
2. The existing policy sees the minority groups' need for English as also linked to family status, so an additional response is to provide special measures to help minority students to adjust to the majority society, such as aides, tutors, psychologists, social workers, career advisors, and so on.
3. The existing policy sees the minority group's need for English as linked to disparities in esteem between the group's culture and the majority culture, so additional policy responses are to include multicultural teaching programs for all children, to sensitize teachers to minority needs, and to revise textbooks to eliminate racial stereotyping.

(4) With only rare exceptions and in very limited contexts, language policies for immigrant minorities in North America, Britain, and Australasia, are located at one or other of the three levels just mentioned. But elsewhere, especially in Northern Europe, fairer language policies exist. These provide three more levels of response.

4. The existing policy sees the premature loss of the minority language as inhibiting transition to learning the majority tongue, so an additional response is to provide some study of the minority languages in schools, perhaps as a very early or occasional medium of transitional instruction.
5. The existing policy sees the minority groups' languages threatened with extinction as community languages if they are not supported, so the policy response is to provide the minority languages as media of instruction, usually exclusively in the early years of schooling.
6. The existing policy sees the minority and majority languages as having equal rights in society, with special support available for the less viable languages, so policy responses include:
   - Recognition of a minority language as an official language.
   - Separate educational institutions or school systems for language groups.
   - Opportunities for all children to learn both languages voluntarily.
   - Language support beyond educational system.

(5) Only the very old bilingual or multilingual OECD states have reached level 6 (Churchill, 1986). There is some ambiguity in other countries, like Canada, where policies differ markedly across provincial boundaries and school districts. In general, only francophone minorities outside Quebec and Anglophone minorities inside Quebec have rights approaching level 6 (see Burnaby, 1997).

(6) The U.S. Bilingual Education Act legislation seems to locate the United States firmly at level 4, although the responses of most schools and school districts themselves seem to be at much lower stage. In practice, the United States is located at levels 1 or 2. There seem major obstacles to producing much advance on this, given the fact that English has been repeatedly fostered to create an "American ethnicity," and quite exclusive English-only policies get much wider political support than in other countries (see Ricento, 1997).

(7) Australia is located at levels 4 or 5, on the evidence of its treatment of many users of aboriginal languages and some immigrant language users, although level 3 is perhaps closer to the actual practices in most states (see Clyme, 1997). New Zealand has begun to move towards the enrichment levels 5 and 6, but only for its ancestral Maori minority. In its language policy for immigrants, New Zealand is still located at levels 1 or 2 (see Watts, 1997).

(8) Its major Celtic areas apart, Britain has much in common with the United States. Britain is at level 3 in the attitudes to multiculturalism that curriculum specialists advocate, but it is only at level 1 in its treatment of immigrant minority language users. Immigrant community languages in Britain receive some recognition, but only in the very early stages of schooling to ease transition to English (see Rassool, 1997). Even in this limited response to the needs of immigrant children, there is recognition that it is much better educationally for children to be engaged in discourse that uses their first language than to be sitting in silence listening to others use a language that is not yet their own.

◆ ***Cooperative Exercise: Language Minorities***

After reading "*Language Minorities*" by Corson (1999), place the following expressions into the correct column according to their part of speech. Are there any that could go into more than one column?

S   NP   Aux + VP   AdjP   AdvP   PP

language policies
are receiving
worldwide attention
because of the population shifts
over the last two or three generations
these shifts highlight language issues
went
unnoticed
in those countries
were
always
significant language minorities
from his studies
saw
major changes
everywhere
to language minorities
he saw the most potent factor
the recent development
of opinion
the more open and tolerant treatment
have resulted
other distinctive structural arrangements
are being set
broadly speaking
three main types

◆ ***Writing Assignment***

Write a short essay in your Language Notebook in response to one or both of these prompts. Save your essay(s) for later use.

1. What language policy do you think would be best in your state? If it were adopted, what implications would there be for education in your local area?

2. Policy 6 in the Corson reading specifies "language support beyond educational system." What does this refer to? What language support outside the educational system is available to non-English speakers in your local area?

Introspection

Look at your essay(s) carefully and proofread for spelling, punctuation, and nonstandard or non-SWE usage. With several paragraphs of your essay, without drawing trees, try to match these symbols (S, NP, Aux, VP, AdjP, AdvP, PP) with the appropriate portions of your text. Are there any missing constituents? Make a note of any questions or problems you have.

TEACHING TO LEARN

Auxiliary Problems

The following sentences are typical of errors that students who are learning English would make. Use the structure of the auxiliary in the tree diagrams to help you decide what the problems are in each one. There are often several ways to change the sentence. What alternatives are there, and how do they differ? Use metalanguage.

Do the first examples as a class, then do the rest in pairs, each taking turns explaining to the other one way to correct the sentence.

Examples: Hasan can will go.
Lorenzo has study.
Amalia is pretty yesterday.

1. The ship going to the port city.
2. Carol have go to school for a long time.
3. The students may can going on the field trip.
4. Giorgio taken his car to the repair shop.
5. Hamlet is writing by Shakespeare.
6. Susana and Alfi was need at home.
7. Sam go to class every day last week.
8. Onasis go to school and study hard every day.
9. They can went the day before yesterday.
10. The English 117 class is gone on a field trip.

LEARNING TO TEACH

Reciprocal Teaching

Description: In reciprocal teaching, learners assume the role of teacher and "instruct" their peers on a grammar point. To do this, learners take responsibility to learn the material, put it into their own words, monitor their partners' understanding and learning, and receive feedback on their performance. Reciprocal teaching requires social and linguistic skills and embeds grammar firmly in communication. It is a foundation for peer editing.

Goals

Subject area goals: Verbal and social skills in speaking and listening

English language awareness goals: Structure or usage

Descriptive grammar goals: Variable metalanguage and development of the ability to explain grammar points

Procedural goals: Verbalization, explanation, and correction of usage problems

Assessment: Teachers monitor reciprocal teaching as it is going on. Learners receive feedback from their partners on how successful their explanations are.

Methodology: There have been many examples of reciprocal teaching in this book (the "Teaching to Learn" sections). For further practice, each individual student should write a reciprocal teaching activity with a grammar point that was difficult for him or her to master. Then do each activity with a partner.

13

Transformed Sentences

All the sentences discussed so far have been affirmative declarative sentences. The phrase structure rules generate affirmative declarative sentences in a straightforward manner. However, not all sentences are affirmative and declarative. Some declarative sentences are **negative,** some sentences are yes/no or <u>wh</u>-word questions (**interrogative**), some are commands (**imperatives**), and some are **exclamations.** The grammar generates these sentences in a different way.

NEGATIVE SENTENCES

Generating negative sentences from phrase structure rules by themselves is problematic. The issue is that the word *not,* the main negative sentential adverb, occurs in one special place in the auxiliary, but the other constituents of the auxiliary change positions around the word *not.* In Chapter 12, we generated adverb phrases as part of the verb phrase and then stated that they also occur elsewhere. To specify the position of the adverb *not* is even more complex. Recall the structure of the auxiliary while you examine these sentences:

> *The elephant is not caressing the monkey with its toes.*
>
> > *Not* is after *be* but before *-ing V.*
>
> *The elephant may not be caressing the monkey with its toes.*
>
> > *Not* is after *may* but before *be-prog V.*
>
> *The monkey has not been caressed by the elephant.*
>
> > *Not* is after *have* but before *-en be passive V.*

The only consistent pattern is that the word *not* always seems to appear just after the first element in the auxiliary, no matter what it is. Even though this is an easy generalization to state in words, it is hard to specify in a phrase structure rule with rigid word order. A more flexible kind of rule will state the generalization.

The tense element in the auxiliary and a main verb is another vexing complication: *The elephant <u>doesn't</u> caress the monkey with its toes.* The questions raised about this sentence are many:

◆ Why isn't the negative sentence *The elephant caresses <u>not</u> the monkey with its toes?*

231

◆ Why is the *not* before the main verb?

◆ Where did the *does* come from?

Negative Transformation

We resolve this problem by using flexible rules, called **transformations,** that allow words and phrases to move and change locations. A transformation takes one affirmative declarative tree structure produced by phrase structure rules and transforms it into a tree structure of another kind, such as negative, interrogative, or imperative. Transformations are best written in words to maintain flexibility.

Negative Transformation

In the lexical Line, insert the word *not* after the first element <u>after tense</u> in the auxiliary, no matter what that element is and even if the element is empty or 0. Also the negative transformation treats the main verb *be* as a part of the auxiliary. (It cannot distinguish between *be* as a main verb and *be* as an auxiliary, so it treats all instances as auxiliaries.)

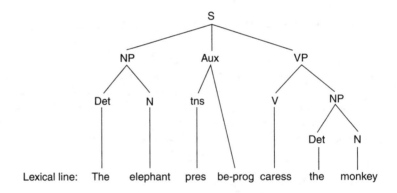

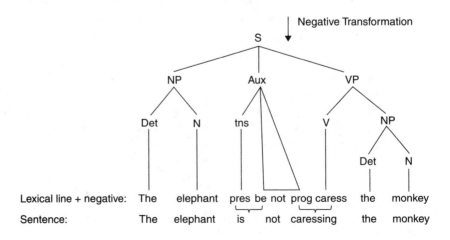

STOP AND PRACTICE
_____

Now you can draw these tree diagrams with the negative transformation already applied. Use the triangle so that you do not need to make a commitment to any precise structure of the auxiliary after the negative transformation has been applied. Show the effects of the morphological rules to the lexical line + negative to derive the final sentence:

1. The monkey cannot hug the bear.
2. The monkey may not be hugging the bear.
3. The monkey may not have been hugging the bear.
4. The bear may not have been hugged by the bear.
5. The monkey had not hugged the bear.
6. The monkey had not been hugging the bear.
7. The monkey is not sweet.
8. The monkey is not being sweet.

Do Insertion Transformation

In sentences that have only a tense element in the auxiliary, the affirmative declarative structure looks like this:

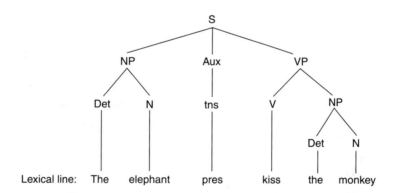

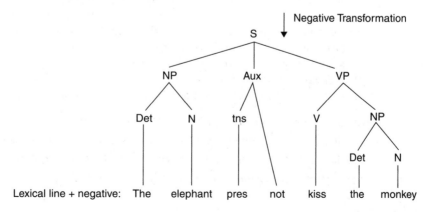

In an affirmative sentence, after morphological rules combine *pres* and *kiss,* the sentence is *The elephant kisses the monkey.* The auxiliary has only tense; the element "after" tense is empty or 0. To form the negative sentence, the negative transformation inserts *not* after the first element after tense in the auxiliary (which in this case is 0), so the *not* goes after tense.

The word *not* separates *pres* from the verb *kiss,* so the morphological rule that would combine them is blocked. At this point, the resulting sentence would be the incorrect **The elephant pres not kiss the monkey.* A new transformation repairs this problem, because the sentence should be *The elephant <u>does not</u> kiss the monkey.*

Do *Insertion Transformation*

In the case of a "stranded" tense morpheme in the lexical line, (e.g., a tense morpheme separated from its main verb by *not*), insert *do* right after the tense. (This transformation does not apply to *be* as a main verb because that is treated as an auxiliary.)

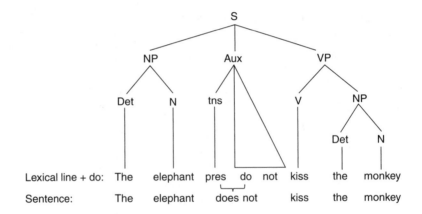

Derivations

Drawing a tree diagram for each transformation as it applies to a lexical line quickly becomes tedious. The shortcut we use is called a **derivation.** If you draw each tree in your imagination and copy off the lexical line for each into an ordered list as each transformation applies, you have a derivation. Thus, in order to construct a derivation for a sentence, you need the ability to imagine the tree in your mind's eye. However, if that metalinguistic ability does not come to you quickly enough, simply draw the tree. Here is a sample derivation for the previous sentence:

> lexical line: *The elephant pres kiss the monkey* →
> lexical line + negative: *The elephant pres not kiss the monkey* →
> lexical line + *do*: *The elephant pres do not kiss the monkey* →
> Sentence: *The elephant does not kiss the monkey.*

──────────────── STOP AND PRACTICE ────────────────

How is the negative sentence formed in each of these cases? Which transformations apply? To answer, translate each sentence into what it would be as output of phrase structure rules. Then show how the transformations apply to get the correct negative sentence. The first one is done for you:

9. The students watched television.
   lexical line: *The students past watch television*
   lexical line + negative: *The students past not watch television.*
   lexical line + *do*: *The students past do not watch television.*
   Sentence: *The students did not watch television.*
10. Their favorite show was cancelled.
11. They had watched it for many years.
12. They missed it.
13. Other shows were entertaining. (main verb = *be*)
14. The boys watched sports.
15. The girls were interested in sports.
16. The students wanted to read magazines.

──

QUESTIONS

There are four types of direct questions, that is, direct requests to another person for a response or for certain information.

Intonational Questions

These questions are phrases or declarative sentences pronounced with rising intonation at the end, symbolized by the question mark:

On Main Street?

In here?

You (are) going?

You heard what he said?

He didn't know?

You knew about what?

Tag Questions

The addition of a tag at the end of a declarative sentence makes a tag question:

You are going, <u>aren't you?</u>

You heard what he said, <u>didn't you?</u>

He didn't know, <u>did he?</u>

You knew about this, <u>didn't you?</u>

Tag Formation Transformation

To do a tag formation transformation, follow these steps:

  a. Make a pronominal copy of the subject and place it after the lexical line.
  b. Make a copy of the tense element and the first element of the auxiliary (the modal or the auxiliary verb) or the main verb if it is *be* and place it after the lexical line.
  c. If the lexical line is affirmative, the tag is negative and vice versa:

  lexical line: *Kermit pres be a frog*
  lexical line + tag   a: *Kermit pres be a frog he*
  lexical line + tag   b: *Kermit pres be a frog pres be he*
  lexical line + tag   c: *Kermit pres be a frog pres be not he*
  Sentence: *Kermit is a frog, isn't he?*

STOP AND PRACTICE

Following the example, write derivations for the following. You may abbreviate the derivation by collapsing the tag question into one application of a, b, and c at the same time if you wish. What do these sentences tell you about negative transformations and *do*-insertion transformations?

  17. Ashley has become a famous singer, hasn't she?
  18. Ashley Campbell is going to Canada, isn't she?
  19. She won't return to New York for five months, will she?
  20. She wants to perform in Ontario, doesn't she?
  21. She didn't travel alone, did she?

Yes/No Questions

Yes/no questions are formed by moving a portion of the auxiliary to the front of the sentence:

  Are you going?
  Did you hear what he said?

A TEACHING MOMENT

Other languages have very simple tag questions. Sometimes the word for "no" or "yes" follows that declarative sentence. In Spanish, the word *verdad?* (*truth*?) follows the declarative sentence. English learners often need practice with the unusual structure of tags because they are common in conversation. They are not frequent in writing outside of fiction, informal letter writing, and the like.

Did he know?

Didn't you know about this?

Subject/Auxiliary Inversion Transformation

Invert the subject of the lexical line and the tense plus the first element of the auxiliary (either a modal or an auxiliary verb) or the main verb *be:*

lexical line:	*Elmo Wheeler pres can swim faster than his brother*
lexical line + subject/auxiliary:	*pres can Elmo Wheeler swim faster than his brother*
Sentence:	*Can Elmo Wheeler swim faster than his brother?*

──────────────── **STOP AND PRACTICE** ────────────────

Write derivations for the following yes/no questions. Remember to start at the lexical line from the phrase structure rules, but do not draw trees unless you get stuck. Note that negative transformations and *do*-insertion transformations also apply here:

22. Was Elmo Wheeler going to dive into the pool?
23. Wasn't he a faster swimmer than his brother? (*Than* is a preposition)
24. Does he consider the water too cold?
25. Doesn't he want to warm up?

Wh-Word Questions

Information questions use pronouns such as *who, what,* or *whose; wh*-adverbs such as *where* or *how,* and *wh*-determiners in noun phrases such as *what man* or *whose car:*

Where are you going to study next year?

What did you hear about that university?

What did you learn about on the Internet?

What major did you pick and why did you pick it?

The *wh*-word is generated in its typical pronoun, adverb, or determiner place by the phrase structure rules:

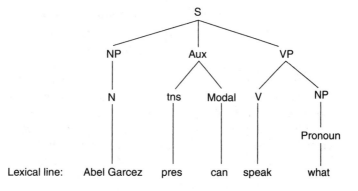

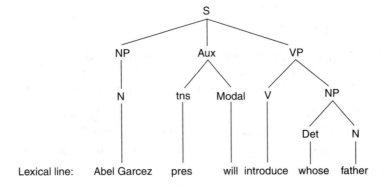

Wh-questions require the subject auxiliary inversion transformation, but in addition, the *wh*-word moves from its original place to a new place in the front of lexical line by a transformation called *wh*-movement.

Wh-*Movement Transformation*

Move the *wh*-word (or its phrase) to the front of the lexical line:

> lexical line: *Abel past be 1 passive hug by who(m)*
> lexical line + subject/auxiliary: *past be Abel passive hug by who(m)*
> lexical line + *wh*: *Who(m) past be Abel passive hug by*
> Sentence: *Who(m) was Abel hugged by?*

> lexical line: *Abel past hug who(m)*
> lexical line + subject/auxiliary: *past Abel hug who(m)*
> lexical line + *do*: *past do Abel hug who(m)*
> lexical line + *wh*: *who(m) past do Abel hug*
> Sentence: *Who(m) did Abel hug?*

> lexical line: *Abel past speak to who(m) for 20 years*
> lexical line + negative: *Abel past not speak to who(m) for 20 years*
> lexical line + subject/auxiliary: *past not Abel speak to who(m) for 20 years*
> lexical line + *do*: *past do not Abel speak to who(m) for 20 years*
> lexical line + *wh*: *who(m) past do not Abel speak to for 20 years*
> Sentence: *Who(m) did not Abel speak to for 20 years?*

To derive the alternative sentence *To whom didn't Abel speak for 20 years?*, *wh*-movement applies to the whole phrase that the *wh*-word occurs in. In fact, the phrases that move are prepositional phrases *(in what way, with whom)*, noun phrases with a *wh*-determiner *(what language, which sport)*, or adjective phrases *(how long, how far)*. See Figure 13.1 for a review of all transformations.

Do **Insertion Transformation**

In the case of a "stranded" tense morpheme in the lexical line, (e.g., a tense morpheme separated from its main verb by *not*), insert *do* right after the tense. (This transformation does not apply to *be* as a main verb because that is treated as an auxiliary.)

Negative Transformation

In the lexical line, insert the word *not* after the first element after tense in the auxiliary, no matter what that element is (even if it is 0). The negative transformation treats the main verb *be* as a part of the auxiliary. (It cannot distinguish between *be* as a main verb and *be* as an auxiliary, so it treats all instances as auxiliaries.)

Tag Formation Transformation

    a. Make a pronominal copy of the subject and place it after the lexical line.
    b. Make a copy of the tense element and the first element of the auxiliary (the modal or the auxiliary verb) or the main verb if it is *be* and place it after the lexical line.
    c. If the lexical line is affirmative, the tag is negative and vice versa.

Subject/Auxiliary Inversion Transformation

Invert the subject of the lexical line and the tense plus the first element of the auxiliary (either a modal or an auxiliary verb) or the main verb *be*.

Wh-**Movement Transformation**

Move the *wh*-word or its whole phrase to the front of the lexical line.

Figure 13.1 *Review of all transformations.*

————————————————— **STOP AND PRACTICE** —————————————————

How are these questions derived?

    26. What has Brad Her been playing for 10 years?
    27. How long will Brad continue to play professionally?
    28. What sport doesn't he play?
    29. Which team does he play for?
    30. When did he start the sport?
    31. Whose father will he introduce at the sports banquet?

————————————————— **STOP AND PRACTICE** —————————————————

Identify which of the previous transformations were involved in these sentences. Then do derivations for sentences 36–41:

    32. Are you learning a lot of grammar in this class?
    33. You are learning a lot of grammar, aren't you?
    34. You are not learning much literary style.

35. What are you learning?
36. What aren't you learning?
37. Do you like grammar?
38. You like grammar, don't you?
39. What do you like?
40. We don't appreciate language prejudice, do we?
41. What don't we like?

IMPERATIVE SENTENCES

You

Imperative sentences are commands for someone or something to do or not to do something. There are two types of commands. The first is for a second person (singular or plural *you*):

> *Get in the car.*
>
> *Be good.*
>
> *Don't be naughty.*
>
> *Don't dawdle.*
>
> *Don't (you) ever say anything.*
>
> *Grab that hammer, will you?*
>
> *Please don't eat the daisies.*

Imperatives are unique among English sentences because they do not need an overt subject, but if they have a subject, it is always *you*. Even imperative sentences with no overt subject seem to be directed at *you*. Their verb form is simple; it cannot have inflectional morphology, as shown by the ungrammatical imperatives **Studied for the exam!* or **Being good!* The meaning of the verb form in the imperative is present or future time.

Imperatives with the main verb *be* form their negative with *don't*, as in *Don't be silly.* This is unlike declarative and interrogative sentences, where *be* is always treated as an auxiliary. If the imperative is affirmative, it might have a tag question with *will* or *would* that softens it. Commands also occur with *please:*

> *Close the door, will you?*
>
> *Please close the door, will you?*

These details suggest that we could derive imperative sentences from sentences with *you* as a subject and *will* or *would* as a modal auxiliary. An **imperative transformation** (which is not formalized further) then deletes the subject, the tense, and the modal after the tag formation transformation has applied (if it does apply).

Let's

Let's is a contracted form of *let us,* so this command is a suggestion for the speaker as well as others to do something. *Let* is already an imperative form, and *us* is a first-person plural object pronoun, but this expression does not maintain the original meaning of *let* as *permit* or *allow:*

> *Let's have a party.*
> *Let's not spend any money on this.*
> *Don't let's spend any money on this.* (dialectal)

Distribution

According to Biber et al. (1999 pp. 219–222), imperatives of both types are far more common in conversation than they are in fiction, news reporting, or academic prose, which makes sense because speakers are more likely to give orders in conversation. However, some imperatives that do appear in academic prose. The last example here is a shortening of *let us suppose,* which would be more formal:

> *In looking for the answers, <u>let us begin</u> with those citizens who have been around for the longest time, the elderly and those in later middle age.*
> <u>*Note*</u> *that x may occur free and bound in P.*
> <u>*See*</u> *also Section 5.2.*
> <u>*Let be*</u> *the breeding population of blowflies at time t and let y be the number of eggs produced.*
> <u>*Suppose*</u> *we believe that the snow is what is muffling the sound of the traffic.*

EXCLAMATIONS

Exclamations are common in conversation and very uncommon in academic prose. One type of exclamation is a phrase or insert with exclamatory intonation or punctuation. Exclamatory sentences sometimes have inverted subjects and verbs, as in the first one here:

> *Oops! The garbage! <u>Here comes the garbage truck</u>!*
> *Help! The car! It's rolling down the hill!*

Other exclamations are singular or plural noun phrases with various introductory expressions, such as *what a* or *what* (or *such/such a* in some dialects). Some exclamations extract the noun phrases out of whole sentences and preface them with the introductory expression:

> *What a big challenge!*
> <u>*What a challenge*</u> *we are facing!*
> *What great students!*
> <u>*What great students*</u> *you are!*

> **A TEACHING MOMENT**
>
> **Exclamation**
>
> English learners do not always understand when to use *what* (with plural or mass nouns) or *what a* (with singular count nouns). In addition, teachers need to point out and practice the inverted explamations:
>
> *Here comes the judge!*
> *There goes the economy!*

EXPLORING CHAPTER PERSPECTIVES

◆ *Discussion Questions*

Read the text of the National Public Radio interview with Mr. Will Fitzhugh titled "Students Not to Write History Term Papers Anymore."
Discuss the answers to these questions.

1. Did you write any term papers in middle or high school, or was your writing limited to fiction? Describe your experience. Did you feel adequately prepared for your writing tasks in college or in your professional life?

2. What were Mr. Fitzhugh's main points? Do you agree or disagree with them?

STUDENTS NOT TO WRITE HISTORY TERM PAPERS ANYMORE

December 3, 2002
Reprinted by permission of National Public Radio

JOHN YDSTIE, host: This time in the school year traditionally begins the run up to midterm exams, but one thing many students won't be doing in the next few weeks is writing a history paper. A new study finds that fewer teachers are assigning term papers, once a staple of the high school curriculum. Will Fitzhugh is the publisher of *The Concord Review*, a nonprofit journal devoted to publishing the best high school history essays from around the country and the globe.

Good morning, Mr. Fitzhugh.

MR. WILL FITZHUGH (Publisher, *The Concord Review*): Good morning.

YDSTIE: Why aren't more teachers assigning history papers?

MR. FITZHUGH: Well, like many things, there are a variety of reasons, but one of the most important ones, at least in our study it showed, that 95 percent of teachers believe that history research papers are important or very important; most of them don't have the time to coach the students or to correct the papers.

YDSTIE: Mm-hmm. Teachers don't have the time. How are they spending their time, or what do they need time to do?

MR. FITZHUGH: Well, to take a somewhat extreme example, somebody once told me that there are teachers in the country with 150 students; that is, five classes of 30 students. If that teacher assigned a 20-page research paper to all of her students when they came in, the teacher would have 3,000 pages to read and correct and make comments on. And there's no way that a teacher can do that, while teaching five classes a day.

YDSTIE: Some teachers have decided to only assign term papers to their honor students. Is that the right approach?

MR. FITZHUGH: Well, I wouldn't deprive honor students of a chance to write a serious history paper, but I think every student should have the experience of reading one non-fiction book and writing one reasonably serious research paper before they receive a high school diploma.

YDSTIE: What do students get out of it, though? I mean, how many students are going to face a time in their life when they need to write an 11-page or 12-page paper and footnote it in the way that's required? Is it really a skill that's useful?

MR. FITZHUGH: Well, I might have had some questions about that a few years ago, before I learned that Ford Motor Company, for instance, has instituted writing classes for its engineer and college graduates because they can't write memos, reports, they can't do basic writing. And the same is true at Boston Scientific Corporation and a number of law firms that have associates coming out of law school who can't write well enough to do the work of the firm.

YDSTIE: Traditionally, we have laid the burden at the feet of English teachers. Are you saying that history teachers are as responsible for teaching their students to write as their English teacher colleagues?

MR. FITZHUGH: Well, my experience has been that English has pretty much decided that fiction is their bailiwick. So that leaves history as the place where you read non-fiction and write non-fiction term papers. The problem with employers is not that they expect their new college graduate hires to write books, but if they go a conference and write a memo when they come back, nobody can understand what the memo says. And that's why they're instituting writing classes. It's basic writing skills, expository writing. I mean, probably if they asked them to write a poem when they got back, they would find that the employee had more experience. That's not what they're looking for.

YDSTIE: Well, thank you very much, Mr. Fitzhugh.

MR. FITZHUGH: You're welcome.

YDSTIE: Will Fitzhugh is the publisher of *The Concord Review*, a non-profit journal that publishes the best high school history essays from around the country and around the world.

◆ *Cooperative Exercise: Students Not to Write History Term Papers Anymore*

A. **Individual Work.** In the text, underline all questions and negatives. Isolate the subject and finite verbal of each and take it back to its earliest lexical line. Then apply transformations to derive the cited question. An example is done for you.

Why aren't more teachers assigning history papers?

lexical line: *teachers are assigning history papers why*
lexical line + negative: *teachers are NOT assigning history papers why*
lexical line + subject/auxiliary: *are NOT teachers assigning history papers why*
lexical line + *do*: *N.A.*
lexical line + *wh*: *why are NOT teachers assigning history papers*
Sentence: *Why aren't teachers assigning history papers?*

B. **Pair Work.** Compare your answers. Together with your partner, identify all noun phrases in the passage and their role in the sentence. Be especially careful to identify gerunds (nouns derived from verbs with the addition of –*ing*) and distinguish them from present participles.

Note: A noun phrase that follows another noun phrase and renames it is called an *appositive*. Here is one example, can you find others? The appositive is underlined; what it renames is in boldface print:

A new study finds that fewer teachers are assigning term papers, <u>once a staple of the high school curriculum</u>.

C. **Class Work.** Go over anything that caused you problems.

◆ *Writing Assignment*

Write a short essay in your Language Notebook in response to one or both of these prompts.

1. Do you agree with Fitzhugh that "English has pretty much decided that fiction is their bailiwick" and "if [employers] asked [an employee] to write a poem . . . , they would find that the employee had more experience."

2. Do you think that history, math, and science teachers are qualified to teach expository writing? Why or why not? What kind of writing assignments could be assigned in those classes?

Introspection

Proofread your essays and make any necessary corrections. In your essays, underline all your finite verbals and prepositional phrases. Make sure <u>not</u> to underline particles. If you find a lot of particles, can you think of other verbs to express your ideas?

| TEACHING TO LEARN |

Negative and Interrogative Sentences

The writers of these sentences need feedback. They might be colloquial, nonstandard, or nonnative usages that are not appropriate in academic language. Identify what type of problem each sentence presents and suggest a correct standard English version. Try out your suggestions on your partner.

1. My mother no went to work today.
2. Those guys don't know no better.
3. Sandra and her friends don't studied very hard for the test.
4. They can't hardly speak English.
5. Don't nobody say that again.
6. I don't go nowhere unless I can go in my RV.
7. Do you can drive to school?
8. Where you are going?

| LEARNING TO TEACH |

Minilectures, Minilessons, and Miniconferences

Description: There are three minis in grammar instruction: inductive or deductive *minilectures* (because grammar instruction must be presented clearly and concisely), *minilessons* (when short explanations and immediate application are prompted by a question or problem raised in a writing workshop or classroom), and *miniconferences* (because learners need individual feedback on their writing and attention to global or stigmatizing errors).

Goals

Subject area goals: Writing improvement/structure and usage

English language awareness goals: Standard Written English and Academic English conventions

Descriptive grammar goals: Forms and labels

Procedural goals: Self-editing and proofreading

Assessment: Video- and audiotapes and assessments of learning outcomes help a teacher assess the effectiveness of lectures, lessons, and conferences.

Methodology: Go to your university's writing lab or learning center where student writers receive tutorial assistance and get permission to observe a tutorial session. While observing, make notes on what issues come up, what and how the tutor explains, what and how the writer understands, and so on. What is your assessment of the success of the tutorial?

14

Complex Sentences

To avoid monotony, good writers vary their sentence structures, making their sentences complex. **Complex sentences** contain a main sentence and at least one subordinate sentence within their structures. In these complex sentences, the subordinate sentence is underlined:

> *That Elmo chased Big Bird is self-evident.*
> *It is wonderful that Big Bird never gets older.*
> *The boys and girls are unhappy that Cookie Monster eats all the cookies.*
> *When Elmo speaks to Big Bird, everyone tries to listen in.*
> *The people that live on Sesame Street are lucky.*
> *The people that we watch on television are not always nice.*

What these subordinate sentences have in common is that they begin with *that* or a *wh*-word, such as *when,* or words labeled **complementizers** or **subordinating conjunctions.** Sometimes the complementizer is deleted, as in this sentence:

> *The people we watch on television are not always nice.*

Like simple sentences, subordinate sentences have subjects and predicates, and their verbs are finite. There are four main types of subordinate structures, each slightly different in its syntactic structure and function in the sentence. The function determines the name of the clause: noun clauses, predicate adjective complements, adjective clauses, and adverb clauses.

NOUN CLAUSES

Embedded declarative statements or questions that function as subjects or objects within their main sentence are **noun clauses.** The phrase structure rules we already have must be revised in order to generate these sentences. Our first new rule allows for a special kind of sentence (S', read as "S-bar") to be inserted under a noun phrase variable, NP. This captures the intuition that the noun clause, although it is a subordinate sentence, functions as a noun phrase in the sentence. The second new rule explains that the S' contains both a complementizer (Comp) and a regular kind of sentence (S):

2. NP → $\left\{ \begin{array}{l} \text{(Det)} \quad \text{(AP)} \quad \text{(N)} \quad \text{N} \quad \text{(PP)} \\ \text{Pronoun} \\ \text{S'} \end{array} \right\}$

9. S' → Comp S

Note: Comp is a variable that stands for words such as *that, when,* or *who.*

REVISED PHRASE STRUCTURE RULES E

1. S →   NP   Aux   VP

2. NP → $\left\{ \begin{array}{c} \text{(Det)} \quad \text{(AP)} \quad \text{(N)} \quad \text{N} \quad \text{(PP)} \\ \text{Pronoun} \\ \text{S'} \end{array} \right\}$

3. Aux → tns   (M)   (have-perf)   (be-prog)   (be-pass)

4. VP → $\left\{ \begin{array}{l} \text{V} \quad \text{(Non–finite)} \quad \text{(NP)} \quad \text{(PP)} \quad \text{(AdvP)*} \\ \text{V} \quad \text{(AdjP)} \quad \text{(PP)} \quad \text{(AdvP)*} \end{array} \right\}$

5. PP →   P   NP

6. AdjP → (Adv)   Adj   (Adv)

7. AdvP → (Adv)   Adv   (Adv)

8. tns → $\left\{ \begin{array}{l} \text{Past} \\ \text{Pres} \end{array} \right\}$

9. S' → Comp S

Note: Adverb phrases also occur elsewhere.

Embedded Statements

These nine basic phrase structure rules generate many English sentences, including these complex sentences with noun clauses:

> <u>*That teachers work hard*</u> *is obvious.*
> *Alicia thinks* <u>*that the world is flat.*</u>

In the first sentence, the noun clause is the subject of the sentence, and deleting the complementizer is impossible because the sentence would be difficult for the listener to understand:

> *<u>*Teachers work hard*</u> *is obvious.*

However, when the embedded noun clause is an object, the complex sentence without *that* is okay:

Alicia thinks <u>the world is flat.</u>

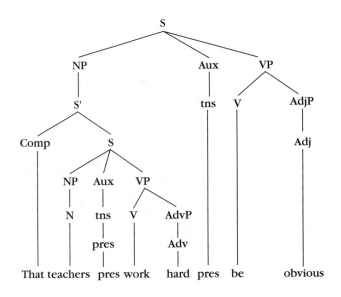

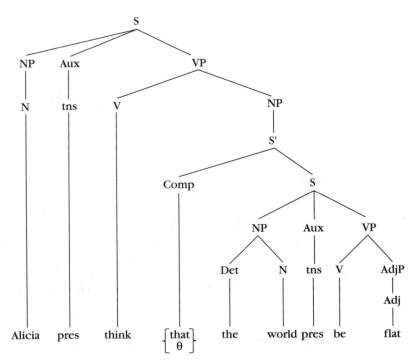

Embedded Questions

Embedded noun clause questions fit into a main sentence that often (but not always) has a questioning, wondering, or uncertain main verb. Embedded questions are **indirect** *wh*-questions or yes/no questions. In embedded *wh*-questions, the *wh*-word is the complementizer; in yes/no questions, the complementizer is *whether* or *if*:

> *I asked the guard <u>what the prisoner said.</u>*
> <u>*When the song was written*</u> *is immaterial to me.*
> *Tomas wondered <u>if monkeys use language.</u>*

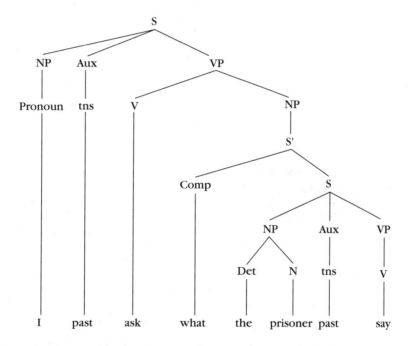

Another type of embedded question involves an infinitive, which looks a bit odd, but a more detailed analysis would take us beyond the subject matter of this book:

─────────────── **STOP AND PRACTICE** ───────────────

Draw tree diagrams for these sentences:

1. Gerardo discovered that his library book was overdue.
2. He thought that he had returned it already.
3. He couldn't remember who the author was.
4. He had forgotten where he put the book.
5. He didn't know what the fine would be.
6. He asked the librarian what to do.

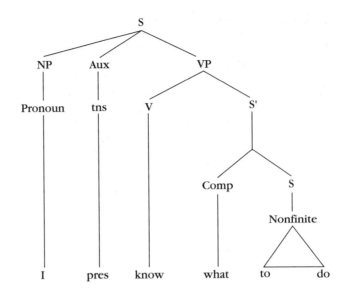

<table>
<tr><td>**A TEACHING MOMENT**</td><td>**Embedded Questions**</td></tr>
</table>

A TEACHING MOMENT

Embedded Questions

Embedded *indirect questions* in English have the same structure as any other noun clause. Their structure is not like direct questions because no inversion of the subject and auxiliary takes place and there is no *do* insertion:

> I *don't know* <u>what he is doing.</u> (What is he doing?)
> *There is doubt about* <u>where he can go.</u> (Where can he go?)
> We *don't know* <u>why he goes there.</u> (Why does he go there?)

However, direct questions and embedded questions in Spanish have the same structure, with subject/verb inversion:

> Que hace (é l)?
> No se' <u>que hace (é l).</u>

Some Spanish speakers learning English, even very advanced ones, transfer this syntactic characteristic to their English and produce sentences that are slightly "off":

> *I *don't know* <u>what is he doing.</u>
> *There is some doubt about <u>where can he go.</u>
> *We *don't know* <u>why does he go</u> there every day.

ADJECTIVE CLAUSES

Adjective clauses were formerly known as relative clauses, taking their name from the relative pronouns *who, whom, which,* and *that* and the posessive determiner *whose,* which serve as their complementizers. These are called adjective clauses because, like adjectives phrases, they modify a head noun from inside a noun phrases. That is, in a main sentence with an adjective clause, the S' modifies from inside noun phrase:

2. NP → { (Det) (AdjP) (N) N (S')   (Adjective clauses)
           Pronoun
           S'   }   (Noun clauses)

Two Types of Adjective Clauses

RELATIVE PRONOUN = SUBJECT		RELATIVE PRONOUN = OBJECT	
	Pro		Pro
the man	*who works*	*the man*	*who(m) I work with*
the chair	*which is green*	*the chair*	*which I sat on*
the idea	*which stands out*	*the idea*	*which you had*
the girl	*who studies*	*the girl*	*who(m) you met*

Relative pronoun = subject adjective clauses have the relative pronoun as the *subject* of the verb following it. *Who* is the subject of *works,* *which* is the subject of *is, which* is the subject of *stands out, who* is the subject of *hugs,* and so on:

   the man who works   *the idea which stands out*

   the chair which is green   *the girl who studies*

Relative pronoun = object adjective clauses have the relative pronoun as the *object* of the verb following it. *Who(m)* is the object of *work with, which* is the object of *sat on, which* is the object of *had,* and *who(m)* is the object of *hug.* Notice also that the verbs in these adjective clauses have other pronouns (*I* or *you*) as subjects:

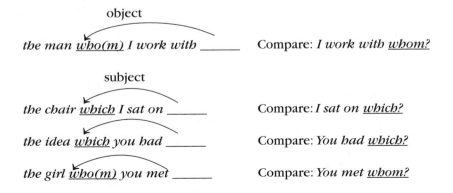

object

the man who(m) I work with _____   Compare: *I work with whom?*

subject

the chair which I sat on _____   Compare: *I sat on which?*

the idea which you had _____   Compare: *You had which?*

the girl who(m) you met _____   Compare: *You met whom?*

A TEACHING MOMENT	

Whom

Whom (and its cousin *whomever*) is a relative pronoun that is rapidly falling out of active use for many people. However, there may be times when you might want to use it or at least know when it is being used correctly. *Whom* is used only in adjective clauses when the relative pronoun is the object of a verb or preposition:

They are the people whom we met _____.

If the preposition stays with the relative pronoun as the two sentences are combined, *whom* must occur:

He is the man. I work <u>with him.</u>
He is the man <u>with whom</u> I work.

In this case, neither *that* nor 0 may occur:

*He is the man with that I work.
*He is the man with I work.

Note also these embedded noun clauses with *who/whomever*:

I love <u>whoever will love me.</u> (*whoever* is the subject of the noun clause)
I will applaud <u>whomever you applaud.</u> (*whomever* is the object of the noun clause)

Either type of adjective clause (with some exceptions discussed later) permits another relative pronoun, *that.* In fact, most grammar checkers in word processing programs mark the use of *wh*-pronouns, prompting the writer to change them to *that.* (This may hasten the demise of *wh*-relative pronouns over time.)

Also, some of the sentences (Relative Pronoun = Object) allow a **zero relative pronoun:** *the man __ <u>I work with,</u> the chair __ <u>I sat on,</u> the idea __ <u>you had,</u> the student __ <u>you met.</u>* The reason for this is that in these sentences the verb has a subject already. If the relative pronoun is the subject it cannot disappear because then the verb would have no subject at all.

Phrase Structure

The structure of adjective clauses is similar to noun clauses, but the S' is part of the noun phrase instead of the whole noun phrase. Which type of adjective clause does this tree show?

To understand this sentence, we must realize that the relative pronoun (*who* or *whom*) refers back to the word *author* and connects it semantically with the "missing" object of the verb *like,* as shown by the arrow in the diagram. Another way to express this idea is to say that the word *who(m)* moves out of its position as direct object

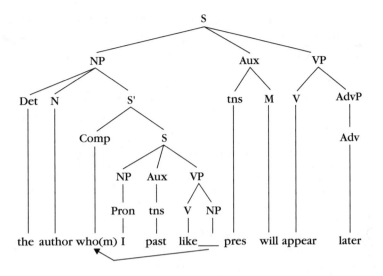

and into the complementizer position by means of the same *wh*-movement transformation that operates in *wh*-word questions.

In the following relative pronoun = subject adjective clause, we associate the word *author* with the relative pronoun *who* and the "missing" subject of the verb *appear* in order to understand the sentence. The *wh*-movement transformation moves the word *who* out of the subject position in the subordinate sentence and into the complementizer position even though there is no noticeable effect on the sentence:

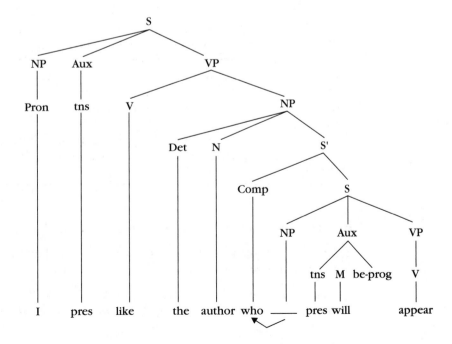

Like other subordinate constructions, adjective clauses can also appear with infinitives: *I don't have any neighbors <u>with whom to bunk tonight</u>*.

REVISED PHRASE STRUCTURE RULES G

1. S → NP Aux VP

2. NP → { (Det) (AdjP) (N) N (S')
          Pronoun
          S' }

3. Aux → tns (M) (have-perf) (be-prog) (be-pass)

4. VP → { V (Nonfinite) (NP) (PP) (AdvP)
          V AdjP (PP) (AdvP) }

5. PP → P NP
6. AdjP → (Adv) Adj (Adv)
7. AdvP → (Adv) Adv (Adv)

8. tns → { Past
           Pres }

9. S' → Comp S

─────────── **STOP AND PRACTICE** ───────────

Draw tree diagrams for these sentences:

7. Autumn is a season that pleases most people.
8. People appreciate the vivid colors the leaves turn.
9. The leaves which we saw on our drive were lovely.
10. We picked up some leaves that had fallen from a tree.
11. The leaves we picked up were yellow, red, and brown.
12. We took the leaves that were red to our home.
13. The drive we took in the country was fun.
14. We took a tour with some people who like autumn colors.
15. The people with whom we traveled were friendly. (The whole prepositional phrase with the *wh*-word is in the Comp.)

Nonrestrictive and Restrictive Adjective Clauses

We can also divide adjective clauses into two types based on their purpose or meaning in the complex sentence:

Laslo, <u>who is my long-lost cousin,</u> is coming to the reunion.

The boy <u>who is my long-lost cousin</u> is coming to the reunion.

Pronouns and Appositives

In sentences with a pronoun (usually *we* or *us*) and an appositive, people are sometimes confused about the choice of subject or object pronoun form, but the rule "form follows function" should apply. Removing the appositive is a good way to know which pronoun is standard usage. There are often no commas in this construction:

<u>We English teachers</u> *have declarative knowledge of grammar.* (*Us English teachers)
They awarded the grammar prize to <u>us English teachers.</u>

The first sentence contains a **nonrestrictive** adjective clause, and the Comp must be *who(m), which,* or *whose* and never *that.* Nonrestrictive adjective clauses add a little additional information to a referent (*Laslo*); we presume prior knowledge because of the proper name. The nonrestrictive adjective clause is set off from the rest of the sentence with commas because the information is optional. In addition, the commas convey a sense of the way we say the sentence, with pauses before and after the adjective clause.

The second sentence is the more typical case; the adjective clause restricts the noun phrase to a specific boy. **Restrictive** adjective clauses tend to occur with definite or indefinite noun phrases and not proper names. Technically, the information is optional, but the sentence is bland and uninformative without it because we do not know which boy the sentence is about. That is why the adjective clause is not set off with commas—it is an integral part of the sentence.

Appositive Constructions

Deleting the relative pronoun and the verb *be* as in the underlined portion of the following sentences produces an **appositive** construction. The deletions leave behind a simple noun phrase *(my long-lost cousin)* that renames and refers to the juxtaposed noun phrase. There are pauses in speech around this construction, represented in writing as commas:

Laslo, <u>my long-lost cousin,</u> is coming to the reunion.
The boy, <u>my long-lost cousin,</u> is coming to the reunion.

PREDICATE ADJECTIVE COMPLEMENTS

Predicate adjective complements have an S' inserted inside an adjective phrase:

1. AdjP → (Adv) Adj (S') (Adv)

	AdjP
Tony will be	*very glad <u>that you visited.</u>*
Jerry will be	*even more happy <u>that you left.</u>*
Marisol got	*so excited <u>that she jumped for joy.</u>*

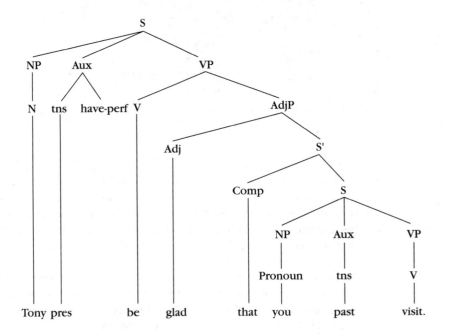

Sometimes predicate adjective complements are infinitives.

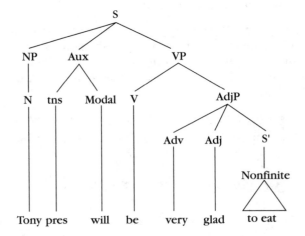

REVISED PHRASE STRUCTURE RULES H

1. S →   NP   AUX   VP

2. NP → $\left\{ \begin{array}{l} \text{(Det) (AdjP) (N) N (S')} \\ \text{Pronoun} \\ \text{S'} \end{array} \right\}$

3. AUX → tns   (M)   (have-perf)   (be-prog)   (be-pass)

4. VP → $\left\{ \begin{array}{l} \text{V (Nonfinite) (NP) (PP) (AdvP)**} \\ \text{V AdjP (PP) (AdvP)**} \end{array} \right\}$

5. PP →   P   NP
6. AdjP → (Adv)   Adj   (S')   (Adv)
7. AdvP → (Adv)   Adverb   (Adv)

8. tns → $\left\{ \begin{array}{l} \text{Past} \\ \text{Pres} \end{array} \right\}$

9. S' → Comp S

STOP AND PRACTICE

Draw tree diagrams for these sentences:

16. We are extremely happy to meet you.
17. We were very unhappy that your plane was late.
18. We are so sorry that you lost your luggage.
19. The luggage handlers are careful to return all luggage.
20. The airline is proud to serve you.
21. I am too tired to complain.

ADVERB CLAUSES

The last type of embedded sentence, the adverb clause, is so named because it modifies the main sentence as a whole, giving the time, sequence of events, or other adverbial information. Adverb clauses can appear in final or in initial position in the sentence:

Bobby ate breakfast <u>before she went to class.</u>
<u>After she got to class,</u> she remembered her homework.
<u>Unless she was wrong,</u> her homework was still on her desk.

The easiest way to generate adverb clauses is to insert a S' as a type of adverb phrase. This set of rules reviews all the embedded sentences we have studied in this chapter:

2. NP → $\left\{ \begin{matrix} \text{(Det)} \quad \text{(AP)} \quad \text{(N)} \quad \text{(S')} \\ \text{S'} \end{matrix} \right\}$ Adjective clause
                                                                      Noun clause

6. AdjP → (Adv) Adj (S') (Adv)   Predicate adjective complement

7. AdvP → $\left\{ \begin{matrix} \text{(Adv)} \quad \text{Adv} \quad \text{(Adv)} \\ \text{S'} \end{matrix} \right\}$
                                                                      Adverb clause

10. S' → Comp S

A tree with an adverb clause looks like this:

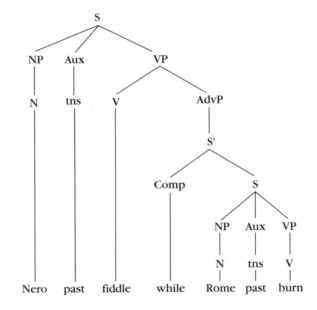

Adverb clauses appear initially in the sentence *While Rome burned, Nero fiddled.* In this case, a transformational rule removes the adverb phrase under the verb phrase and attaches it to the top S. The displacement explains why we often find a comma separating the S' from the rest of the sentence as in the following tree diagram.

───────────────── STOP AND PRACTICE ─────────────────

Draw tree diagrams for these sentences:

22. The film crew found the homeless people while they were scouting a new location.
23. As soon as the crew saw them, they filmed them. (Hint: Treat *as soon as* as a multimorphemic lexical unit, i.e., one word.)
24. After the film had been shot, the crew left.

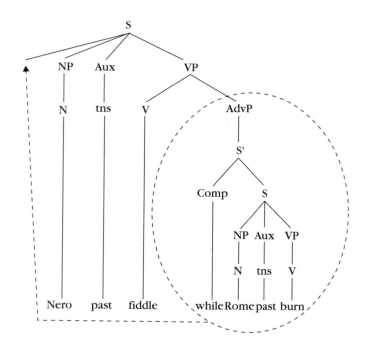

25. The film went on a news show when it had been edited.
26. Harriet donated her money by phone as she watched the homeless people on television.

SOME ADVERB CLAUSE COMPLEMENTIZERS

TIME	CONTRAST	CAUSE	INTENTION	CONDITION
after	*although*	*as long as*	*in order that*	*as long as*
as	*even if*	*because*	*so that*	*if*
before	*unless*	*inasmuch as*		*provided/-ing that*
now that	*while*	*since*		
since	*whereas*			
until				
when(ever)				
while				

A TEACHING MOMENT

Sentence Fragments

In Chapter 5, we saw that conversations in Standard Spoken English often include sentence fragments consisting of phrases or subordinate sentences. This error transfers to writing if writers compose sentences with subordinate sentences that are not connected to their main sentences. The use of fragments is becoming more common among some popular authors, but students should probably avoid using them:

The Provost has cancelled classes today because of the inclement weather. <u>Which is exactly what I was hoping for</u>.

I will be able to add several pages to my term paper. <u>Because I have extra time</u>.

PHRASE STRUCTURE RULES I

1. $S \rightarrow$ NP   Aux   VP

2. $NP \rightarrow$ $\left\{ \begin{array}{l} \text{(Det)} \quad \text{(AdjP)} \quad \text{(N)} \quad \text{N} \quad \text{(S')} \\ \text{Pronoun} \\ \text{S'} \end{array} \right\}$

3. $Aux \rightarrow$ tns   (M)   (have-perf)   (be-prog)   (be-pass)

4. $VP \rightarrow$ $\left\{ \begin{array}{l} \text{V} \quad \text{(Nonfinite)} \quad \text{(NP)} \quad \text{(PP)} \quad \text{(AdvP)**} \\ \text{V} \quad \text{AdjP} \quad \text{(PP)} \quad \text{(AdvP)**} \end{array} \right\}$

5. $PP \rightarrow$ P   NP

6. $AdjP \rightarrow$ (Adv)   Adj   (S')   (Adv)

7. $AdvP \rightarrow$ $\left\{ \begin{array}{l} \text{(Adv)} \quad \text{Adj} \quad \text{(Adv)} \\ \text{S'} \end{array} \right\}$

8. $tns \rightarrow$ $\left\{ \begin{array}{l} \text{Past} \\ \text{Pres} \end{array} \right\}$

9. $S' \rightarrow$ Comp S

─────────────── **STOP AND PRACTICE** ───────────────

Identify what type of clause the fragment is. Then draw a tree diagram with it inserted in its place as a subordinate sentence. You may need to make some other structural changes:

27. I spent the summer picking fruit. Until I quit for school.
28. I had to pick pluots. Which are a hybrid of plums and apricots.
29. Maybe you don't know much about picking. That it's a very difficult job.
30. My parents are proud. That I am at college.

EXPLORING CHAPTER PERSPECTIVES

◆ *Discussion Questions*

Read "The Role of Language in Learning" by Corson (1999, pp. 85–90). Discuss the answer to these questions.

1. What are the five main points from this selection? Write them in your Language Notebook to share with your classmates.

2. Do you agree that "our ability to think depends on the many previous dialogues that we have taken part in?" What does that statement mean? What is an example of it?

3. What lexical and syntactic characteristics of this text identify it as Academic English?

THE ROLE OF LANGUAGE IN LEARNING

David Corson

Reprinted by permission of Lawrence Erlbaum Associates.

(Emphasis added)

(1) Curriculum theorists of a generation ago put together ideas that still shape the curriculum in every English-speaking country. Moffett's (1968) book *Teaching the Universe of Discourse* helped set the scene with the key idea that our ability to think depends on the many previous dialogues that we have taken part in. Research in a range of disciplines now confirms the accuracy of that key idea. It puts language and discourse at the very heart of education.

(2) The same ideas drew people's attention to the fact that schools make too little use of students' own language, especially their informal and expressive talk and writing, as a learning resource in the classroom. And . . . these ideas are just as applicable to the education of second-language learners of English as they are to students of English as a first language. Specifically, the following four points are supported widely in studies of the observed behaviors of students and teachers:

◆ Language develops mainly through its purposeful use.
◆ Learning usually involves talking, writing, representing, and moving.
◆ Learning usually occurs through talking, writing, representing, and moving.
◆ The use of discourse is basic to intellectual development.

(3) Here . . . discourse refers to the full range of meaning-filled events and sign systems that we encounter in life. But the words of a language are the most common systems of signs that people meet. Although many systems of signs, inside and outside education, have shared meanings, words provide most of the important symbols for forming and refining thought.

(4) Up to middle childhood, English-speaking students are rather similar in the words that they need to use and which they choose to learn. Later, things change. After 12 years, children begin to acquire the shared meanings of tens of thousands of new words, along with the other signs that they need to succeed at higher levels of formal education. *The foundation*

(*continued*)

for that academic learning is laid in children's early life experiences, especially in the contacts with the culture of literacy that are offered in quality early childhood education.

Language Development and the Early Childhood Years

(5) It is no surprise, then, that early language development is the secret to intellectual growth, including later language development and educational success itself. The most important foundation for any system of education is a strong and universally available system of early childhood education beginning at around 3 years of age. Yet for all their wealth and educational commitment, many English-speaking constituencies still lack this universal provision, and the educational outcomes are inevitably lower than they should be.

(6) We know that later attainment leaps when children have preschool education (Royal Commission on Learning in Ontario, 1995). In fact, the huge benefits for later education of early childhood education are among the most widely attested findings in educational research. In answer to the question "Does early childhood education do any good?", a broad range of longitudinal studies in Europe and the United States followed students' careers throughout their schooling. They found these lasting beneficial effects for school learners who had early childhood education at 3 and 4 years:

- ◆ Improved cognitive performance and achievement throughout education.
- ◆ Greater aspirations for education, motivation, and school commitment.
- ◆ Decreased delinquency, crime, and lower arrest rates.
- ◆ Decreased incidence of teenage pregnancy.
- ◆ Increased high-school graduation rates.
- ◆ Higher enrollments in postsecondary education.
- ◆ Lower rates of unemployment.

(7) The main factor in all this is the opportunity for using discourse that quality early childhood settings offer. We can tell what schools need to be doing at every level by looking at what good early childhood education already offers. What it offers is the widest possible exposure to experience-based language use.

(8) *Indeed, shared experiences provide the best basis for interaction with students at any age and from any culture.* Clearly the nature of these experiences will change across age groups and cultural settings. Thus the culture of the child has to be in the mind of the teacher. Clearly, too, the nature of the experiences that can be shared changes as children grow older. For example, teachers working dialogically with the very young like to know about past events in the children's lives, and they need to have shared some concrete experiences with the students for them to talk about together, and so expand their learning. Skilled teachers working dialogically with older students try to get inside the more abstract ideas in their students' minds that represent their developing theories about the world. Once they are informed in this way, teachers use this shared experience as a basis for interaction.

(9) Through their interactions with classmates and teachers, students are introduced to new meanings, and they get constant opportunities to use talk in making those meanings their own. Moreover, this is as true for students using a first or a second language. For young immigrant students, it is much better educationally to be engaged in discourse that uses their first language than to be sitting in silence listening to others use a language that is not yet their own. . . To meet the complex demands of present-day education, students need

frequent opportunities to interact in small-group discussions that focus on the exploration of new concepts. They need regular opportunities to work together around shared media, to shape new media creations, and to interpret the creations of others.

(10) Central to all this is the key role that language has in learning. *Indeed, a school language policy is really a school learning policy.*

A School "Language for Learning" Policy

(11) For my purposes in this chapter, language includes eight human activities that link directly with learning and with the growth of knowledge:

◆ Listening: attending to the oral language of others and giving meaning to it.
◆ Speaking: expressing meaning to others in oral language.
◆ Reading: attending to the written language of others and giving meaning to it.
◆ Writing: expressing meaning to others in written language.
◆ Moving: using facial expression, gesturing, and movement to express meaning.
◆ Watching: attending and giving meaning to the movements of others.
◆ Representing: Using visual effects to express meaning to others.
◆ Viewing: attending and giving meaning to visual effects created by others.

(12) This list includes four language activities that everyone sees as part of the core language curriculum. But the last four activities have really come into their own only in recent decades. In many young people's lives, and in most present-day jobs, these last four now assume an importance that gives them a core place in curriculum planning. In the contemporary world, these basic competencies of *media literacy* increasingly support human thought itself.

(13) As an instrument for thought and social interaction, language helps us in all the many areas that education aims to develop. Just an introductory list of these areas shows the help that language offers:

◆ It helps us direct attention to items or events.
◆ It helps us maintain that attention.
◆ It helps us in classifying things in our experience.
◆ It helps us relate these things to one another.
◆ It helps us impose order upon the world.
◆ It helps us express our feelings about that world.
◆ It helps us recall events by offering a framework for our memories.
◆ It helps us put old information together in new ways.
◆ It helps us make inferences and speculate about conclusions.
◆ It helps us share and negotiate our meanings.

(14) All these activities are basic to learning in a school curriculum, and it is not easy to be successfull anywhere in the social world without them. *Taken together, they suggest why language stands at the center of the many interdependent cognitive, affective, and social factors that shape learning.*

(15) Indeed, a number of key theorists and researchers have extended our insights into issues just like these. The work of Vygotsky, Bruner, and Bakhtin often comes to mind whenever education intersects with research in the different language disciplines. And the complementary ideas of these noted figures have become influential in education theory and practice (Measures, Quell, and Wells, 1997). But rather than looking directly at their ideas, I prefer to use the conclusions of educators whose work is a little closer to today's classrooms.

(continued)

(16) Barnes, Britton, and Torbe (1986) are well-known figures in language curriculum development, and their ideas on teaching that curriculum are much influenced by the earlier figures. Not surprisingly, they are in broad agreement about the links between language, learning, and knowledge. First, Torbe describes his stance on knowledge and learning as somewhat contrary to the orthodox view, which holds that we can judge successful knowledge acquisition has taken place when the students have "got it right." He believes that those who see learning like that find it difficult to accept another very different model: *a model of teaching and learning that values risk-taking, welcomes conjecture, and sees error-making as inevitable and necessary.* In brief, he concludes that what all learners have to do is "discover for themselves."

(17) Barnes's work centers directly on talk as used by teachers and students in schools. From his wide-ranging studies, Barnes concludes that certain views on what knowledge is seem to be linked with matching views on the role of language in learning. In particular he contrasts a transmission view of knowledge with an interpretation view. The first is concerned with the acquisition of information, and the second with cognitive and personal development. Barnes sees the assumptions behind most approaches to teaching falling somewhere on a continuum between these two views. The transmission view is concerned mainly with the students' performance, and the interpretation view with their struggle to understand. *Barnes concludes that talk helps learning in any activity that goes beyond the rote demands of transmission.* It helps learning whenever there is a need for understanding, especially an understanding of processes. Because of the evolving nature of any interpersonal context in which speakers contribute, respond, and change their expressed thoughts and attitudes, meaning is continually created and re-created over stretches of discourse. This is the dialogic way of coming to know ourselves and others, and of coming to understand the world. Its central place in education has been clear since the days of Socrates, yet most classrooms still operate in ways that block its widespread use.

(18) Finally, Britton is interested in expressive writing and in the use of interactive activities for developing quality in written work. He believes that part of the very nature of human learning is that it proceeds by anticipation: We tackle a problem forearmed with alternative possible solutions. More than this, learners bring whatever they already know with them and they interpret it in the light of new evidence. *He suggests that it is through language that understanding develops in technical fields, because language brings our commonsense concepts to a point of engagement with the technical concept.* For Britton, when expressive talk is used as a means of education, students are able to bring their commonsense views into the learning context. They are asked to present them in language ready to be set alongside other impersonal and objective public statements.

(19) Taken together, ideas like these prompted fundamental changes to classroom practices. These changes have been proceeding in English-speaking countries since at least the mid-1970s, and almost everywhere teachers have gradually been adjusting their approaches. Nevertheless, the spread of these changes has been patchy, not least because those responsible for the education of teachers have not always been proactive in urging reforms. *This means that teachers often vary greatly in their readiness to acknowledge the central role of language in learning, even teachers with similar experience working in the same school setting. So just changing some of these teacher attitudes, or reconciling them with one another, is often the first challenge for a language policy to address.*

◆ *Cooperative Exercise: The Role of Language in Learning*

Individual Work

Take two numbered paragraphs from the Corson selection and underline all the embedded sentences. Identify what type of subordinate sentence they are. Are there any you cannot identify?

A. **Pair Work.** Go over your answers to see if you agree. For any that you disagree on, discuss until you reach a resolution

B. **Class Work.** Discuss any controversies.

◆ *Writing Assignment*

Write a short, well-organized essay in Academic English in your Language Notebook in response to one or both of these prompts.

1. Do you agree with Corson's contention that universal preschool would benefit learning? Why or why not? What is keeping your state from implementing universal preschool?

2. Do you agree that teachers (science, history, math, and so on) have been slow to recognize the central role of language in learning? Why or why not?

Introspection

Proofread your essays and make any necessary corrections. In your essay(s), underline the embedded sentences you can find and identify them. If you have few embedded sentences, can you expand or combine your sentences to contain more?

TEACHING TO LEARN

Sentence Fragments

With a partner, take turns identifying the sentence fragments in the example of Standard Written English on the next page, "Language Prejudice." Say what type of phrase or subordinate clause the fragment is and suggest an editorial change to eliminate the fragment unless it seems appropriate to the text. What other stylistic changes would you make?

LEARNING TO TEACH

Modeling

Description: For learners to become autonomous in proofreading and editing, grammar and usage-related activities must transition from teacher centered to student centered. The sequence is first **modeling**, then **guided practice**, and finally **free application** by the learner. This section discusses a modeling technique.

The instructor projects a specially written example or a learner's paper (with permission of the author and removing the name) so that all learners can see it. After focusing on the good points of the paper, proceed to discuss how the paper could be more effective. Instructors verbalize the critical thinking that goes into proofreading and editing. All the while learners note usage problems, solutions, and suggestions for improvement in their Language Notebooks so that they can use the notes when proof-reading and editing their own writing. As they see and participate in the process more than once, they internalize it.

Goals

Subject area goals: Writing improvement

English language awareness goals: Review of Standard Written English and Academic English usage, style, organization, and other writing conventions in the context of authentic student-produced writing

Descriptive grammar goals: Metalanguage and explanation focused on learners' needs

Procedural goals: Proofreading and editing applications

Assessment: Teachers may give students anonymous surveys to fill out about the usefulness of the modeling technique, or they may analyze the improvement in learner writing.

Methodology: Make a overhead transparency of one of your essays from this book or another class. Give your transparency to your partner, who proofreads it and edits it, marking suggested changes on it. Give it to your instructor, who will choose several papers to use in the modeling procedure, commenting on the original paper and the corrections that were made by the partner.

Language Prejudice

I take issue with Brookman's guest column entitled "Hello? Is anyone out there speaking proper English?" Brookman betrays some inaccuracies in her understanding of English spelling and grammar. Not to mention her condescending tone.

First off spelling. Our spelling system is a conservative system, which was frozen in time long ago. And which doesn't match our present day pronunciation well. Many people, not just people who work in discount stores and grocery stores, spell according to the sound of the word.

Judgmental Attitudes

Are bad spellers dimwitted Philistines? Or just people who have failed to master an unpredictable system that relies heavily on visual memory? Or people who don't have spell-checkers handy?

Next, words. Don't be judgmental about young people, including store employees, who don't have extensive vocabularies and may not recognize a word like *gourmet*. Vocabulary learning is developmental. The older the person, the larger the lexicon.

Saying *rode* instead of *ridden* reflects people's regional background or socioeconomic origin. Not their intellectual abilities. Saying *weaved* instead of *woven* is following a tradition in English to make irregular verbs regular over time. Like *dreamed* versus *dreamt* or *hanged* versus *hung*.

Then those pesky place names. Place names are notoriously difficult to pronounce. It's a cheap shot to criticize the way someone pronounces a place unknown to them. Examples from my area: Butte des Morts, Fond du Lac, Oconomowoc, Waukesha.

Linguistic Realities

Language is social. Its commonalities bind us together. Language is also individual. Because we don't speak the same way. Some people find this inevitable language variation interesting. Not threatening or repugnant.

Language changes over time. Otherwise we would all speak as the characters in Chaucer do. Some people think that language change is degenerative. Other think that change is neutral. Not frightening, not stupid.

Also, to think that spelling errors and nonstandard grammar are problems that have emerged in the past 40 years is to deny that there's been a thriving and lucrative spelling and grammar book publishing industry for centuries. This is not a recent "dumbing down" problem.

The fact is that mainly upper and middle class people already speak a native dialect similar to Standard English. Lucky for them that our school standard approximates their native speech, making learning easier for them.

On the other hand, the dialects of other populations tend to diverge from Standard English. Such as rural people, second-generation immigrant groups, the urban working or lower socioeconomic classes and minorities.

Those who do not grow up speaking standard English in their homes often have a harder time when they get to school. Because they are also grappling with language differences. It especially hinders learners if their teachers consider them stupid or ignorant because of their speech.

Finally, it is absurd to connect spelling errors and nonstandard grammar to tasteless television, Disney movies, office workers improperly trained in technology. And then to a "slovenly misuse of their brain (leading) to cruelty and stupidity of all sorts: addiction, racism, child abuse, street crime, and demagoguery."

Have you ever misspelled a word? Have you ever committed a grammar mistake? Let he who is without sin cast the first stone. Or him.

15

Compounds and Nonfinite Phrases

This chapter deals with other ways writers add complexity and variety to sentences. One way makes use of conjunctions (like *and* and *or*) to concatenate two or more words, phrases, or sentences within one sentence. A second way is to add absolute expressions (underlined in the following) to a main sentence. Absolute expressions involve a nonfinite verbal, but sometimes there is no verb at all:

> *<u>Driving to work</u>, I saw the billboard.*
> *<u>My car a mess</u>, I turned in at the carwash.*

Finally, a third method modifies constituents in the sentence with nonfinite verb phrases.

COMPOUND CONSTITUENTS

Almost any phrasal or lexical constituent of a sentence may conjoin with another of the same type using **coordinating conjunctions:** *and, or,* and *but.* For example; we join two or more nouns, verbs, adjectives, adverbs, prepositions, particles, and even some determiners:

> *<u>Fred and Ginger</u> danced all night.*
> *They <u>swirled and hopped</u> all over the dance floor.*
> *Ginger felt <u>happy, excited, and energetic</u>.*
> *Fred swung Ginger <u>quickly but carefully</u> around.*
> *He swung her <u>up and out</u>.*
> *They danced <u>in and out</u> of the ballroom.*
> *Fred whirled Ginger around <u>two or three</u> times.*

Coordinating conjunctions also join phrases and clauses:

> *<u>The thin man and the chubby woman</u> are light on their feet.*
> *Ginger <u>took a few steps away and turned around</u>.*

> ## A TEACHING MOMENT
>
> ### Subject–Verb Agreement
>
> If the conjoined constituents function as the subjects of the sentence, there can be some difficulties with subject–verb agreement. For example, two singular subjects conjoined by *and* have a plural verb, but two singular subjects conjoined by *or* have a singular verb because the subject is either one or the other but not both. This makes sense logically, but it is not always characteristic of Standard Spoken English (SSE), so learners may need assistance with conjoined subjects and correct verb agreement in Standard Written English (SWE) and Academic English (AE):
>
> My uncle and aunt are going to travel to Ohio.
> *Either my uncle or my aunt are going to travel to Ohio.
> Either my uncle or my aunt is going to travel to Ohio.

Fred felt <u>very happy and very lucky</u>.
Fred swung Ginger in a circle <u>very quickly but carefully</u>.
They danced <u>in the ballroom or on the terrace</u>.
The people <u>that danced</u> and <u>that felt happy</u> were in love.
<u>While they were dancing</u> and <u>when we saw them</u>, they were ecstatic.

When *and, but,* or *or* conjoin two or more main sentences together, the resulting sentence is **compound:**

<u>I forgot my lunch money</u> and <u>you forgot yours too</u>.
<u>I usually remember to bring my money</u> but <u>you often forget to bring yours</u>.
<u>You need to remember your money tomorrow</u> or <u>you will be in trouble</u>.
<u>I need to bring my lunch money</u> and <u>you need to bring your own</u>, or <u>we won't be able to go on the field trip</u>.

In the case of coordinated words, phrases, or sentences, the coordinating conjunction appears only at the beginning of the last conjunct. Generally, the conjoined constituents have no comma between them if there are only two. If there are more than two, there is an optional comma before the conjunction:

I bought apples, eggs, a loaf of bread, and a bag of peanuts.

Conjunction by Phrase Structure Rule

We can formalize this information by stating a very general phrase structure rule with a **supervariable X,** a variable which stands for all syntactic variables: lexical variables, (N, V, Part, Prep, and Det), phrasal variables (NP, VP, AdjP, AdvP, and PP), and the clause

---

A TEACHING MOMENT

Conjoined Sentences

I forgot my lunch money and you forgot yours too.
Compound sentences with two identical or nearly identical conjuncts joined with *and* have alternatives that can be difficult for English learners because they use the helping verb *do* or an auxiliary plus *too/also* or *so/neither/either*:
I *forgot my lunch money and* you did too.
Inverted: I *forgot my lunch money and* so did you.
I *couldn't remember it and* you couldn't either.
Inverted: I *couldn't remember and* neither could you.

---

and sentence variables (S' and S). The rule states that any part of speech can occur more than once and that the last constituent is preceded by the conjunction (conj).

X → X^ conj X,
where ^ means that the category could appear more than once

This rule abbreviates these trees and, of course, more:

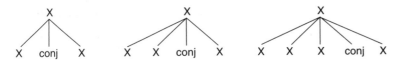

Substituting syntactic variables into the trees yields these trees and more:

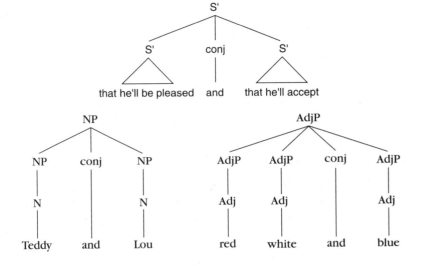

FINAL PHRASE STRUCTURE RULES

1. S →   NP   Aux   VP

2. NP → $\left\{ \begin{array}{l} \text{(Det) (AdjP) (N)   N   (S')} \\ \text{Pronoun} \\ \qquad \text{S'} \end{array} \right\}$

3. Aux →   tns (M) (have-perf) (be-prog) (be-pass)

4. VP → $\left\{ \begin{array}{l} \text{V   (Nonfinite)   (NP)   (PP)   (AdvP)*} \\ \text{V   AdjP   (PP)   (AdvP)*} \end{array} \right\}$

5. PP →   P   NP

6. AdjP → (Adv)   Adj   (S')   (Adv)

7. AdvP → $\left\{ \begin{array}{l} \text{(Adv)   Adv   (Adv)} \\ \text{S'} \end{array} \right\}$

8. tns → $\left\{ \begin{array}{l} \text{Past} \\ \text{Pres} \end{array} \right\}$

9. X → X^ conj X,

   where ^ means that X could appear more than once

10. S' → Comp S

Note: Adverb phrases also occur elsewhere.

───────────────── STOP AND PRACTICE ─────────────────

Using the final phrase structure rules, draw trees for the following conjoined constituents. These are not complete sentences, only phrases:

1. Santa and his merry elves
2. out of sight and out of mind
3. study in the library, go to a movie, or eat in a restaurant
4. whether you tell me the answer or you write it on the paper
5. intelligent and well-prepared enough
6. extremely kindly and cordially indeed

───────────────── STOP AND PRACTICE ─────────────────

Using the final phrase structure rules, draw trees for the following whole sentences:

7. We prefer to choose from two or three different cakes.
8. We like to eat our cakes, but we want to have them too.
9. You might call me on my cell phone and tell me your answer.
10. The balloon flew into the air and toward the horizon.
11. You should be concerned, worried, and very alarmed about people's misspellings.
12. That teachers work hard and that they earn psychic income are two true statements.

> ## A TEACHING MOMENT
>
> ### Parallel Structure
>
> Generally, only identical types of constituents can be conjoined, but sometimes, especially in speaking, people conjoin elements that they perceive to have the same function in the sentence. For example, if two constituents are descriptive, people may feel that they can be conjoined even if they are different types of phrases:
>
> > The temperature was _below zero_ and _very frigid_.
> > He likes _to eat_ and _finding new restaurants to eat in_.
> > They don't know _the procedure_ or _how to find out what it is_.
>
> Good writers avoid mismatched conjoined expressions and revise them so that they are **parallel:**
>
> > The temperature was [_subzero_ and _frigid_.]_{Adjective Phrases}
> > He likes [eating and _finding new restaurants to eat in_.]_{Gerunds}
> > He likes [to eat and _to find new restaurants to eat in_.]_{Infinitive Phrases}
> > They don't know [_how to do it_ or _how to find out how to do it_.]_{Noun Clauses}

Conjunction Through Punctuation

It is not always necessary to use conjunctions to join sentences. Instead, closely related sentences can be joined by punctuation, most commonly a semicolon but sometimes a colon. Both the semicolon and the colon are common in news reports and AE, but they are rare in informal writing styles:

> But the presence of English in Indian country did not lead to an automatic acceptance of English fluency on the part of the tribes; ancestral languages continued to be the codes-of-choice for many tribes until the middle of the twentieth century: even today, students from Navajo, Mississippi Choctaw, Crow, some of the pueblos, and other tribes enter kindergarten or grade school for the first time with only nominal fluency in English. (Leap, 1993, p. 147)

When two sentences are conjoined with a semicolon, they often have a transition word in the second sentence, as in the first example in the following. Transition words used this way are sentential adverbs, and they can also appear after a period, as in the stylistic alternative in the second example:

> *The writers on the main panel described the steps they had to go through in order to write productively each day; in addition, they spoke about their daily joys and perennial frustrations.*
>
> *The writers on the main panel described the steps they had to go through in order to write productively each day. In addition, they spoke about their daily joys and perennial frustrations.*

A TEACHING MOMENT

Comma Splice

Spoken English, of course, has no punctuation; it is something to be concerned about only in writing, so it can cause significant problems. In informal writing, people sometimes conjoin two sentences with a comma instead of a semicolon. This error is called a **comma splice** because two sentences that can stand alone are spliced together with a comma. In formal writing style, instead of using a comma, writers should use the semicolon or a conjunction, or separate the two sentences using a period and a capital letter. And, as a writing teacher told me once, it is best to use only one semicolon per page or less.

In Spanish writing, many writers prefer a style with long and complicated sentences rather than the shorter and less complex sentences usually preferred in English (but see Leap, 1993). Also, there is a tendency toward conjoining sentences with a comma. Writers who are proficient in Spanish may transfer this punctuation to English, and comma splices may be common.

A TEACHING MOMENT

Parallel Structure

With correlative expressions, SWE and AE require parallel structure:

> I *dislike both the color and how it jumps out at you.*
> Preferred: I *dislike both the color and its vibrancy.*

Correlative Conjunctions

Two words that join identical constituents in a parallel structure are correlative conjunctions: *both . . . and, not only . . . but (also), either . . . or*, and *neither . . . nor.*

> *We both can and will succeed where others have failed.*
>
> *Not only did he win the game, but he gave the others a sound thumping. [Note the inversion in the first conjunct.]*
>
> *The flowers will either die from lack of water or naturalize.*
>
> *Neither fame nor fortune were his for the asking.*

ABSOLUTE EXPRESSIONS ▬▬▬▬▬

MacArthur (1992) defines an **absolute expression** as "a term indicating that a word, phrase, or clause stands apart from the usual relations with other elements in a sentence" (p. 6). Most examples involve nonfinite verbals, but some do not, and they can occur at the beginning or at the end of sentences. Only a few absolute expressions are

A TEACHING MOMENT	**Dangling Modifiers**

Absolute expressions without overt subjects must match their main sentence in subject, or else they will "dangle":

Obsessed with computer games, their parents forced them to set time limits on their playing.
Realizing that conservation was a must, the lights were turned off.
A total mess after the storm, I turned in at the car wash.
With dinner prepared, the candles were lit on the table.

common in SSE, such as *weather permitting* or *present company excluded*. This description is extremely broad and therefore somewhat unhelpful to the student of grammar, so it may be best to define absolute constructions by example:

PRESENT PARTICIPLE

With subject:	*The war having begun, all citizens were asked to conserve energy.*
With *with*:	*The table was beautiful, with candles shining on dark wood.*
Without subject:	*They turned off their lights, realizing that conservation was a necessity.*
Without verb:	*His car (being) a total wreck, he decided to use mass transit.*

PAST PARTICIPLE

With subject:	*The student, his floppy disk tightly clutched in his hand, appeared at my office door.*
Without subject:	*Obsessed with computer games, Lalo became interested in programming.*

INFINITIVE

With subject:	*Noah freed the animals from the ark, each one to go forth and multiply.*
Without subject:	*To be consistent, each section of the report needs to have a title.*

NO VERBAL	*The girls sat studying together, their hair in curlers.*

INFINITIVE PHRASES

We have already seen a couple of inventive uses of infinitive phrases in subordinate structures:

Predicate adjective complement	*He is proud to be a teacher.*
Noun clause-embedded questions	*I don't know how to do it.*
Adjective clauses	*Jan found a box in which to put her cookies.*

Infinitive phrases also turn up in other locations serving other functions in a sentence. Infinitives refer to situations or complex concepts, or they can describe or modify:

INFINITIVE PHRASE AS REFERENTIAL NOUN PHRASE

With subject: *For Jenny to go to college is my fondest wish.*

Without subject: *To seek prosperity was the goal of many immigrants.*

Extraposed, with dummy subject *it*:   *It is my fondest wish for Jenny to go to college.*

                                          It was the goal of many immigrants to seek prosperity.

DESCRIPTIVE INFINITIVE PHRASES

Adjectival function: Her desire <u>to meet the actor</u> led to her downfall.
                          There was no one <u>to stop the tragedy from happening</u>.

Adverbial function: They went to school <u>to learn</u>.
                          She spoke to him *to* <u>convince him to go</u>.

LOOKING FORWARD AND BACKWARD

Section 3 has presented phrase structure rules, transformations and derivations, and morphological rules as grammatical mechanisms for understanding the dynamic but consistent structure of a variety of English phrase and sentence types. The rules are discovery procedures to help students of grammar intuit the structure of sentences they see in texts everywhere because their metalinguistic awareness is now well honed. From the simple declarative sentence to the compound complex sentence, the same system is responsible.

However, this book does not cover everything; in fact, you may not have learned everything presented here. Nevertheless, whatever you have learned, you are now in a good position to start teaching about language using the language awareness curriculum with subject area goals, language awareness goals, descriptive grammar goals, and procedural proofreading and editing skills. The more you teach, the more you learn. The more you learn, the more you see and hear in the language around you. Be an informed consumer—and lover—of language.

EXPLORING CHAPTER PERSPECTIVES

◆ *Discussion Questions*

Reread the Corson reading in Chapter 14.

1. What does Corson mean when he says that "shared experiences provide the best basis for interaction with students at any age and from any culture"?

2. Corson lists eight activities at the interface between language, learning, and knowledge. What does each of these mean? Can you think of any more activities that stand at the interface?

◆ *Cooperative Exercise: The Role of Language in Learning*

A. **Individual Work**

In the Corson text, underline all instances of coordinating conjunctions. Identify what constituents are conjoined and their part of speech.

B. **Pair Work**

a. Compare your answers with a partner.

b. Identify all prepositional phrases.

c. With your partner, find any infinitives and identify what type of use it is.

d. Find any instances of absolute expressions and identify what type each is.

◆ *Writing Assignment*

Write a short essay in your Language Notebook in response to one or both of these prompts:

1. What relationship is there between Corson's ideas of universal preschool to early and late development of metalinguistic awareness?

2. Which of Corson's ideas are most relevant to teachers as they think about implicit and explicit grammar learning and instruction in their classrooms?

Introspection

Proofread your essays and make any necessary corrections. Take a 50-word selection of your own essay. Identify all parts of speech, all phrases, all main and subordinate sentences, and any other syntactic features you have used. How complex is your prose? How does it compare to Corson's use of AE?

TEACHING TO LEARN

Dangling Expressions

In "dangling" expressions, the subject of the modifier does not match the subject of the main sentence. With your partner, go over these sentences, taking turns identifying if the sentence has a dangling expression or not. If it does, explain it to your partner and suggest an SWE alternative that does not dangle. You can either add a subject to the modifier or rephrase the main sentence (e.g., change active to passive):

1. As a child, he learned to speak four languages natively.

2. The train overcrowded, we had to stand up during the trip.

3. Found guilty of murder, the judge sentenced the man to years in prison.

4. When finished cooking, you need to take the roast out of the oven.

5. Warned of the danger, the sharks frightened the swimmers.

6. Speeding down the street at 80 miles an hour, the car careened out of control.

7. To understand the problem, both factors need to be considered.

8. As a boy, his parents encouraged him to play all sports.

9. Always a wonderful host, Mark welcomed his guests at the door.

10. While cooking the potatoes, the water should never evaporate completely.

LEARNING TO TEACH

Editing Workshop

Description: For learners to become autonomous in proofreading and editing, grammar and usage-related activities must transition from teacher-centered to student-centered. The sequence is modeling, guided practice, and free application by the learner. This section discusses techniques to support guided practice and free application for peer and self-proofreading or editing. (Two techniques supporting guided practice and free application that we have already discussed are the grammar log and modeling.)

Proofreading and editing workshops usually take place in a writing lab or in a classroom. In any case, teachers provide learners with interaction, monitoring, and feedback. They also provide editing checklists or allow learners to construct their own editing checklists based on their notes from modeled proofreading and editing activities or drawn from their grammar logs. In addition, there should be ample resources in the form of dictionaries and other language reference books, which learners should know how to use.

Goals

Subject area goal: Writing improvement

English language awareness goals: AE/SWE usage and style

Descriptive grammar goals: Variable, generated by learner needs and teacher/student interaction

Procedural goals: Proofreading and editing, that is, finding needed changes, recalling or researching corrections, and making corrections

Assessment: Teachers assess whether learners improve in their proofreading, editing, and writing. They can also conduct student surveys.

Methodology: Based on your grammar log and feedback from instructor, make up your own personal grammar checklist for you to use to proofread and edit any paper before handing it in. Do you have a problem with dangling constructions, parallel structures, or comma splices? What other usage problems do you have?

CULMINATING GRAMMAR PROJECT

1. Answer these questions about the following quote from Recinto:

"For example, to understand the goals of the Bilingual Education Act of 1968, one needs to understand why that legislation was passed when it was passed, whose interests were being served, what the general policy framework was with regard to minority languages and speakers of those languages, what sort of support was or wasn't provided to implement the legislation, what the prevailing social attitudes were at the time regarding bilingual education, and so on."

    a. Identify the part of speech of each word and multiword lexical unit. Do not guess. Use diagnostics. Be as specific as you can (e.g., instead of writing "pronoun," write "first-person singular personal pronoun").

    b. Identify each noun phrase, verb phrase, adjective phrase, adverb phrase, prepositional phrase, and infinitive phrase.

    c. Identify what tense, aspect, voice, and modal each auxiliary and verb phrase has.

    d. Identify all the embedded sentences and label what type they are.

    e. Explain the parallel structure in this sentence.

2. Find your own complex sentence from AE from a textbook of your own (not this one) and prepare the same cooperative activities and an answer key. Gear your activities to a high school advanced placement or honors English class.

Other Suggested Final Projects

1. Return to the Hairston survey in Chapter 8 and redo it. Do you understand more of the errors and feel more confident about the corrections?

2. Look up the language arts standards in your state or region again. Do you know all the descriptive grammar metalanguage used and the usage problems listed?

3. Select a 25-word text from a work of fiction or poetry. Identify all the parts of speech, all the phrases, and all the sentences, including subordinate sentences. What interesting challenges do you find? Is the text different syntactically from an academic prose text?

4. Refer to the guidelines in Chapter 4 and write a lesson plan with a descriptive grammar goal and a procedural goal. Identify your grade level and class composition. Hand in both a sequence of activities and a matrix.

5. Refer to the guidelines in Chapter 4 and write a lesson plan with a language awareness goal that ties into a subject area goal from literature. For example, if your subject area goal is to read *Huckleberry Finn*, the language awareness goal might be an examination of the dialects used by different characters and how that contributes to our image of the character. Hand in both a sequence of activities and a matrix.

6. Refer to the guidelines in Chapter 4 and write a lesson plan that includes all four types of goals: subject area goals, language awareness goals, descriptive grammar goals, and procedural goals. Hand in both a sequence of activities and a matrix.

Bibliography

Aitchison, J. (1987). *Words in the mind: An introduction to the mental lexicon.* Oxford, UK: Basil Blackwell.

Allen, J. (1995). *It's never too late: Leading adolescents to lifelong literacy.* Portsmouth, NH: Heinemann.

Andersson, L., & Trudgill, P. (1990). *Bad language.* Cambridge, MA: Blackwell.

Andrews, L. (1993). *Language exploration and awareness: A resource book for teachers.* New York: Longman.

Barber, C. (1994). *The English language: A historical introduction.* Cambridge, UK: Cambridge University Press.

Barnitz, J. (1997). Emerging awareness of linguistic diversity for literacy instruction. *Reading Teacher, 51*(3), 264–266.

Barnitz, J. (1998). Linguistic perspectives in literacy education. *Reading Teacher, 51*(7), 608–611.

Barnitz, J., Gipe, J., & Richards, J. (1999). Linguistic benefits of literature for children's language performance in teacher education contexts. *Reading Teacher, 52*(5), 528–531.

Bertrand, N., & Stice, C. (2002). *Good teaching: An integrated approach to language, literacy, and learning.* Portsmouth, NH: Heinemann.

Biber, D. (1988). *Variation across speech and writing.* Cambridge, UK: Cambridge University Press.

Biber, D., Conrad, S., & Reppen, R. (1998). *Corpus Linugistics: Investigating language structure and use.* Cambridge, UK: Cambridge University Press.

Biber, D., Johansson, S., Leech, G., Conrad, S., & Finegan, E. (1999). *Longman grammar of spoken and written English.* London: Pearson Education.

Blackmore, A., Pratt, C., & Dewsbury, A. (1995). The use of props in a syntactic awareness task. *Journal of Child Language, 22*(2), 405–421.

Bowey, J. (1986). Syntactic awareness in relation to reading skill and ongoing reading comprehension monitoring. *Journal of Experimental Child Psychology, 41*(2), 282–299.

Broadview Press Editorial Board. (1988). *Common errors in English.* Lewiston, NY: Broadview Press.

Burt, M., & Kiparsky, C. (1972). *The Gooficon: A repair manual for English.* Rowley, MA: Newbury House.

Burt, M., & Kiparsky, C. (1974). Global and local mistakes. In J. Schumann & N. Stenson (Eds.), *New frontiers in second language teaching* (pp. 71–80). Rowley, MA: Newbury House.

CAHSEE. (2002). California Department of Education, California High School Exit Exam Standards and Assessment Division. Available: http://cahsee.cde.ca.gov. (2002, August).

California Department of Education. (1998). English-language arts content standards for California public schools, kindergarten through grade twelve (adopted by the California State Board of Education, December 1997). Sacramento.

California Department of Education Reporting. (2002). Spring CAHSEE results, press packet. Available http://cahsee.cde.ca.gov

Carson, R. (1956). *A Sense of Wonder.* New York: Harper and Row.

CBEST. (2003). California Commission on Teacher Credentialing and the National Evaluation Service. California Basic Educational Skills Test. Available: http://www.cbest.nesinc.com/CA_sampleques_teestdesc.htm

Chomsky, N. (1965). *Aspects of the theory of the syntax.* Cambridge, MA: MIT Press.

Clark, E. (2003). *First language acquisition.* Cambridge, UK: Cambridge University Press.

Connors, R. J., & Lunsford, A. A. (1988). Frequency of formal errors in current college writing or Ma and

Pa Kettle do research. *College Composition and Communication* 39, 395–409.

Corson, D. (1999). *Language policy in schools: A resource for teachers and administrators.* Mahwah, NJ: Lawrence Erlbaum Associates.

Cowan, N. (1995). *Attention and memory: An integrated framework.* Oxford, UK: Oxford University Press.

Croft, W. (1991). *Syntactic categories and grammatical relations.* Chicago: University of Chicago Press.

Cumming, S., & Tsuyoshi O. (1997). Discourse and grammar. In T. A. Van Dijk (Ed.), *Discourse as structure and process* (pp. 112–137). London: Sage.

Echevarría, J., & Graves, A. (1998). *Sheltened Content Instruction: Teaching English language learners with diverse abilities.* Boston, MA: Allyn & Bacon.

Egan, M. (1999, May). Reflections on effective use of graphic organizers. *Journal of Adolescent and Adult Literacy, 42*(8), 641–645.

Ellis, R. (1994). *The study of second language acquisition.* Oxford, UK: Oxford University Press.

Ellis, R. (2002). The place of grammar instruction in the second/foreign language curriculum. In E. Hinkel & S. Fotos (Eds.), *New perspectives on grammar teaching in second language classrooms* (pp. 17–34). Mahwah, NJ: Lawrence Erlbaum Associates.

EPT Educational Testing Service. (2003). http://www.ets.org/csu/epttest.html

Frank, M. (1993). *Modern English: A practical reference guide.* Englewood Cliffs, NJ: Regents Prentice Hall.

Gaux, C., & Gombert, J. (1999). Implicit and explicit syntactic knowledge and reading in pre-adolescents. *British Journal of Developmental Psychology, 17*(2), 169–188.

Gombert, J. (1992). *Metalinguistic development.* Chicago: University of Chicago Press.

Graduate Writing Assessment Requirement. (2003). http://www.sjsu.edu/depts/Testing/wstbull.html

Greenbaum, S., & Quirk, R. (1990). *A student's grammar of the English language.* Harlow, UK: Longman.

Hairston, M. (1981). Not all errors are created equal: Nonacademic readers in the professions respond to lapses in usage. *College English, 4,* 794–806.

Harklau, L., Siegal, M., & Losey, K. (1999). Linguistically diverse students and college writing: What is equitable and appropriate? In L. Harklau, K. Losey, & M. Siegal (Eds.), *Generation 1.5 meets college composition* (pp. 1–16). Mahwah, NJ: Lawrence Erlbaum Associates.

Harris, M. (1992). *Language experience and early language development: From input to uptake.* Mahwah, NJ: Lawrence Erlbaum Associates.

Heath, S. (1986). What no bedtime story means: Narrative skills at home and school. In B. Schieffelin & E. Ochs (Eds.), *Language socialization across cultures* (pp. 97–126). Cambridge, UK: Cambridge University Press.

Heine, B. (1993). *Auxiliaries: Cognitive forces and grammaticalization.* New York: Oxford University Press.

Hinkel, E., & Fotos, S. (2002). From Theory to Practice: A Teacher's View. In E. Hinkel and S. Fotos, *New perspectives on grammar teaching in second language classrooms* (pp. 1–12). Mahwah, NJ: Lawrence Erlbaum Associates.

Hopper, P., & Thompson, S. (1984). The discourse basis for lexical categories in universal grammar. *Language, 60,* 703–752.

Hopper, P., & Thompson, S. (1985). The iconicity of the universal categories "noun" and "verb." In J. Haiman (Ed.), *Iconicity in syntax* (pp. 151–186). Amsterdam: John Benjamins.

Jacobs, G., Power, M., & Inn, L. (2002). *The teacher's sourcebook for cooperative learning: Practical techniques, basic principles, and frequently asked questions.* Thousand Oaks, CA: Corwin Press.

Johnson, D., & Johnson, R. (1999). *What makes cooperative learning work.* Cooperative Learning, JALT Applied Materials, Tokyo, Japan: JALT Publications.

Krashen, S. (2003). *Explorations in language acquisition and use.* Portsmouth, NH: Heinemann.

Lakoff, G. (1987). *Women, fire and dangerous things: What categories reveal about the mind.* Chicago: University of Chicago Press.

Langacker, R. (1987). Nouns and verbs. *Language, 63,* 53–94.

Langacker, R. (1991). *Foundations of cognitive grammar: Vol. 2. Descriptive application.* Stanford, CA: Stanford University Press.

Larson-Freeman, D. (1986). *Techniques and principles in language teaching.* New York: Oxford University Press.

Leap, W. (1993). *American Indian English*. Salt Lake City: University of Utah Press.

Lewis, M. (1998). *Implementing the lexical approach*. Hove, UK: Language Teaching Publications.

Massachusetts Curriculum Frameworks. (2003). Massachusetts Department of Education. Available: http://www.doe.mass.edu/frameworks/

Massachusetts Department of Education. (2002, July). Massachusetts Comprehensive Assessment System (release of spring 2002 test items). Available: http://www. doe.mass.edu/mcas

McArthur, T. (1992). (ed.) *The Oxford Companion to the English Language*. Oxford, UK: Oxford University Press.

McQuade, F. (1980). Examining a Grammar Course: The rationale and the result. *English Journal* 69.7 (Oct.) 26–30.

Millward, C. (1996). *A biography of the English language*. Fort Worth, TX: Harcourt Brace Jovanovich.

Nation, K., & Snowling, M. (2000). Factors influencing syntactic awareness skills in normal readers and poor comprehenders. *Applied Psycholinguistics, 21*(2), 229–241.

Newmeyer, F. (1998). *Language form and language function*. Cambridge, MA: MIT Press.

Noguchi, R. (1991). *Grammar and the teaching of writing: Limits and possibilities*. Urbana, IL: National Council of Teachers of English.

North Carolina High School Exit Exam student handbook. North Carolina State Board of Education. (2002, February). Available: http://www.ncpublic schools. org

Ochs, E. (1988). *Culture and language development: Language acquisition and language socialization in a Samoan village*. Cambridge, UK: Cambridge University Press.

Ochs, E., Schegloff, E., & Thompson, S. (1996). *Interaction and grammar*. Cambridge, UK: Cambridge University Press.

Pennycook, A., Phillipson, R., & Wiley, T. (1998). *Panel discussion on the ideological implications of the spread of English*. Sociopolitical Concerns Academic Session, International Teachers of English to Speakers of Other Languages (TESOL) Conference, Seattle, WA, March 18.

Phillipson, R. (1992). *Linguistic Imperialism*. Oxford, UK: Oxford University Press.

Pinker, S. (1994). *The language instinct*. New York: William Morrow.

PSAT/NMSQT. (2003). College Board for Education Professionals. Counselors, PSAT/NMSQT, writing skills questions. Available: http://www.collegeboard.com/psat/counslrs/html/writing.html

Radford, A. (1990). *Transformational grammar: A first course*. Cambridge, UK: Cambridge University Press.

Ricento, T. (1998). National language policy in the United States. In T. Ricento & B. Burnaby (Eds.), *Language and politics in the United States and Canada* (pp. 86–87). Mahwah, NJ: Lawrence Erlbaum Associates.

SAT. (2003). College Board. Scholastic Aptitude Test. Available: http://www.collegeboard.com/student/testing/sat/about/SATI.html

Schieffelin, B., & Ochs, E. (Eds.). (1986). *Language socialization across cultures*. Cambridge, UK: Cambridge University Press.

Seely, C. (1998). *TPR is more than commands—at all levels*. Berkeley, CA: Command Performance Language Institute.

Skutnabb-Kangas, T. (2000). *Linguistic Genocide in Education or Worldwide Diversity and Human Rights?* Mahwah, NJ: Lawrence Erlbaum Associates.

Sorenson, S. (1991). *Working with special students in English/language arts*. Bloomington, IN: ERIC Clearinghouse on Reading and Communication Skills.

Stanford Achievement Test Series (9th ed.). (1999). Harcourt Brace educational measurement promotional booklet. San Antonio, TX: Harcourt Brace.

Taylor, B. (1987). Teaching ESL: Incorporating a communicative, student-centered component. In M. Long & J. Richards (Eds.), *Methodology in TESOL* (pp. 45–60). New York: Newbury House.

Tomasello, M., & Herron, C. (1988). Down the garden path: Inducing and correcting over-generalizations errors in the foreign language classroom. *Applied Psycholinguistics* 9: 237–46.

Tomasello, M., & Herron, C. (1989). Feedback for Language Transfer Errors: The garden path technique *Studies in Second Language Acquisition* 13: 513–517.

Tunmer, W., Herriman, M. & Nesdale, A. (1988). Metalinguistic abilities and beginning reading. *Reading Research Quarterly, 23*(2), 134-158.

Tunmer, W., & Myhill, M., (1984). Metalinguistic awareness and billingualism. In W. Tunmer, C. Pratt, & M. Herriman (Eds.), *Metalinguistic awareness in children* (pp. 169-187). Berlin: Springer-Verlag.

Tunmer, W., Nesdale, A., & Wright, A. (1987). Syntactic awareness and reading acquisition. *British Journal of Developmental Psychology, 5*(1), 25-34.

VanDeWeghe, R. (1993). Spelling and grammar logs. In L. M. Cleary & M. D. Linn (Eds.), *Linguistics for teachers* (pp. 367-370). New York: McGraw-Hill.

Weaver, C. (1996). *Teaching grammar in context.* Portsmouth, NH: Heinemann.

Weaver, C. (Ed.). (1998). *Lessons to share on teaching grammar in context.* Portsmouth, NH: Heinemann.

White, L. (2000). A paradigm change for the teaching of the mother tongues. In L. White, B. Maylath, A. Adams, & M. Couzijn (Eds.), *Language awareness: A history and implementations* (pp. 41-56). Amsterdam:z Amsterdam University Press.

White, L., Maylath, B., Adams, A., & Couzijn, M. (Eds.). (2000). *Language awareness: A history and implementations.* Amsterdam: Amsterdam University Press.

Willis, D. (1996). *The lexical syllabus.* London: Harper-Collins.

Willis, D., & Willis, J. (1996). *Challenge and change in language teaching.* Portsmouth, NH: Heinemann.

Wolfram, A. (1991). *Dialects and American English.* Englewood Cliffs, NJ: Prentice Hall.

Wolfram, A., & Christian, D. (1999). *Dialects in schools and communities.* Mahwah, NJ: Lawrence Erlbaum Associates.

Index